# the mind's mirror

**dream dictionary &
translation guide**

# the mind's mirror

## dream dictionary & translation guide

By Kari Hohne

Published by Way of Tao Books.
P.O. Box 1753 Carnelian Bay, Ca 96140
PaperBird is a division of Way of Tao Books.
www.wayoftao.com
Printed in the United States of America

ISBN 978-0-9819779-1-1

For Jackie, my nursery twin who dreams the same dreams.

# Introduction

Because we rehash daily events when we dream, we usually dismiss the process. However, research shows that the mind is processing this information specifically because it may have impacted us in ways we failed to recognize. When the opportunity to transform comes up against the walls of our beliefs, a more natural sense of self-awareness still finds productive ways of breaking through our conscious barriers. Personal growth is heightened when we take an active approach in understanding our dreams.

Sigmund Freud called dreaming "a peculiar form of thinking." He believed dreams only appeared cryptic as a way to allow transformative information beyond the walls of defense mechanisms and active consciousness. Dreams allow us to understand our existence from a much broader perspective. Since dreaming takes place in a part of the brain that developed before language, this peculiar sensory organ communicates in images. It is as if dreams are the *Mind's Mirror* because they offer an *objective* reflection of who we are. They hold the clues to our unacknowledged desires and hidden potentials.

Therapists use dreams to uncover clues to understand the motivation of a client in crisis. In this way, dreaming becomes an evolutionary mechanism that keeps us evolving in a changing world. Understanding our dreams can have a profound impact on our ability to experience happiness and success.

The challenge we face in understanding the language of dreams is in recognizing that *everything* that appears in the dream is our *reflection*. Other characters portray unacknowledged aspects that we have associated with them. They appear in our dreams as a *representation* of that part of us that is undergoing transformation. Even the landscape, mood and objects will conjure up personal meaning designed to affect us in the same *unspoken way* that art, cinematic drama and music moves us.

Dreams provide a point of view that is unique and strange, but more importantly, can move us emotionally and inexplicably toward a change in perspective. Therefore, while we may not remember our dreams, they are still changing us in profound ways. Dreams usually reveal the exact opposite of what we believe to be true about ourselves. Using the *Mind's Mirror* to understand the unique language of your inner world will become an indispensable tool for heightening self-discovery.

Many times our dreams will portray archetypes or universal symbols that derive from our ancient stories or what psychologist Carl Jung called the collective unconscious. I too, have observed how clients undergoing transformation will dream in patterns that include the themes that are found in world mythology.

We may dream of meeting a Trickster character who traps us in our inconsistencies. In later stages of dreamwork, the Wise Woman or Wise Man guides us. We can accompany the Unknown Child as a representation of the birthing of new aspects. Trickster, or the bizarre character who presents us with something unusual, upsets the status quo of the psyche to turn it topsy-turvy. The Wise one acts as a spiritual guide and represents our connection to our deeper insight. Finally, giving birth or accompanying and Unknown Child can represent the birth of our new and emerging identity. *The Mythology of Sleep: The Waking Power of Dreams* is an excellent companion guide to this book. It explores the common themes and settings that appear in mythical adventures and dreams.

## Facts About Dreaming

- You may think that you do not dream, although research shows how REM or rapid eye movement demonstrates how EVERYONE dreams.
- To remember your dreams, simply make an effort to start paying attention to them. Once you begin observing how clues come forward that can accelerate growth, looking at the dream for direction will aid in your ability to recall your dreams.
- Researchers explore how the mind functions like a computer in its "back up" and "recycle bin" processes. As another sensory organ, you revisit experience, explore potential and release outworn perspectives. This is how dreaming becomes the steward of a healthy psyche.

2

- When you are "stuck" in a transformative cycle, the dream always reveals "the way through."
- If your dream recurs, it should be given careful consideration. Once you understand it, you will see that it will not recur.
- If you are awakened during REM sleep, you will be able to remember your dreams in more detail than in the morning.
- The human body is designed with a paralytic feature that keeps your limbs from acting out on your dreams. The body holds an inherent wisdom that allows it to heal itself, which requires no thought or action on your part. Similarly, the process of dreaming can be viewed as a perceptive or parasympathetic "organ" that activates a type of "healing" while you sleep.
- Dreams often present the exact opposite of what you believe to be true about yourself. Often, sharing their content with another person will allow you to recognize how the dream reflects what you may be "missing" about your current situation.
- Understanding your dreams can lead to balance and wellness as well as helping you become more assertive, self-confident, and equipped with a strong sense of who you are.

# Types of Dreams

## Daydreams

You spend an average of 70-120 minutes a day, daydreaming or fantasizing. Between waking and sleeping, you may slip into fantasy at various times of the day where the imagination wanders. Since it is impossible to maintain a high level of focus continuously, as awareness decreases, you lose yourself in fantasy. You may revisit the past and dream of the future. In this way, you travel near the dreamscape, although consciousness still provides interference.

## Lucid Dreams

Lucid dreams occur when you "wake up" while dreaming. Sometimes this sudden sense of knowing you are dreaming allows you to do fantastic things like fly over the houses you see. Many people actually wake themselves up within the dream to remain in this lucid state to explore how they can influence dreams. This ability to achieve the lucid dream state is an important initiation into mastering the power of thought and its ability to influence events.

## Nightmares

The nightmare often causes you to wake up in a state of panic with your heart racing. Yet nightmares are a positive sign that something powerful is stirring within. Sometimes a dream can reflect actual trauma or unresolved crisis, although the nightmare is always a WAKE UP CALL to explore how feelings require processing. Most people who come to me for dream analysis, do so because of a dream of this type. The more graphic and disturbing the dream, the more you will remember and process it. The ground may shake or an intruder may stalk you. In reality you are either getting a wake up call to shift the foundation of your beliefs, or need to explore intimacy so that others are not intruding in your life.

Whether you are attempting to overcome a real life crisis, or transcending *non-rational* fear, dreaming is a "safe place" that allows

4

these ideas to be explored. Perhaps you cannot recognize that *you are on the wrong path,* and so, the nightmare may recur until the situation is resolved. People are relieved to discover that something inside can not only guide them, but also, awakens them to their own self-imposed barriers.

A nightmare can be as simple as *leaving something behind* while you hurry to your destination. It can be as frightening as actually experiencing death or dismemberment as you awaken to the idea of letting go of a past way of being. More than any other dream, the nightmare will disturb you *so profoundly,* that it cannot be forgotten. It is a *natural* mechanism, which forces you to confront the truth about what you are not facing. Once these fearful feelings are integrated into your transforming identity, the nightmare will not recur.

### Recurring Dreams

Recurring dreams are story lines or themes that repeat themselves over weeks, months and even years. Sometimes they leave you feeling *puzzled* because they seem irrational. *The Mind's Mirror* has a way of forcing consciousness into perplexity, as an important aspect of transformation. Recurring dreams seem to go hand in hand with the nightmare. Since dreams are suggesting what you fail to acknowledge in daily life, whatever you are avoiding or not facing will continue to be the subject matter of your dream, until it is resolved. Like nightmares, once the *puzzle is solved* and the aspect is integrated into consciousness, the dream will not recur.

### Dreams About Healing

Many times vehicle doors or lower and upper rooms of a house will depict aspects of the body, offering a message about your health and well-being. The front door can suggest arms, while the back doors can represent legs. Lighting or electrical circuitry can be neurological, while water problems can suggest psychological, vascular or "plumbing" issues. The top floor of a building can represent the head, while the rooms below can suggest various parts of the lower body.

Protecting a "treasure" can signify repression at the root of illness, while searching for a key is often the clue to wellness. If you are experiencing "dis-ease", *where* it is taking place in the body is as

5

important as *why*. If the left leg is suffering, look for its representation in dreams of ground floor doors, or lower left portion of a structure or vehicle. Sometimes before a physical manifestation will appear, you are warned in advance of over indulgence or things that can impact your wellness. Many therapists recognize repression at the root of illness. Since dreams portray what you are repressing, they are a profound tool in achieving wellness and balance.

### Prophetic Dreams

The "dream cycle" is a lot like "myth cycles." In our ancient stories, the hero is tested in various landscapes, finding clues at special places in an effort to uncover the truth about both, their *identity* and *destiny*. Similarly, the changing landscape and clues within a dream cycle captures the essence of *why* we dream. When a dream is observed to "morph" into different landscapes, the dream is described: *"as if it was the same dream, but then it changed..."*

The dream cycle usually presents the idea of *time* in three stages:
a) The first cycle shows you as "the hero" facing a *current* challenge.
b) The second cycle shows the *past* and the part it played in creating this condition.
c) Finally, the third cycle offers bizarre clues that are actually finding their way into consciousness in any way they can. These clues provide direction as to how you can transform to meet the *future*. This portion has *unusual* images that will allow you to discover your *real* identity and therefore, your destiny.

In the first cycle, you are exploring the *conflict* at hand and given the symbolism that can help you understand it objectively. The second cycle usually portrays a sudden change of landscape. This portion usually portrays family members and symbolism from the past. It describes how the current crisis was created by the ideas you cling to. The third portion of the dream is usually most bizarre as *the transforming aspect of the psyche* pushes you beyond your static sense of self. The final cycle often can be viewed as prophetic because when it is compared against future events, you discover actual events that validate the dream content.

Dreams are *The Mind's Mirror* because they have a special predisposition for reflecting aspects of you in a way that is *puzzling* or *strange.* The "newness" or bizarre imagery of the dreamscape provides the innovative perspective that is necessary for transformation. The final cycle of the dream offers information about the "missing link" in overcoming conflict or crisis.

Understanding your dreams will make more sense to you when once you recognize how dreams have an *uncanny* way of breaking into your consciousness through the medium of sleep. The synchronistic aspect of the final setting may simply be the result of how your unconscious mind knows what is coming, before you consciously piece the information together.

## Life Changing Dreams

During periods when you are actively undergoing transformation, you will experience Great Dreams or Cosmic Dreams, which are rich in mythological associations. They often portray a meeting with universal archetypes such as The Great Mother or Wise Man. These dreams can fill you with such emotion and appear so vivid that you remember longer than normal dreams. In many ways, you would call them life changing. Revisiting these dream themes to contrast the symbolism against ancient mythology can present you with a more profound understanding of its message. Life Changing Dreams usually occur when you are actively approaching change with an open mind.

# How to Recall Your Dreams

- Prior to sleep, make a conscious decision to remember your dreams and ask for guidance. This actually improves your ability to remember a dream.
- A healthy and balanced diet in addition to a regular sleep routine will improve dream recall.
- Have a notebook or tape recorder next to your bed to immediately record the dream.
- Since dream imagery takes place in a different part of the brain, you will notice how allowing your thoughts of the day to intrude will make accessing dream content more difficult. Train yourself to stay with the dream, prior to thinking about what you need to do that day. If nothing else, capture the sense of emotion that the dream invoked, and use that as a thread to allow the dream imagery to return.
- Write down as many details as you can remember. It is not important to catch every aspect because many portions of the dreamscape will say the same message in several different forms. Start slowly, capturing the mood, landscape, and as many details as you can recall. The dreamscape lends itself well to association so even if you are not sure of the accuracy of the symbolism, in the beginning you can use whatever words or images come to mind. This will allow you to start recognizing the profound input that always emerges from the unconscious.
- Once you are able to easily recall your dreams, start looking for the less obvious symbols, like time of day, lighting, colors and numbers.
- You dream of the type of things that consciousness would rather keep "below the surface." Do not become frustrated when you are unable to recall the content. If accessing this information were easy, it wouldn't have been the subject of your dream. Sometimes finding the appropriate words appears

difficult, so try *drawing* images. *Explore the "flavor" of your dream and the feelings it created.*

- The most important part of dream processing is the practice recording information **without analyzing it.** Approaching the content as objectively as possible to record the details will allow you to analyze it later. Even while it may appear nonsensical to you, discussing the content with a friend or partner can sometimes help you to understand it.
- Remember that the subconscious speaks "cryptically" specifically to allow repressed information to come forward so record everything.
- Assume that the dream knows more than you do. Gather the imagery and symbols and let the dream become your guide. The dream is trying to offer a fresh perspective about what you are failing to acknowledge in your daily experiences. Once the dream's message begins to unfold, try to apply it toward your life.
- Those aspects of the dream that appear the most bizarre will in time, provide the most profound clues about your identity and how to understand the way forward.

### Analyzing the Dream

*Approach the symbolism objectively* and identify the setting, characters, symbols and theme of the activity. It will usually take a series of dreams before you begin to see how conflict and its resolution are being described by your unique associations. Since the story is unique to you, the symbolism will also be personal, although the Dream Dictionary can lead you in the general direction.

*Trust that the information is relevant* and is being revealed to you in the only way it can be expressed. The dream may appear just beyond the grasp of your memory. You can begin to observe how concrete belief structures ward off this emerging information. You dream from a more fluid awareness, and must use a similar free flowing consciousness when retrieving the content.

9

*Explore the dream in pieces*: a) I was in a *car* that drove *off* a *bridge*; b) I was at a *train station* with a *strange man* and *forgot my baggage*; c) There were *several children playing* in a *garden* where I walked *through a door* into *strange house*. All of this symbolism is describing essential elements of where you stand in relation to your growth. The *car* describes your *"drive to move forward"* or motivation. The *train station* is an aspect of growth that shows your desire to *go somewhere new* or transform. The *unknown* characters represent *unrecognized* aspects of *you*. The *strange man* can be the idea of *unrecognized masculine* traits, like being assertive or moving toward independence, while the *children* can portray *young* or emerging sides of you, which is also represented by the *unknown house*. *Forgetting baggage* or *"the things"* you carry with you is a common theme from the aspect of growth. The other symbolism will reveal how you are approaching change and what is necessary to move forward.

*Without pre-judging the content,* write it down immediately. Look at the words individually and objectively. You will see that in most cases, they are saying the exact opposite of what you believe to be true about yourself.

*In dreams, all symbols have relevance,* no matter how ridiculous they may appear. Besides things, look for colors, time of day and numbers.

## Questions to Consider

### What is the setting and how does it capture the dynamics of your current situation or *inner* landscape?

You may dismiss the dream because it appears to rehash the day's events. Since dreams often present what you are *not* acknowledging during the day, look for something that the dream appears to be highlighting. Instead of presenting the situation as you experienced it, recognize the elements that made it appear different: *"It seemed like...it* was the store I was in yesterday *but..."* The dream's *metaphorical* associations are the key to identifying its hidden message.

If you are dreaming about the situation, then there is some relevant aspect about it that you are missing. Experience always teaches you something and you are given a *second chance* to apply its message productively. Understanding that something is being brought to your attention, respect this input with an open mind, by looking at the situation again. Dreams do not merely replay what you have already observed and concluded. The fact that the event is in your dream, suggests that how you processed it may have been incorrect.

### Who are the characters in the dream?

You may dream of Susie and Mark, but how would you describe these individuals? What side of *"you"* are these characters representing? All symbols and characters describe how you are growing into and letting go of the mask that you wear. Each subject's characteristics will reflect your existing or changing identity over time. They represent the side of you that you have *unconsciously* associated with them, *whether or not you are aware of it*. Who is Mark? *Mark is angry all of the time.* Who is Susie? *Susie is a good mother and cares for everyone but herself.*

Look at your circumstances as if Susie is personifying *that* part of you that is unrecognized. Mark might embody anger that you are not acknowledging. When looking at the dream from this perspective, *what*

11

*are you saying to yourself through these characters?* What part of your current way of interacting are you not acknowledging? All characters represent stagnant, evolving or non-integrated aspects of you. Even when characters die or are threatened, they represent the dying away of outworn ways of expressing yourself on the road to authentic empowerment. Birth and children are usually describing the nature of how you are changing.

### Can the dream be tapped for inspiration or intuition?

Dreams are not always solving conflicts. With practice, you can actually prepare yourself to receive information from the unconscious. Before you sleep, think about the type of input you require. Perhaps you are an artist and want to explore something in a new way. Many people allow their dreams to guide them in moving forward and making changes. As you approach on new project at work, perhaps you require inspiration. If you prepare your mind before sleep and observe your dreams for input, you will be quite surprised with what comes forward. Regardless of how abstract the images appear, work with them until you understand their message. Keeping track of your dreams, you will observe intuitive details about future events that will help you prepare yourself for approaching changes.

### Have you explored the opposite meaning of the dream?

It is natural to approach dreams from the standpoint of regular experience, although what comes out in the dream is *the opposite of what you believe.* Just as you hadn't really thought about how you would describe "Mark as being angry all of the time," you probably didn't realize that you are angry too. If you dream about an *intruder* and feel afraid that *you are being invaded,* it is not a message about taking precautions but is actually a message about being *too reclusive.* Perhaps you may need to be *more open* or intimate so that others aren't *intruding* into your life. If you dream of *being naked* and feel embarrassed or ashamed, you may have been wearing the *costume* of an *unnatural persona* and are exploring removing this *clothing* that only hides your human and natural side. During the day, you may have revealed yourself in a way that left you feeling vulnerable. The dream allows you to explore *why* this process was difficult for you. More importantly, dreaming is a *natural mechanism* that keeps you evolving.

The dream suggests the feelings you need to face and integrate within your life. In a dream, you may be going to an event and *cannot find* certain clothes (sense of identity,) shoes (sense of direction) or wallet (sense of self-worth). Dreams often present a message about the way you cover yourself to mask your more real nature. You dream of a *landslide* and become fearful of the future when the dream is actually exploring the need to *shift your foundation*. The concrete platform you stand upon needs to give way, so new growth can occur.

### Can the dream become a model
### as you learn about yourself through others?

Just as all characters represent unrecognized aspects of you, real life situations are always a growth opportunity to explore unrecognized aspects. Like dreams, the people you meet may be helping you to express evolving aspects of *who you might become* or *what you need to discard*. Don't be quick to judge and dismiss difficult encounters. What can the experience teach you about yourself? Why was *this person* put on your pathway? Is the encounter challenging you to recognize an aspect of yourself you are not acknowledging? The encounter is propitious, because you always attract the things you need. Like a spinning leaf that encounters a trapped log in the river, if two things are doing similar things, it is only a matter of time before they meet in the great river of life.

## Common Dream Themes

**Houses and Buildings** are structures that often represent your "inner architecture" as a representation of your inner world. The *attic* signifies higher thought or spiritual ideas. It can also suggest the ideas you store and collect or how you must "climb upward" or raise consciousness to sort through what you no longer need. The *basement* is usually the subconscious or the area underneath, which you keep "below the surface." Unknown or *undiscovered rooms* in a house will suggest aspects of you, which are unknown, but are currently being explored. The *living* room is a social place, where you explore your nature as you meet others, while the *bed* can be a place of exploring sexuality. The *bath* room is where you "get naked" and is associated with "coming clean," or being truthful with yourself. The *family* room houses the dynamics inherited through family interaction, while the *hearth* or *fireplace* often symbolizes your sense of heritage and what you hold sacred. Watching something burn in the fire is the same thing as processing and releasing these tendencies.

*Hallways* are places of transition, where you meet others in "neutral space" and often appear when you are exploring choices. The *front yard* or *garden* is what you are cultivating for "public view." The *back yard* is suggestive of more organic aspects, which *are not made obvious* to others. You will often discover or *search* for something in the *bushes* or *shadows*, as a way of exploring the correctness of your behavior.

*Public Buildings* often appear as rickety structures that seem to go in bizarre directions, representing how you grow into social circumstances not yet created. They can be places in which you are lost, or searching for something (transformative clues) on a specific *floor* or level of consciousness: past beliefs below, emerging ideas on the ground floor, and other floors that might be associated with the number it represents: *see numbers.*

*Doors* can mean many things: boundaries and unblocking your potential, while knocking is often sexual. The *front* door leads you into the world, while the *back* and *side* doors allow for an "escape" or for the

15

"intrusion" of characters who will teach you about yourself. If you *open a door*, you are taking an objective approach into the unknown. When the *door is inside of a professional building*, it can suggest potential or exploring transitions in your career.

A *church* can house spiritual beliefs, but can also suggest how irrational ideas based only on faith are holding you back in some way. Sometimes you will be looking for a *key* in a church that suggests how a self-criticism may be trapping your organic nature as a physical symptom or dis-ease.

A *school* suggests learning experiences or being measured against others in your abilities. In the same way, a *gymnasium* is a place of competition in a more physical way. A *factory* is a place of "mass production" or the attitudes that you "assemble" to fit in. It can also suggest what you are currently "making" out of experience. A *hospital* is a place of personal crisis; or where you seek "critical" care, as in understanding the incapacitating nature of your critical tapes. Hospitals can also represent "new life" or the place where you are "born" into a new way of being.

*Hotels, Airports* and temporary or transitional places while traveling suggest experimenting with temporary attitudes as a way of understanding yourself differently. The *floors* of these structures are also indicative of levels of awareness associated with the transition. You stand on the ground floor of current awareness and travel upward to achieve your ideals, or downward to find the things holding you back.

**Vehicles** and **Places of Transportation** reveal your motivation and *the condition* in which you are currently moving forward from the standpoint of autonomy. The type of vehicle, and whether or not you are driving, in control or being driven, will portray your present sense of autonomy, and how reliable it is. *Danger* and the idea of *crashing* suggest how you are not in control of where you are going and are therefore, feeling uncertain about your direction. Being *stopped by police* or *traffic lights* are indicative of conscious controls such as self-discipline and conscience.

*Boats, ships* and *trains*, in which you are a "passenger," suggest how you are following a proven course that is not self-directed or easily changed. Travel over *water* is indicative of emotions and how the "flow of events" or "current" leads you forward. Being a passenger on a ship often represents situations that feel beyond your control. The water can be *dark, calm* or *choppy* in relation to how you feel about where you are going in life. Fellow passengers can shed light on the transforming elements of your nature.

A *bicycle*, because it is propelled forward by *your actual effort*, can suggest vitality and issues related to health. As a child, perhaps you learned to ride by balancing while you moved forward, suggesting balancing motivation with other elements in your life. *Bumper cars, go-carts* and other *jalopies* suggest how you are moving forward, sometimes in comical ways.

*Airports* and *train stations* are places of transition, and therefore are associated with hopes and ambitions. You can "fly" to your destination through expanded awareness and ambition, or find your compartment or "place" on a train that follows a "proven track." You can be going *up, down* or in *circles,* as a way of pointing you toward inspiration, overcoming repression, or revisiting the past. (See **Placement and Perspective** in the dream dictionary).

**Archetypes and Universal Characters** portray how the many characters that appear are always representing some aspect of *your* transforming identity. Police stop you in dreams when you are doing something "illegal" or when an evolving aspect is transcending the critical or disciplinarian tapes of conscience. Babies will represent the birthing of your new identity, while the death of someone suggests elements, which must "pass on." You might know you are somehow responsible for this "death" by feeling victimized or pursued. You can be "suddenly saddled" with the responsibility of caring for an "Unknown Child," which suggests how you are not quite sure what to do with this "new identity."

Intruders appear when you believe you are being invaded, or when you have unwittingly been revealed by approaching intimacy with apprehension. You can encounter universal characters or Archetypes, such as the dark one, monster, devil or Shadow, which will always represent that part of your power, which appears frightening or unknown to you. Women being "kissed" by a monster in dreams will often coincide with the onset of menstruation and menopause, or those times in life when her body demonstrates a power beyond her control. Meeting this character always coincides with monumental stages of her development. Accessing the power this character holds over you often represents a power that remains dormant, which can lead to integration and wholeness. The Wise Woman or Wise Man are often reflective of intuition and how it guides you.

The **Persona** is the mask you wear into the world, and in dreams, your evolving identity takes form as your Persona depicted by the many characters you meet. These characters can also portray new and evolving "costumes" that you are trying on as you move forward.

The **Shadow** embodies your rejected and repressed aspects. At some point, you may have decided some part of you is unacceptable because it suggested weakness, a fear of fitting in with the group, or unresolved anger that you refuse to "own." In actuality, these aspects become the fodder of dreams, and how they explore untapped potential on the pathway to discovering your *real* nature. The Shadow is often represented by the Intruder, Pursuer, or Monster. (See **Shadow** in the dream dictionary.)

The **Anima / Animus** represent the female and male aspects of the opposite sexes. Men and women possess feminine and masculine traits and in dreams, the anima may appear to a male as a highly feminized figure. The animus is the male "protector" or attractive man who appears to the female. Men may dream of doing feminine things, like wearing a dress, while a woman may do things that would be considered masculine like dominating or mounting another woman. These types of dreams are actually coaxing the male toward sensitivity, while the woman may be exploring empowerment through a dream of domination.

These qualities emerge as a reminder of how the female must develop her assertive or masculine potential, while the male must be sensitive or introspective in expressing and blending sensitivity into his masculinity. Both the female and male qualities are necessary in authentic empowerment and balance.

The **Unknown Child** symbolizes your innocence and untapped or budding potential. It represents vulnerability and helplessness, but also aspirations and insight into how you may integrate potential by understanding the symbolism associated with the child. As you evolve, you sometimes dream of accompanying a baby or young child suggesting this "new" and emerging side of your Persona. The fact that you may not know where the child came from, or what you should do with it, suggests the way that *who you are becoming* today is constantly growing or experiencing rebirth as you grow to meet the future.

The **Wise Man** acts as a guide or helper in dreams. You may meet a religious icon, an old man as a teacher, father or some other unknown authority figure. Often, they will say special words of wisdom and offer guidance. This figure represents the higher self and your ability to transcend difficulty. It is important to record the message or symbols associated with this character as a way of understanding your way through the transformative landscape. Representing masculine or productive elements, they often present the keys to your social success.

The **Great Woman** can appear as a real mother or grandmother, suggesting your nurturing and wise qualities that are rising to the surface. Offering reassurance or direction, Jung also thought the Old Woman represented the "unattractive" aspects of the feminine, appearing as a Witch or old Bag Lady. In this case, she can be associated with the duality of how the mother is the giver of life at the same time that she is jealous of how you become self-sufficient. Representing your critical tapes turned inward, meeting the Old Woman as a negative character can help you move beyond repression and dis-ease. Meeting the positive figure usually coincides with the male moving actively toward intimacy, or the female moving toward increased self-esteem.

The **Trickster** is the cosmic jester of the dreamscape and portrays the comical way that the psyche seeks to break through in bizarre ways. Manifesting in many forms, he stands at the psychic crossroad, pointing like the scarecrow in the Wizard of Oz. His antics may seem ridiculous, although his clues are most profound in helping you break out of the status quo. There are many roads and the right road is sometimes just the pathway exposing the contradiction inherent in your absolutes. See **Archetypes and Universal Characters** in the Dream Dictionary for more information.

**Landscape or Scenery** can offer messages related to how you see clearly in the *day* or by *light* (conscious) or whether you are not facing something in the *night* or in the *dark* (unconscious). In the *forest* (subconscious,) you often meet a character or *archetypal guide* who can

19

offer clues to your transformative processes. *Trees* are stationary and rooted, suggesting the details of your genetic heritage.

You can climb a *mountain* to gain a wider view, while it can also represent how you can remain a prisoner to your beliefs. The *desert* returns you to an uncomplicated or barren landscape where you can discover the roots of your sustenance. The *sea* or *seashore* is the home or barrier of the unconscious, where you can discover the treasures (fish/sealife) that can be brought forward as clues to your evolutionary journey. *Natural disasters* like *earthquakes, tornados, floods* and *tsunamis* suggest the transformative power or your emotions rising to the surface to transform what you believed to be static.

**Being Naked or Exposed** suggests how you are exploring or exposing the deeper or hidden sides of your being. As you move toward intimacy, you may have dreams of being *undressed in public* or relieving yourself in a *bathroom without walls* as the result of having your natural side exposed. As a child, you may have dreamed of *going to school in your underwear* when what you most wanted was to abide by the golden rule. In proportion to the rules you impose on yourself, you will find that dreams lead you toward the freedom to be real. To *"get naked"* or *"relieve yourself"* in public, you are allowing for the movement of other aspects that had not previously found expression. This sense of being vulnerable, suggests how intimacy and exposing yourself is the only way of moving toward authenticity.

Being exposed can also take place in dreams in which you feel *trapped*. If this brings all you *fear* to the surface, then the symbolism is doing exactly what is necessary so you can understand it. If the dream focuses on a *snake*, shed your skin and learn to express your natural drives; if it is a *burglar*, then face intimacy openly so that nothing is stolen. When some part of you is being *revealed*, stalked or *discarded*, you "get naked," confront the truth of "what you fail to see," and learn to "let go of the protective covering that can no longer serve you. If you are frightened, it is simply a call to overcome your fear of being who you are. If you are ashamed, you may need to overcome whatever is keeping you from being a natural creature in a natural world.

**Losing Teeth** is a common dream that occurs at monumental points in life. Just as you lose your baby teeth as a child, wisdom teeth as an adolescent and perhaps all of your teeth when you grow old, teeth are associated with letting go of old ways of "chewing on things." The way you approached situations in the past will no longer do. Teeth can also represent credibility. As you smile, you can suddenly look stupid because your *teeth are falling out*. This demonstrates how losing teeth can be an aspect of the *Trickster*, or transformative mind, humorously tricking you toward more authentic behavior. When you are about to say "the same old thing," you are left mumbling with a mouth full of teeth, representing "the old way" of chewing or digesting experience. Whatever you were about to say in the dream would definitely not be considered the truth, in light of who you are becoming.

**Water Dreams** are the most common dreams because water represents emotions, and how you feel about the changes that are taking place around you. To dream of *turbulent seas*, suggests a sense of crisis associated with your transformation. Usually when you have this type of dream, later you will dream about being on a similar ship in calmer waters. This is a dream cycle that portrays the growth you have achieved. In all of our ancient stories, water is the mysterious reservoir where the hero is to retrieve a treasure. Similarly, *raging water* is the difficulty that often initiates you into a process of self-discovery, where the reward is your ability to retrieve a *treasure below the surface*. Floods can undermine the foundation of your beliefs until you are forced to let go of what you think you need, in the pursuit of simple survival. Water can represent health and wellness since it is also the elixir of life.

**Dreams About Flying** occur during exhilarating or empowering points in life. While you are dreaming, you may suddenly "wake up," as consciousness realizes *anything is possible*, and so you fly. This is an aspect of the psyche exploring potential and self-imposed limitations. At the same time, dreaming of "waking up" and starting the routine of the day, only to realize it was a dream, portrays the need for a "wake up" call in breaking your routine.

**Police Dreams** occur when one aspect of your evolving identity is challenged by the "peacekeeper" or the "patrolling" aspect. Sometimes the message is important: *slow down*. At other times, the police will come to "inspect" the changes you are making, representing your disciplinary tapes. Associated with the "inner critic," encountering police is often occurring because you may actually need to step out of the lines to transform.

# THE DREAM DICTIONARY

# A

The letter "A" in a dream can symbolize your desire for recognition and accomplishment as in getting an 'A' on a test, or being A number one. Alternatively, it is a symbol that resembles an arrow and can be pointing out something or pointing you in a specific direction related to the dream. Associated with arriving, "A" can be a message about embarking on a new, more fulfilling path. since it begins the alphabet, A is often associated with beginnings. It is a letter that can suggest abundance and fullness and how you attract experience with your attitude.

**Abandoned:** Dreaming of being abandoned or left behind shows your attempt to let go of outworn behavior or characteristics. It can reflect an identity crisis as you move into a new situation with fears of not fitting in. In a sense you are abandoning your old identity in preparation for a transformation. If the dream focuses more on being left behind, there is a sense of exploring where you are in relation to other's expectations of you or life stages.

**Abbreviation:** When a combination of letters or an abbreviation appears in your dream, the message can relate to someone you know with those initials. Some aspect or characteristic associated with them is being examined and perhaps adopted or discarded in your expression. Explore whether the letters sounded together resemble a word. For example: IM can suggest 'I am' or 'Instant Message' as in not taking the time to think before you respond. DN can sound like 'the end' or can represent Down in its abbreviation so say the letters over and over to see if another word manifests. B can suggest 'be' and R can represent 'are.' Explore the individual letters in the dictionary. See also **People** and **Name.**

**Abdomen:** Since emotions are associated with "gut feelings," dreams of the abdomen represent feelings you are not acknowledging. The *condition* of the abdomen and whether or not it is yours, suggests whether you are owning or integrating your gut feelings. See **Anatomy and Body Parts.**

**Abduction:** Being abducted shows how you may be allowing your real nature to be 'kidnapped' by fear or the pressure of others. The threat of being abducted by aliens and UFOs is a common dream theme arising from peer pressure or doing things that go against your sense of Self. Being threatened by a sinister character can portray the Shadow, which represents the unacknowledged but powerful part of your nature that you are not allowing to have expression. In a sense, you are 'kidnapping' yourself or repressing some aspect of your nature. Being kidnapped by anything portrays the internal conflict created when one side of you is evolving, yet is blocked by your more ingrained or critical nature from the pressure of conformity. You may dream of abduction any time you feel developmental pressure of this type. See also **Alien, UFO, Shadow** and **Archetypes and Universal Characters**.

**Aborigine:** Dreaming of an aborigine reflects the more natural, 'uncivilized' side of you that seeks expression aside from social restraints. Dreaming of foreign persons can be a way of exploring life from a more foreign perspective. Visiting foreign cities can symbolize a change in outlook and changes to your sense of values. If commerce is involved, the dream can be exploring work issues that might be viewed in a new light. If it is a cafe in a foreign country, you are exploring new ways of finding fulfillment.

**Abortion:** To dream of aborting or stopping some type of procedure or mission shows your inability to make some type of change. If it involves a baby, then there is a sense that a new or emerging identity is being abandoned. Dreaming of having or caring for a baby shows the emergence of a new side of you. If you dream of abortion, it will suggest your unwillingness to change, open or transform. If someone else is having the abortion, then the issue will be more related to the side of you this person represents. See **People**.

**Above:** Seeing something above you in a dream can represent your aspirations. The upper area of a house can symbolize conscience or

26

spiritual ideas. The upper floors related to a stairway or elevator can show how you explore upward movement in your career. See also **Placement and Perspective.**

**Abroad:** Dreaming of going abroad or into a foreign country shows changes taking place within you as you expand your outlook. Taking an airplane can symbolize widening your aspirations. The foreign place you are traveling to needs to be considered in terms of the adjectives you would use to describe this place. As a representation of those qualities being broadened within you, the city personifies new and unexplored potential. See also **Foreigners**.

**Abscess:** A wound in a dream can portray issues of hurt that you are not facing. An abscess carries the idea that something is festering and needs to be 'cleaned up' so healing can begin. As a play on words, explore whether the idea of abscess is really suggesting being obsessed or holding onto something. See also **Wound** and **Decay.**

**Absorb:** A dream that focuses on something that absorbs can be a message about your current focus. You can be 'absorbed' in one thing at the expense of something else. It can also symbolize being drained or the sense that you are not allowing for the free expression of feelings because of its association to 'wetness.'

**Abyss**: Seeing an abyss captures the idea of how you approach the unknown depths within you. An event may have triggered the idea that there is more going on inside than you realized. The abyss can also represent reaching an apex and the need to make changes that make you feel like you may have to go 'down' or 'backwards' in order to continue. It can be a symbolic representation of not having all the facts in order to see clearly. See also **Valley** and **Canyon.**

**Accent:** When something is said in a dream with a noticeable accent or slur- consider what is being and said and by whom for information about what is being dismissed by habit or routine. A waiter with a foreign accent would be portraying the exploration of nourishment and fulfillment in a way you hadn't considered. What other elements about this waiter might provide clues about possible fulfillment in work? Having a neighbor with a foreign accent or meeting a foreigner can represent a more exotic/different side of you that is being developed. If a person is speaking in a dream in an unintelligible sort of way, it can be personifying a way of expressing yourself that is not authentic or not truthful. If the person is intoxicated, you might explore whether drinking is a crutch for your free expression. See **Alcohol** and **Foreigners.**

**Accident:** As you grow, you can feel insecure about where you are going. In fact, you go through many changes because situations force you to change. The accident is a way of exploring insecurities about how you are moving forward. The details surrounding the accident will reflect whether or not you feel in control and autonomous in moving forward.

It is important to note that the accident dream is not necessarily a warning of being on the wrong path. The mishap merely reflects the colliding aspects of where you are in life, and where you feel you should be. Accidents can symbolize your fears as you confront or collide with your other needs. Ambition can be thwarted by fear, or the need to make changes can collide with the feeling of being stuck.

Since a boat relies on the current, wind and outside elements to go forward, accidents involving water suggest the way emotions are driving you. Water accidents can portray fears about how circumstances feel beyond your control and are leading you forward.

Choppy water can be a message about feelings you are not confronting that would better serve you if you approached how you feel honestly. Calm water can portray the ways you attempt to go with the flow to master your forward movement.

Accidents involving motorized vehicles represent insecurities about your motivation and ambition. If the accident involves a car, it portrays insecurities about the choices you are making. If the accident involves a plane, you may feel insecure about aspirations as you embark in an upward direction. An accident by train can show the disappointment you feel in light of other's expectations of you. Tracks have been laid down for you, although you have a sense of not being able to follow them.

If you are driving or are responsible for the accident, you may be questioning your direction, but still feel autonomous and

28

empowered. If someone else is driving or has caused you to be in an accident, this other character should be considered in relation to their influence on your autonomy. This dream shows the power you give away and the key to how it holds you back.

Example: a mate driving you in a dream reveals the power you have given this person to make decisions for you. A parent driving you shows the power they hold over you because you allow it. Whomever drives you in a dream holds the key to what drives you in life. If the character is not involved in your life, then consider what part of you they might represent and how this aspect may be undermining your ability to move forward. Accident dreams usually occur when you are attempting to become more empowered, self-actualized and self-directed.

If the accident involves natural events or is the result of a natural disaster, it can be a way of dissolving your current foundation or belief structure to allow for more 'natural' changes within you. If the house is involved, it suggests certain areas of your life that are undergoing transformation. See also **Houses and Buildings** and **Natural Disasters**.

**Accountant:** The character that appears in your dream associated with finances can represent issues related to self worth. We often dream about money matters when we are feeling insecure about our finances to the point that we are not facing these feelings during the day. This type of dream can be a wake up call to get your finances in order so you can feel less stressed about it. The other symbolism can shed light on the feelings you may be exploring related to self worth through this character. See also **People**.

**Acid:** As a chemical or solvent that destroys or burns, acid reveals the way natural elements or your environment is affecting you. Suggesting a type of alchemy or transformation, acid does not make something disappear, it only 'reduces' it to its base or organic elements. Acid demonstrates how painful feelings may be festering on the surface and threaten to break through 'skin' or surface awareness. Through the transformation, you will discover the basics of what is really important to you. See also **Burning.**

**Acne:** Whenever a dream focuses on the face - it can be a message about 'keeping face' or credibility. Generally your appearance in a dream is a way of exploring self esteem or your self image. If something on your face (like a pimple or acne) diminishes your attractiveness, you may be exploring the idea that you are not expressing your true self or acknowledging your own beauty. If you are picking a pimple or trying to remove a blemish - the message can be about releasing ideas or feelings that are undermining your self image.

**Adolescent:** A teenager or adolescent is a character on the threshold of puberty and responsibility. Interacting with a person of this age can portray the ideas and feelings adopted at that point in your life. The type of interaction will show your current relationship to your sexual feelings or social responsibility as you explore changes. The adolescent in a dream is also symbolic of the development of an emerging side of you. This theme generally begins as accompanying an Unknown Child or giving birth to a baby as a representation of rebirth. When the child becomes an adolescent in the dream, it shows the growth and assimilation that is taking place when you are 're-parenting' yourself. See Unknown Child under **Archetypes and Universal Characters** and **People** and **Family**.

**Advertisement:** Seeing something on an ad or in a commercial can be a way of objectively exploring something prior to integrating it. New ideas or perspectives will sometimes appear 'out there for public view' as a way of testing it out. Seeing something in the news or in an advertisement is usually the first step in integrating difficult issues, such as the traits you may have adopted from your parents, but cannot 'own.' See also **Newspaper.**

**Affair:** A very common dream scenario involves dreaming that your partner is intimate with someone other than you. Although you may feel that your intuition is telling you something, remember that dreams use other people and their qualities to portray you. Consider the qualities of this interloper and whether or not it might represent an aspect of you that is being explored. As you make changes, you may feel insecure about the effects it will have on your relationship. You may dream of your partner with someone 'new' as a representation of the new you.

Although you may be in a fulfilling relationship, you can dream of intimacy with past partners. At some point in your life, you projected the power for self love upon your mate. It is as if they hold/held the power to make you feel good about yourself. Consciously you may feel that you are functioning independently in a current relationship, but since you dream of what you are not facing, the appearance of an 'old flame' can be activated when you feel uncertain about your value in a current relationship. These past partners embody the idea of self love - they appear as we explore and merge (sexual intimacy) with this potential to love ourselves. This must occur independently from the feedback we are currently receiving.

Since dreams allow for the free exploration of feelings, it is common to dream of sharing affection, sex or intimacy with people other than your mate. As you 'role play' by experiencing the different aspects of yourself, it can be portrayed by various characters, where you sometimes behave in a masculine way (mounting/dominating.) You are merely exploring your desire to be more aggressive. You may dream of being unusually sensitive or affectionate with another woman, or in a feminine way, as a way of 'embracing' or exploring the idea of increased sensitivity. The side of you this person represents and how you approach them in the dream, will feel 'clandestine,' only in proportion to how you are currently not 'embracing' or integrating this side of yourself in waking life. See also **Love** and **Anima/Animus.**

**Afraid:** Dreams are a safe environment to explore insecurities and fears. In fact, the vast majority of dreams involve some type of conflict. Dreaming allows difficulties we are facing to be 'acted out' through symbolism. Much inner shifting and growth occurs even while we are not remembering our dreams. When facing crisis, we are told to 'sleep on it.' When we wake up the situation always looks different. This is because much processing goes on in the dream state. Fear too, is diminished in this way.

When you wake up remembering the dream or feel afraid, you carry the strangeness of the dream back into consciousness. Often the bizarre symbols will stay with you as you explore its possible meaning.

Dreaming specifically arouses emotion as a wake up call (not necessarily bad) and feeling fear is a strong motivator for change. Even the most frightening dreams are a good sign that something powerful is stirring within and seeking expression. See **Nightmare** and **Shadow.**

**Ahead:** Seeing something ahead of you in a dream can portray your sense of where your path is leading you. If you are following a car then you may be moving ahead by following others without a clear sense of direction. Following a group of people would have the same message, especially if you are getting on public transportation. Explore the symbol that appears up ahead as a way of understanding how its activation or integration becomes a clue to how you can move forward successfully. If it is an abandoned **house**, it can symbolize outworn ideas; a **tree** can represent family dynamics that need to be considered. If the symbol appears dangerous, the dream is coaxing you toward initiation - where overcoming your sense of fear can set you free.

Usually what appears threatening in a dream is the personification of your fear. Understanding the symbol in its most positive light can help you overcome your fear. For example, a snake symbolizes shedding an old skin in preparation for rebirth; and abyss or ravine shows that you have reached an apex and may need to 'climb down' or learn new skills prior to climbing back up. See also **Placement and Perspective.**

**Air:** When air is the subject of a dream, something may be floating or suspended in a way that is portraying your current state of suspense. The object that is suspended can offer clues about how to move forward.

The air can be clear or dirty as a reflection of whether you may need to 'air something out' or to 'clear the atmosphere.' The temperature of the air can describe feelings of coolness or feeling 'hot' as in unprocessed anger. Filling something with air will often make it bigger, representing growth or expansion. Being unable to breathe is the same as feeling like you are not living in a healthy way or feeling that you are not getting what you need in life. See **Sky.**

**Air Raid:** See **Cover** and Airplane under **Vehicles and Places of Transportation.**

**Airplane and Airport:** The airplane, as a transportation symbol, signifies motivation and direction. Its association with flying can represent aspirations or your ability to 'soar.' You will usually dream of trying to catch a plane when you are making changes to your aspirations. This type of dream also occurs when you are attempting to let go of negative conditioning to feel more self assured. Missing a plane can symbolize a fear of failing. A plane that threatens to crash is another way of exploring your insecurities in light of the goals that you have set for yourself.

Airports and train stations are places of transition, and while the train depicts how you are breaking away from the tracks that were laid down for you as expectations of others, the airport represents ambition and is a place where you can 'fly' through expanded awareness and insight. Danger and the idea of crashing can reveal your insecurities about your ambitions. but does not necessarily mean that you will crash land. The dream is just allowing you to explore your insecurities so you might make necessary changes. It also allows you to strengthen your commitment to what you are trying to achieve.

Waking up within a dream to attempt the impossible, like flying can also be expressing a sense of power and accomplishment. It encourages the idea of how closely experience is tied to thought and beliefs. The flying dream generally occurs during periods of successful achievement or heightened inspiration. See **Vehicles and Places of Transportation.**

**Alcohol:** If you dream of drinking alcohol, you may be exploring the idea of alcohol dependency. We usually dream of what we are not acknowledging. Being drunk can also suggest 'intoxication' or feelings of exhilaration that you are not expressing during daily life. Alcohol is a mood altering substance, which allows you to express your unbridled nature. The purpose of dreams is to face the truth about what we fail to acknowledge and help us to express our true nature. If alcohol or being drunk is the theme of the dream, you may have lost your feelings of sensitivity when relating to your environment. If you are dreaming of rubbing alcohol, you may be aware that a type of healing requires that you take difficult or painful steps.

**Aliens:** Dreaming of UFOs or being threatened by aliens portrays how you are exploring aspects of yourself, which you find difficult to 'identify with.' Your sense of being different from the group (and how you feel about it) will be portrayed by how 'foreign' the characters appear in your dreams.

Unlike family (genetic or inherited self-dynamics,) friends, people (acquaintances that change you,) and even aborigines (the more organic side of you,) aliens would be considered natural creatures, they are just 'not from around here.' Being abducted by aliens is actually suggesting how you are being 'kidnapped' by your fear of conformity because you are not being authentic. Fitting in with the group often comes at the price of your real nature. A robot would also be offering a message that you are not being authentic or are just going through the motions to fit in. See also **Galaxy** and **Flying Saucer**.

**Ambulance:** The ambulance ties together the idea of crisis, the need to be nurtured and as a vehicle, guidance in making directional choices. Like dreams of calling Nine One One, or seeing something written in red ink, the ambulance can bring a high level of needed focus to the idea that you feel you are in a 'state of emergency,' not physically but perhaps spiritually or emotionally. You may feel out of control of directional decisions or may need to become more self directed.

If the ambulance is unusual, the required change you may need to make - is not necessarily something you have tried before. The aspects surrounding the ambulance need to be considered for added insight about how you are moving forward in life. If the ambulance crashes into your vehicle, it suggests how fear and insecurity may be keeping you from moving forward. If the ambulance is carrying belongings or other unusual items, explore what those symbols represent to understand how carrying something (like an idea) is taxing your autonomy. See **Vehicles and Places of Transportation**.

**Amulet and Necklace:** Rich with mythological significance, being given an amulet, stone or necklace can represent insight that can shed light upon your unique talents or abilities. At the same time, your heart can be blocked by the idea or value you place on such a public display of what you hold to be precious.

34

**Amusement Park:** This is a place where children overcome a sense of fear in exchange for excitement, By returning to a childlike state of innocence, you are exploring taking risks in an effort to find happiness and exhilaration in social situations. The funhouse, mirrors and rickety rides offer a playground for self-reflection as you move forward. Being on a ride that is out of control can symbolize relying on something or someone to achieve success. It can also represent the idea that you are moving too fast or taking unnecessary risks in what you are doing. See Jalopy under **Vehicles and Transportation** and Rickety Structures under **Houses and Buildings**.

**Anatomy and Body Parts:** The parts of the body appear commonly in dreams because we are so 'body conscious' in daily life. Some parts grow and fall out, like teeth, fingernails and hair. They represent growth and where you stand in relationship to your sense of time and the need to let go of outworn ideas.

You lose your **teeth** during monumental times of life and in the same way, losing teeth will depict a threshold, or turning point. Teeth falling out can also be a message about credibility, or saying something that does not express the truth of what you feel. **Fingernails** and **hair** grow and need to be trimmed, suggesting both wisdom and how it must be pruned at times, to promote healthy growth. Hair can represent vanity and self-reflection, regardless of where it appears on the body. **Eyebrows** frame your way of viewing things and 'move' as a way of suggesting how you express yourself or respond. Plucking, grooming, shaving and brushing hair reflects changes in how you view your 'beauty' or self-image. Making changes to your hair can symbolize a change in attitude. Grooming someone else's eyebrows or hair can suggest adopting characteristics of what this person represents. It can also show the influence they have on you.

The **head** is the seat of your personality and way of thinking. If the head is not yours, or separate from the body, it suggests a disconnection between what you are saying and doing. The **mouth** portrays both, communication skills, and how you may need to 'chew' things over to digest them. The **jaw** has more of an emphasis on what you say, but can also represent holding firm. You can '**nose**' your way into something that perhaps, 'doesn't smell right.' You can '**face**'

35

something or give 'ear' to the truth in dreams where the ears offer an objective way of seeing how you fail to listen.

Beauty is in the '**eye**' of the beholder in terms of self esteem. You may experience a real 'eye opening' message when seeing an eye is the same as disowning the sense of 'I' and so, the message gives you an objective view of an eyeball. In this way, sensory symbols are usually a message about being more observant or responsive in daily life.

The **chest** and **abdomen** house your feelings and suggest issues related to emotions. The **arms** signify empowerment and your ability to provide, give and take, while the **legs** take you forward in life and represent movement, direction and following a path that better reflects who you are. Dreaming of impaired arms and legs can portray issues that are holding you back or not allowing you to move freely and take what you need. **Hands** and **fingers** are an extension of the arms, signify trying to 'grasp' something or to take what you feel you need. As an extension of the legs, **feet** provide balance and may symbolize getting 'cold feet' or putting the 'foot in the mouth.' See **Shoes.**

**Skin** represents the most obvious aspect of who you are, and can symbolize the self from a sense of surface awareness, as in 'only skin deep.' Focusing on something on the skin can represent something bugging you. The **back** often portrays responsibilities, while **bones** and **blood** portray basic traits that are at the core of who you are, or what lies below the surface: bones being solid and structure oriented, and blood being your essence or life force. Seeing blood on any object is an objective way of exploring feelings that remain below the surface. See **Blood.**

**Genitals** have associations that transcend the simple idea of sexual feelings. Breasts often relate to how you explore self-nurturing ideas, while female genitalia for a woman will signify her essence or connection to life. To a man, female body parts suggest sensitivity, while he explores his 'underdeveloped' traits associated with femininity, like sensitivity or intuition. Male genitalia observed by a woman often has associations with becoming more assertive or aggressive. For a man, his genitals represent his life force and sexuality. See also **Anima and Animus**.

**Ancient:** When a symbol appears to you as being 'ancient,' it can have different meanings. First, being 'old' or 'antique' can suggest a part of you associated with the symbol that is outworn, or no longer true in terms of the person you are becoming. Ancient buildings can portray ideas constructed in the past that still influence you today. Ancient artifacts will have associations with the symbol discovered (see **Vase, Stone, Amulet, Jewels** and **Chest.**) Secondly, when you discover something ancient and profound as a treasure, it suggests finding a deeper connection to experience by exploring inspiration or spiritual beliefs. Many people explore deep transformation through imagery that is associated with temples (that house our beliefs) or artifacts (as a representation of what we carry, even while it is old). As we change, fundamental aspects remain unchanged by time. Life peels away the layers that reveal your ancient or unchanging nature. This 'ancient' symbol can represent the core of who you are that is timeless and valuable, offering clues to your real identity and destiny. Explore whether the dream is suggesting letting go of the outworn or tapping the part of you that is valuable yet buried.

**Anesthetic:** Where alcohol allows your emotions to be expressed freely, an anesthetic 'dulls' the senses. Without being able to feel, you are hiding pain in a way that might keep you from understanding and processing your feelings so you can grow. Dreaming of being drugged, drowsy or sleepy suggests how repressed parts of you are seeking the first stages of expression. Dreaming that someone else has drugged you shows the power you have given this person to have control over you. Often this other person represents the **Shadow** or how one side of you undermines the power of another, as in aggression undermining feelings, or fear undermining assertiveness.

**Angels:** Like birds, angels can represent the higher aspects of the mind breaking through to offer inspiration or direction. No matter what transpires in life, you have a sense of this higher self within you that can carry you through all difficulty. If the angel offered a message, it should be given careful consideration. Angel dreams often occur with messages about the future. See **Prophetic Dreams**.

**Anger:** A person who can process anger easily will feel anxiety in a dream, but not anger. If you are clearly angry in your dream, then look for how you might be repressing anger in daily life. This is an emotion, which we learn early to repress, and each of us processes anger in different ways. Therefore, you may dream about other characters acting with anger against you. This is the only way the person 'who is never angry' will have of processing and integrating this 'unpleasant' emotion. A ferocious animal attacking you is a clear example of how anger is portrayed in a dream. Since you cannot own the emotion during the day, you experience it as something 'wild and uncontrollable' attacking you in the dream.

**Anima-Animus:** The Anima and Animus represent female and male aspects being activated in the opposite sexes. Men and women possess feminine and masculine traits equally and in dreams, the anima may appear to a male as a highly feminized figure. The animus can appear as the male 'protector' or associate who appears to the female in dreams. Men will dream of doing feminine things, like wearing a dress, while a woman may do things that would be considered masculine like dominating or mounting another woman. Both are exploring the opposite traits of their gender in an effort to adopt them. These type of dreams are coaching the male toward sensitivity, while the woman may be exploring empowerment through a dream of domination. These qualities emerge as a reminder of how the female must develop her assertiveness or power to provide for herself, while the male must develop sensitivity or introspection in expressing and blending his feminine side into his masculinity. Both the female and male qualities are necessary in authentic empowerment and balance.

Often this Archetype will appear as someone in a dream that wants to be intimate - while you thwart these unsolicited advances. Since this energy is seeking integration and expression - their behavior can show how this is emerging within you. Sharing intimacy with this Archetype portrays how these qualities are being adopted or integrated. Having them tease or question you, while approving or disapproving of your response can be a type of initiation into authenticity. There is also a **Shadow** side to this Archetype. Since the Shadow represents qualities that remain outside of awareness because they were deemed unacceptable, often there will be something quirky about this Archetype when it first makes its appearance. It can present as a **Trickster**, challenging you to confront your inconsistencies in thought. Or, this character can appear bizarre or handicapped as you examine the dysfunctional expression of its energy.

Dreams of this type show a sequence of meeting an unusual character of the opposite sex who wants to be intimate. They may bother or challenge you, or you may dream of an immediate attraction as you move to adopt the qualities this character represents. The intimacy stage shows the actual integration or acceptance of these qualities as you move toward a higher level of self actualization. See also **Archetypes and Universal Characters**.

**Animals:** The mammalian side of the brain developed when we evolved from our nocturnal existence to become social creatures. This was a time when emotions and facial expressions developed, which are associated with parenting and social exchanges. Similarly, in dreams, animals often symbolize emotions, expression and the response of your more 'wild,' uncivilized, yet natural self. This part of your nature can be at odds with the inner critic that coaxes you toward conformity.

Since we view animals as acting spontaneously toward their urges without social restrictions, animals often represent normal urges that are breaking through conscious controls. If you dream of being threatened or attacked by an animal, some part of your emotions or behavior (usually anger or sexual feelings) may have erupted or surfaced in way that felt like it 'came out of the woods.' You do not 'own' the energy and so it threatens you. If the animal's teeth are a focal point, there is a sense that these emotions or feelings will cut through skin awareness to have expression. As frightening as these dreams may appear, they are merely the way your natural expression comes up against your desire to 'be good' or follow the rules. All symbols in a dream personify aspects of you and the animal appearing in a dream is no different.

**Wild animals** portray the need to express your authentic feelings in an unbridled way, while domesticated animals portray how you have been conditioned to guard them.

**Apes, chimps** and other **primates** can suggest mimicking social behavior or acting mischievously as a way to stir up a response in others. **Gorillas** are more powerful and unpredictable, reflecting the power of emotion and urges to break through social restraints. **Bears** too, can represent sudden protective responses, or defense mechanisms active in daily life. Bears are associated with childhood and maternal influences.

**Cats** portray your instinctual and sensitive nature that avoids domestication, and is somewhat manipulative. **Dogs** are 'faithful' and loving, representing the easy expression of feelings and love in your relationship with others. The **Wild Dogs**, like **jackals** and **coyotes**, guard the way into the hidden realm of the subconscious. Meeting their snarling teeth portrays your own fears about digging within to discover the truth about how you feel. These types of dogs can appear as Archetypes when you are going through a transformative process. Carnivorous animals can signify how you can be 'eaten up' by being afraid to allow your emotions free reign.

**Elephants** 'never forget' and are enormous emotional beings. They portray the power of your emotions to trample over ideas that hold you back. Often, dreams of elephants can reveal long held emotional pain that is coming to the surface. Beasts of burden such as the **donkey** and **ox,** suggest being saddled or yoked to responsibility, while the 'animal-ness' of this symbolism suggests that it is unnatural or too self-restrictive. The **pig** is a symbol of satisfaction and enjoyment, sometimes at the expense of all else. In many myths, pigs are sacred and represent the family. **Lions** and tigers reflect masculine and feminine aspects of the power of sexuality. Both are blindly driven to devour for sustenance, and can portray the power of your innate drives that appear beyond your control when you take what you feel you need.

Domesticated animals, like the **cow** and **bull** can represent territorial issues, where the cow is motherly and passive, while the bull is father-like and aggressive They suggest the care-giving qualities of your parents and how you have adopted these qualities through domestication. The bull offers additional insight, in that it explodes when it sees 'red,' representing feelings that remain below the surface. It can be a symbol of exploring how you are currently processing anger and what part your parents played in 'bequeathing' this trait to you. Additionally, the cow is a cosmic and sacred symbol of expanded awareness and evolution.

The **horse** is associated with 'spirit' and exuberance, suggesting the enthusiasm to 'win' or race forward. Of all the animals, the horse will sometimes reflect communication taking place between what you think and what you feel, since there is a belief that horses are 'psychic' or respond instinctively to our thoughts as we ride them. The zebra is a unique creature and it is said that no two **zebras** have the same pattern, therefore reflecting the uniqueness of spirit.

**Goats** and **rams** portray drives associated with sexuality, impishness and playful curiosity, while sheep and lambs 'follow the herd' and are corralled, suggesting that you feel that you are being too passive in a situation. **Deer** can signify the gentleness of the soul and your innocence and vulnerabilities. **Rabbits** can reflect reproduction, intuition and a sense of sacrifice since they are low on the food chain.

**Ground burrowing** animals represent both hiding and digging beneath the surface. The soft eyed (innocence) of many of the furry (protective) and burrowing (hiding) creatures, like **squirrels, rabbits** and **groundhogs** are rich with symbolism related to 'emotions stirring below the surface.' The **fox** may represent your 'craftiness' in hiding your real feelings or an inability to commit or make choices. **Rats** and mice are often considered to be 'pests' or associated with what is 'unclean' or forbidden. Rats can be 'stowaways,' hiding in ships, or in the shadows, representing abandoning something, sneaking around or escaping like a 'dirty rat.' Used in scientific laboratories, both can symbolize 'experimenting' with expressing natural urges.

The **Hippopotamus** presents a sort of hybrid, in that it is an animal associated with diving beneath the water, where its large size is indicative of the enormous emotions that can be submerged. See Alligator and Crocodile under **Reptiles.**

**Ankle:** The ankle, as a symbol ties together the idea of feet (the path) and the leg (taking a stand or the power of will.) It provides for flexibility portraying your sense of direction. To twist your ankle in a dream can suggest looking at alternatives or making a few changes to your path. See also **Anatomy and Body Parts**.

**Answer:** When characters respond or give you an answer in a dream, it is usually because you are not acknowledging something important. You can see it as "you" saying something to yourself. Some side of you is questioning what you are doing and the answer should be explored as a type of direction that you are not considering.

If we ask a character something in a dream and they do not answer, the dream is exploring the idea that we are out of sync in some type of change. The anxiety that is often associated with dreaming occurs because you dream of what you are not facing. Anxiety is important because it stirs emotion and brings a necessary change in perspective 'to the surface.' In this way, a puzzling answer or statement is made, which leaves you feeling something. Feeling uneasy is the first step toward making the necessary change.

Answer dreams usually coincide with times when you are on the wrong path or being encouraged to follow another. The words may appear irrelevant and you may find yourself waking up from a bizarre dream with only the feeling of being 'disturbed.' The waters of consciousness are now stirred, to allow for a more objective way of approaching your circumstance. See also **Fear.**

**Ant:** An ant or other insect can appear in a dream when you are not dealing with a situation that is bugging you. The small size of this insect can also portray vulnerability or feeling insignificant. Seeing ants working industriously can personify following a course that perhaps is not your own. See also **Insects.**

**Antique:** Heirlooms suggest your heritage or family traits that you protect. Antique furniture can portray the ideas that you rest upon that would be associated with the past. If there is something faulty in the furniture - these ideas can no longer be 'stored' or you can no longer rest on them (as in furniture). An antique piece of jewelry can personify what you feel is valuable and precious about yourself - and also your desire for offspring. An antique carving or archeological artifact captures both the idea of the past and what is buried 'underground' or within the subconscious. Some aspect of this artifact is a representation of you. See also **Ancient.**

**Anus:** A dream that focuses on the anus is a symbol about elimination. Whatever symbol is associated with it needs to be considered as a message about letting go, or coming to terms with a type of integration that is blocked. Also see **Anatomy and Body Parts**.

**Anxiety:** Human beings are 'self-organizing' systems forced to interact with an environment that is always changing. We seem to use the dream state as 'training wheels' in exploring and making any changes. Life's natural movement toward entropy is unfolding all around us, even while we try to achieve stasis and a sense of the familiar. In higher organisms (like humans) this pursuit of stasis is achieved through the nervous system. Dreaming offers a sensory vehicle to process anxiety in a safe environment. Anxiety is a common theme in dream specifically because it is one of the most important reasons for dreaming. When disturbing things happen in our dreams, they are meant to do just that: disturb consciousness and help us to let go. See **Nightmare, Answer,** and **Attack or Being Chased**.

**Apes:** This animal is most like a human, yet we use the word 'ape' to describe how we mimic others. It might be a clue that you are following the crowd and at the expense of expressing who you really are. The ape is also unpredictable and amusing, and can personify the **Trickster** within you - jarring you from taking yourself so seriously.

When the Ape appears frightening it can symbolize the power of your body that doesn't feel under your control. For example, it is common for a woman going through menopause to experience this power as a frightening Ape. In some ways the Ape will personify your idea of your most uncivilized and wild/natural power - that part of you that is purely instinctual. See also **Gorilla** and **Animals**.

**Apocalypse:** Like many of our ancient myths, battles can take place between the various worlds or levels of existence, which end in an apocalypse or end of the world scenario. These types of dreams occur when the 'old way' of doing something must come to pass so that a 'new world' can be created in its place. See **Natural Disasters** and **Landscape and Scenery**.

**Apple:** The apple can be associated with the idea of desire and something that is forbidden. Since we are told to 'eat an apple a day' for health, the apple can be a symbol of necessary healing. A dream that focuses on an apple can be a symbolic portrayal of how you are moving to satisfy your needs for fulfillment, but feel somewhat guilty in doing so. See **Food.**

**Archetypes and Universal Characters:** When we move through various stages of change, we will have different types of dreams. Conflict oriented and **Chase** dreams occur while we explore the necessary transformation or integration that must occur. The **Natural Disaster** type dream, **Crow, Raven, Phoenix** or **Fiery Ram** often appear to symbolize archetypes representing sacrificing the past foundation in order to move into the future. As we begin the transformative journey or rebirth, we may dream of accompanying an **Unknown Child**, then find ourselves with an older child as a representation of the birthing, cultivation or re-parenting of new aspects. We might then dream of **natural landscapes** with furniture erected of natural objects as we get more earthy and grounded in who we are and what we need to succeed. Finally, we can meet the **Wise Guide** as a representation of the wisdom that has developed within, and our new ability to be inspired as we grow empowered to become self-directed.

The many characters that appear in dreams represent an aspect of you as you change and grow. **Police** stop you in dreams when you are doing something 'illegal' or when an evolving aspect is transcending the critical or disciplinarian tapes of conscience. **Waiters** and Waitresses appear when you are exploring a more appropriate way of nourishing yourself. **Firemen** can symbolize the defense mechanisms that 'douse' your real feelings and emotions. At the same time, the fireman can be a clue that passion isn't achieving expression. Babies or the Unknown Child will represent the birthing of your new identity, while the death of someone suggests elements, which must 'pass on.' You might know that you are somehow responsible for this 'death' by feeling victimized or pursued, but only you can allow for the death and rebirth. You can be 'suddenly saddled' with the responsibility of caring for this 'Unknown Child ,' which suggests how you are not quite sure what to do with your emerging and 'new identity.'

**Intruders** appear when you believe you are being invaded, or when you have revealed your intimate self with someone and felt uncomfortable. The stalker or intruder can also personify qualities that remain unintigrated but are a key to your empowerment. **Abductors** who try to kidnap you reveal a part of you that you are having difficulty integrating. You may have gotten caught up in a competitive situation that brought forward traits you are not comfortable with and in a sense, you felt 'abducted.' (see **Aliens**) These types of encounters reveal Archetypes, such as the **Animus, Anima**, dark one, monster, devil or **Shadow**, which will always represent that part of your power, which appears frightening or unknown to you.

Women being 'kissed' by a monster in dreams will often coincide with the onset of menstruation and menopause, or those times in life when her body demonstrates a power that is beyond her control. Meeting this character always coincides with monumental stages of her development. Think about the character that attempted to kidnap you or break into "your house." If a woman dreams of an attractive but frightening male in this way, he represents her ability to move fearlessly through the world. Accessing the power that this character holds over you often represents a power that remains dormant, which can lead to integration and wholeness.

The **Wise Woman** or **Wise Man** are often reflective of intuition and how it guides you. These types of characters appear commonly when you are going through a difficult period of transformation. They reveal a profound sense of guidance, but also how you are accessing and becoming more seasoned.

Jung explored common symbols in dreams that possessed universal meaning. While symbols can represent personal issues, our mythologies portray the universal themes that appear commonly in dreams. Jung called these elements Archetypes:

1. **The Persona** is the mask you wear into the world, and in dreams, your evolving nature and potential takes form as your Persona depicted by the many characters you meet. The Persona is also explored through the symbolism of clothing. See **Persona**.

2. **The Shadow** is your rejected and repressed aspects. At some point, you may decide that some part of you is unacceptable because it suggested weakness, fear of fitting in with the group, or unresolved anger. In actuality, these aspects become the power of untapped potential. The Shadow is often represented by the Intruder, Pursuer, or Monster. See **Shadow**.

Freud described repression as how "a shadow falls over the ego," paralyzing its ability to perceive in the present. Through projection, one fails to observe objectively in the moment, but witnesses an overlay where the past is infused over the present. Since you cannot 'own' these qualities, you discover these aspects in others, as the 'enemy.'

As a type of defense mechanism, he believed repression worked to keep the truth inaccessible. He also explored fixation and fetishes as being organized by ideas that evoked a sense of attraction and repulsion at the same time. An urge that initially sought pleasure brought instead, displeasure as the pathway from urge to satisfaction was distorted.

This convergence of feeling is at the root of the intense emotional response or charge that is created when you encounter your Shadow in another. Understanding the Shadow is central to your empowerment and wellness. When you can understand and transcend the initial displeasure arising in this type of encounter, you are able to access the truth of what you fail to acknowledge within.

While Freud hinted at it, Jung pioneered the study of the Shadow and referred to it as the repressed and undeveloped aspects of the personality. Their diverging ideas created a schism between them, demonstrating the enormous power that the Shadow holds over us in our relationships. Although they both explored the unconscious to understand repression, their personal experiences led them to describe its contents differently. Where Freud projected his sexual frustration into his interpretations, Jung came to project his strong need for spiritual freedom. In their encounter, Freud may have been threatened by Jung's sense of freedom and wholeness, while Jung bristled at the idea of such a limited system of interpretation.

Jung described projection as changing "the world into the replica of one's unknown face. The more projections are thrust between the subject and the environment, the harder it is for the ego to see through its illusions." He described the Shadow as those dark, unwanted, and unrecognized qualities of the ego that were deemed negative and ultimately repressed. Understanding the creation, repression and ultimate resurrection of the Shadow, provides a basic understanding of why we dream. While you sleep, those sides of you that remain dormant are given expression. When the dream conjures fear, you can be certain that its symbolism offers clues to your empowerment by integrating the elements associated with the Shadow.

**3. The Anima / Animus** represent the female and male aspects of the opposite sexes. Men and women possess feminine and masculine traits and in dreams, the anima may appear to a male as a highly feminized figure. The animus is the male 'protector' or associate who appears to the female. Men will dream of doing feminine things, like wearing a dress, while a woman may do things that would be considered masculine like dominating or mounting another woman. These type of dreams are coaching the male toward sensitivity, while the woman may be exploring empowerment through a dream of domination. These qualities emerge as a reminder of how the female must develop her assertive or masculine potential, while the male must be sensitive or introspective in expressing and blending his feminine side into his masculinity. Both the female and male qualities are necessary in authentic empowerment and balance. See **Anima - Animus**.

**4. The Unknown Child** symbolizes your innocence and potential. Like the soul, it represents vulnerability and helplessness, but also aspirations and insight into integrating potential. As you evolve, you sometimes dream of accompanying a baby or young child suggesting this 'new' and emerging side of your Persona. The fact that you may not know where the child came from, or what you should do with it, suggests the way that who you are becoming today is constantly growing or experiencing rebirth as you grow to meet the future.

**5. The Wise Man** acts as a guide or helper in dreams. You may meet a religious icon, an old man as a teacher, father or some other unknown authority figure. Often, they will say special words of wisdom and offer guidance. This figure represents the higher self and your ability to transcend difficulty. It is important to record the message or symbols that are associated with this character as a way of understanding your way through the transformative landscape. Representing masculine or productive elements, they often present the keys to your social success.

**6. The Great Mother** can appear as a real mother or grandmother, suggesting your adopted nurturing qualities. Offering reassurance or direction, Jung also thought that the Old Woman represented the 'unattractive' aspects of the feminine, appearing as a Witch or old Bag Lady. In this case, she can be associated with guilt, seduction, dominance and death. This duality suggests that although the mother is the giver of life, she can also be jealous of how you become self-sufficient. Representing your critical tapes turned inward, meeting the Old Woman as a negative character can help you move beyond repression and dis-ease. Meeting the positive figure usually coincides with the male moving actively toward intimacy, or the female moving toward increased self-esteem.

**7. The Trickster** is the cosmic jester of the dreamscape and portrays the unconscious active in consciousness. The psyche has an amazing and clever way of injecting humor into dream symbolism in an effort to jar the status quo. This humorous character straddles the same psychic trading post where inspiration is packaged and sold as spirituality. Manifesting in many forms, he stands at the psychic crossroad, pointing like the scarecrow in the Wizard of Oz. His antics reveal the ridiculous way that you believe you must make choices. There are many roads and the right road is sometimes just the pathway exposing the contradiction inherent in absolutes. In the middle road between good and evil is your willingness jump into the unknown.

The Trickster offers a puzzle and asks you to dance awhile with ambiguity, so life's deeper mysteries can be revealed. Portrayed in a Freudian slip, it is Trickster who plants the whoopee cushion in the psyche, triggering laughter when you know that the time is not appropriate. Humor often arises when you perceive an incongruity.

Cloaked as the Fool or Vagabond, he points to the middle way between absolutes or the conflicting ideas that have stunted your evolution.

The Raven, Crow or Coyote appear in myths asking the hero to sacrifice the body in return for metamorphosis. Often presenting you with a wild card of possibilities, the Trickster of the psyche is not afraid to send you out with mismatched shoes during an important presentation when you are in the 'wrong place.' Teaching a lesson of humility, you find this Jester of the inner landscape, making you laugh at yourself in all of your serious attempts to be certain.

Trickster represents the power of humor that allows you to see your inner contradictions. Instead of finding your 'home in the absolute,' you are forced out like a hobo in search of a train. Humiliated and riding in a boxcar, you encounter everything you believed you'd never see. You have no choice but to shake your head and laugh when the rug is pulled out from beneath your interior house of cards. "Oh my, is this what life feels like down here in the gutter? I can't tell you why, but I suddenly feel alive again."

Trickster inspires the late night comedian who says what nobody else would dare say. He makes you blurt out the comical truth when in all gravity, you have found yourself trapped in your illogical ideas. Trickster inspires dreams of going to school in your underwear, when what you most want is to abide by the golden rule. It is Trickster who removes the bathroom walls, in dreams where you have no choice but to 'relieve yourself' in public. "Let go...be intimate...find your human side and live." He is the breath of fresh air found at the top of the mountain or sometimes, face down in a puddle, in your migratory journey across the psychic landscape.

In myths, what Trickster does is always the opposite of what is considered sacred. Like the process of dreaming, Trickster leads you through stages in mysterious steps to 'trick' you into growth. We see this in American Indian stories that are humorously interwoven with bits and pieces of truth and insight. In the same way, dreams offer a non-rational way of perceiving experience, beyond the defense mechanisms created by rote and reason. Trickster keeps you from taking yourself too seriously. As a powerful and transformative aspect of the psyche, when a character appears that makes you feel uncomfortable or silly, you meet the great shape shifter as the potent and transformative power of Trickster. See also **People** and **Attack or Being Chased.**

**Arm:** The arm is associated with what you are holding or a sense of responsibility. It is also a symbol or actively doing something to have your needs met. The wrist suggests flexibility in meeting your needs. Arms can also represent responsibilities we feel we have - while the dream can be exploring the idea of releasing this sense of responsibility. We are generally aware of our responsibilities - so dreaming of arms that are dysfunctional is how we explore holding when we should release. See also **Anatomy and Body Parts**.

**Armor:** Dreaming of armor is the defensive posture you take to protect your feelings. Being given armor denotes how this behavior may have been adopted as a child. Women will sometimes dream of a gun as a symbol of sexual feelings that feel overpowering. See also **Weapons and Utensils.**

**Army:** Dreaming of being in an army denotes how you are operating with a new sense of discipline or restriction. Being invaded by soldiers portrays insecurities about conformity and authority. Rather than confronting restriction, symbolizing disciplinarian or critical tapes, being a part of an army reflects how you give in to defensive tendencies.

**Arriving and Leaving:** To have the sense that you 'arrive' in your dream can portray your journey toward achievement. You may arrive on time or **Late,** in relation to how you view your journey in life. Awaiting the arrival of someone else will describe an emerging part of you that will soon be 'coming' onto the scene to be transformed or integrated. Leaving or having a dream that focuses on someone else leaving is a way of exploring the idea of closure and transformation. See **Vehicles and Places of Transportation.**

**Arrow:** Dreaming of shooting arrows is usually a way of focusing on your goals or identifying what you are trying to achieve. Interestingly enough, just like the mythical cupid, f you are struck by an arrow, the dream is opening you to intimacy. Anything that penetrates the skin to reveal blood, is symbolizing how feelings come to the surface. If you shoot an arrow and miss the mark, you may not be aiming in the right direction. The dream can be suggesting a necessary shift in focus that will allow you to succeed. See also **Bow.**

**Ascending:** Dreaming of going up shows how you are taking 'steps' toward an expanded way of viewing experience such as a spiritual awakening or a desire to rise above difficulty. See **Placement and Perspective** and **Houses and Buildings**.

**Ashes:** Seeing ashes from a **Fire** is a sense that something important is being reduced to its base elements. This is an organic symbol of allowing the past to be transformed so that you can grow to meet the future. Often the burnt remains can symbolize your inability to let go of responsibilities that are not yours and must disintegrate as part of your rebirth. Like the phoenix that rises from the ashes of the past, this is actually a positive symbol. Ashes in the air, blocking your ability to see signify an inability to let go of the past or to see your way clearly into the future.

**Ass:** Beasts of burden suggest being saddled to responsibility, while the 'animal-ness' of these creatures suggest that it is not natural. The donkey is stubborn and can portray how you fail to see how you are yoked to responsibility that is not really yours. See also **Anus** and **Animals.**

**Atmosphere:** The atmosphere or setting of a dream is an important aspect that can portray the condition of your 'inner' landscape. Being in space can portray uncertainty about your direction - or feeling that you are taking a path that others may not support. It is not necessarily negative. You may feel alone in your decision, but this can be a prerequisite if you are making changes. If the atmosphere is dark - you are exploring ideas that are hidden from consciousness. If the atmosphere feels oppressive, you may need to make more room in your life for your ambitions. A fiery atmosphere can portray anger or the need to express feelings that are bottled up. A cloudy or gloomy atmosphere can represent feeling depression - although an impending storm can be the first sign that new life is stirring within. See also **Air**.

**Atomic Bomb:** The atomic bomb is one of the most searched symbols on our website. Its association with fallout or devastation embodies feelings that can remain below the surface, while capturing your fear of facing the truth of a situation because of the fallout that may ensue. Any explosion signifies the release of repressed anger or emotion of some type. The natural energy released by this 'man-made' device shows the extent of the repression, but also the necessity of releasing feelings so you can be renewed and open to a changing world. In a dream, seeing the explosion of an atomic bomb and its threat of 'radio-activity,' can also warn of the psychological manifestation of physical symptoms due to the inability to recognize and process anger.

**Atonement:** Praying or seeking forgiveness for something often reflects your inability to apply forgiveness toward others and especially yourself. When you forgive, you give nothing away that you really need anyway. When you learn to let the past go, you can release the burden that you carry with you. Receiving a blessing or religious symbol is the stirring of spiritual feelings or finding meaning in adversity.

**Attack or Being Chased:** As frightening as it seems, the chase dream is a common dream theme for the 20 something crowd entering the work

51

force. When we are young, we are uncertain about the 'code of conduct' or the behaviors that are required of us. The fast pace at which we may be forced to adopt new identities in the work place, brings a past way of being in opposition with a new way of being. Being chased reflects the non-integrated aspects of your evolving identity currently in conflict. This dream also happens frequently when we are moving, divorcing or making significant changes to our identity.

Being pursued or attacked is the 'internal drama' of one side of you questioning your behavior as you enter new situations. Like the voice of the parents, who taught you about what you should or shouldn't do, these tapes continue to play as dream characters that emerge each time a new situation calls you to become something you may not be comfortable with.

During daily life, the Shadow or non-integrated qualities within you, can be masked and take form as drama 'out there' when what is really going on is drama 'in here.' Just as these encounters encourage you to grow, dreams challenge you in the same way. The most frightening dreams are simply a call to acknowledge, integrate new characteristics and discard old ones as you evolve. As you grow to meet new situations at various stages of your life, these pursuit dreams become quite common and fade away as your sense of self has become more clearly defined. Similarly, conflict has a way of dissipating in your life once you have 'composed the inner terrain' enough to have developed self-esteem and self-knowledge.

Ferocious animals will attack in dreams, when your emotions have erupted 'beyond your control,' feeling wild and foreign to you during the day. See **Blood** and **Animals**.

Finally, there are times when you are the pursuer or attacker in a dream. Commonly, you will have a dream of attacking someone else or witnessing someone being killed and do nothing about it, even though you would never do that in real life. In the same way that someone dying represents the passing of an old or outworn way of being, not doing anything when someone is 'eliminated' speaks to how you let go of the outworn.

If you see the situation more like an assassination, you might consider whether you are allowing something to continue (such as an affair) that your psyche may see as an assassination of character. How you felt about being the attacker will determine whether 1) there is 'remorse' in the sense that subconsciously, you know you are killing off an important part of you that shouldn't be discarded or 2) 'neutral' because you know that what has passed is no longer necessary. See also **Enemy**, **Murder**, **Death**, **Nightmare** and **Weapons and Utensils**.

**Attic:** The attic is associated with the past and ideas that we have stored away. Upper rooms suggest rising above something or spiritual ideas. The attic suggests ideas that we 'pack away' as in repressed but associated with issues of conscience. See **Houses and Buildings**.

**Attraction and Rejection:** Often you will dream of being attracted or intimate with a famous person or someone other than your mate. Consider the qualities this person demonstrates and how you are exploring whether or not they are active within you. When you dream of an unusual power that someone holds over you, the idea that you are giving your power away to this person is being explored. Dreaming of being rejected in your affections can actually symbolize a need to let go of the side of you associated with this person. If you dream of an unusual way of moving forward as in levitation, you are exploring a new way of feeling lighter in your approach to what had seemed like a difficult situation. Magnetism can also symbolize how things are connected or the circular journey of life where changes take place but the core of who you are remains unchanged. See also **Rejection**, **Anima/Animus**, **Love** and **People**.

**Audience:** Performing in front of others is a common dream because it is a way of working through self-judgment and insecurity. In most cases, there is embarrassment as you meet the severity of your inner critic. When performing in front of others brings joy, this is a measure of your self worth and often coincides with an intense period of transformation, which has culminated in your success. Being unable to perform because you have lost something, suggests that you are on the wrong pathway. Whatever is lost will offer an important clue in understanding your authentic nature and overcoming insecurity. See **Purses, Wallets, Luggage, Jewels and Keys**.

**Authority:** People in our dreams that are considered authority, such as bosses, principals and government officials signify that part of the psyche that organizes and controls the assimilation of new ideas. Often we dream of these figures when we are making big changes, as if some aspect of the psyche needs to approve of a new way of thinking. See also **Police**.

**Automobile:** The automobile is a classic symbol of motivation, and reflects whether or not you are feeling autonomous as you move forward in life. If you are driving and the vehicle is out of control, you may be questioning the choices you are making. If you are riding as a passenger, you may not recognize how you are not taking the reins of responsibility for where you are going. You have given power over to the person driving the vehicle and may be needlessly blaming them for failing. If it is a parent driving you, there may be unconscious attitudes or criticisms you have adopted that are holding you back or diminishing your self-esteem.

These types of dreams suggest the condition in which you are currently moving forward. The type of vehicle, and whether or not you are driving, in control or being driven, will portray your present sense of autonomy. See **Vehicles and Places of Transportation**.

**Autumn:** This is a time of year when all things on the earth turn back for regeneration. Stripped of foliage, all living things return to their roots to be renewed. Autumn in a dream portrays the idea that a period of outward building to achieve success is becoming introspective. Sensing that the season has changed to autumn can coincide with having children moving out of the house or going into retirement. Although the earth moves toward incubation, an enormous amount of energy is building for a springtime to come.

**Avalanche:** Generally snow and ice, the avalanche occurs when a mountain or your solid belief structure gives way. When it is snow, it suggests that hiding beneath a cold exterior will no longer serve you. When it is the dirt of a landslide, it portrays the mountain of a hardened perspective giving way so that a new perspective will rise in its place. See **Natural Disasters** and **Landscape and Scenery**.

**Awake:** To dream that you are awake when you are actually dreaming offers a double dose of the extent to which you may be repressing something. The message is that you need to wake up and face something. When you suddenly 'wake up' to realize that anything is possible and that you can fly, it is an aspect of the psyche exploring potential and self-imposed limitations. To 'wake up' and do something of a daily routine, portrays the need for a wake up call in what you are habitually doing. See **Sleep** and also **Flying**.

**Ax:** This symbol can have associations with having an 'ax to grind' representing both the idea of aggravation and the need to let go. See also **Weapons and Utensils**.

# B

The letter "B" in a dream can explore the idea of how to just 'be,' or how you are currently behaving. Associated with the idea of second rate, or things that are bothersome, the letter "B" can also represent missing the mark or settling for second best. This letter can also be a symbol for boy.

**Baby:** Dreaming of an unfamiliar child or caring for a unknown baby portrays growth or the emergence of a new side of you. You may have a sense of feeling responsible for this unknown child as a representation of the need to care for and nurture this new aspect of you. Dreaming of twin babies can symbolize the emergence of balance, or the fulfillment that comes after a difficult decision is made. See the **Unknown Child** and **Archetypes and Universal Characters**.

**Babysitting:** Anytime you are caring for a child in a dream it can suggest the need to care for a part of yourself that requires nurturing. When you are going through a type of transformation, you may dream of an unknown child that you must care for as a representation of a type of rebirth or awakening of your new potential.

**Back:** Dreaming of the back is associated with responsibility and burdens. Since it is that part of the body rarely seen, it can symbolize what you are not facing or how you are not acknowledging that you are carrying unnecessary burdens. See **Anatomy and Body Parts**.

**Backpack:** Associated with what you carry on your back, the backpack is similar to a purse or wallet representing identity, but is carried with a sense of a burden or responsibility. Used to carry books, it can suggest ideas that are holding you back. The drama surrounding the backpack portrays baggage and whether carrying it is good or bad. See **Purses, Wallets, Luggage, Jewels and Keys**.

**Backstage:** When you dream of something taking place on a stage - you are exploring a more objective view of your passions and desire for free expression. When you go backstage to meet an actor or performer, pay careful attention to their characteristics. They are representing some aspect of you - perhaps a more creative way of expressing yourself. Performers often personify your own desire to be more expressive, demonstrative and passionate. Going backstage can be a way of making an intimate connection with this part of your nature.

**Bacteria**: Similar to sperm, bacteria can represent attraction, where you can become 'infected' or transformed by allowing your biological drives free reign within you. At the same time, infection or 'getting something from others' carries the message of how you are being influenced by those around you.

To dream of watching bacteria in a Petri dish denotes your sense of gaining insight into how you feel about your biological drives. Germs can appear 'unclean' and threatening, or they can portray the sense of how things happen to your body that are beyond your control. It can symbolize sexual feelings, where ideas take hold and simply grow. A virus shows the power of thought and its connection to what unfolds in experience. The fever that is connected to illness shows feelings (possibly anger) that needs to be released.

**Bad Breath:** To dream of having or smelling bad breath can symbolize communication issues that you are not comfortable with. You may be expressing yourself in a way that has made you feel is not clean, pure or truthful. If another character has bad breath - you may not be giving consideration to feelings of resentment. Explore what part of you this character may be representing and whether or not this part of you is achieving expression. See **People, Kiss** and **Mouth**.

**Badge:** A badge is worn to signify the part you play and can be symbolic of your sense of identity, similar to a name badge. Anytime your name becomes the focus of a dream - you are taking steps to express your authenticity. Unlike the hat that crowns your ideas, the badge covers your chest and can sometimes signify trading authenticity to play a part. The type of badge and what it signifies should be considered to understand how the dream is helping you further define who you are. See also **Name.**

**Badminton**: Dreams that focus on games of volleying are usually exploring integration. What adjective would you use to describe the person you are playing badminton with? Could you be exploring this quality as you move toward integration.? The other elements and symbols surrounding the game and equipment can shed more light on whether or not you are achieving this integration.

**Bag:** Since a bag holds the things you carry with you and hold to be valuable, the bag can be a symbol of how you take inventory of what is no longer necessary on your journey. Losing a bag can be a representation of career changes or a change in identity. See **Purses, Wallets, Luggage, Jewels and Keys.**

**Bakery:** Dreaming of desserts can be a way of exploring 'just desserts' or the rewards you are seeking in life. Food symbolizes your need for fulfillment and desserts can represent sexual feelings or how you seek comfort. Something taking place in a bakery can represent new ideas that are 'rising' or 'baking.' If the dream focuses on whipped cream - the association has a more sexual meaning. Since the type of food items prepared in a bakery are not considered healthy or nourishing, you may be exploring escapism tendencies that are not necessarily helping you to become more independent. See **Food** and **Dessert.**

**Balcony:** Dreaming of something taking place on a balcony can be a way of exploring your outlook or aspirations. You may feel the need to widen your perspective to explore opportunities you are missing. If there is a frightening character hiding on the balcony - you may need to explore how you (see Shadow) or someone in your life is holding you back in some way. If the balcony is falling or in need of repair - the message would be about making adjustments that allow you to achieve your ambitions. If the balcony leads to a fertile landscape - you may be going through a powerful transformation that is making you more grounded and authentic. If the balcony overlooks a pool or body of water - you are making strides to understand the deepest part of your nature – See **Unconscious, Houses and Buildings** and **Shadow**.

**Bald:** Like your ideas, hair grows over time and requires that you cut and groom it to keep it healthy. When you dream of being bald, you may have had the sense that your ideas were 'stripped' away from you as your attitude undergoes a drastic change. This could also be the humorous way that your psyche is suggesting that you are being caught in a 'bald face' lie. Seeing a bald man can be a sexual symbol or it can signify old age. A bald woman suggests adjusting sensitivity with a healthy dose of aggressiveness.

**Ball:** A ball is a symbol of wholeness and balance. Dreaming of a game that centers around catching and throwing a ball can represent the idea of integration. There may be two sides of you that require balance in moving forward. Examine the team members or characters. What adjective would you use to describe them? This part of you may need to be understood and integrated. A dream that focuses just on a ball can be suggesting wholeness or the circular aspect of life as in how all things come back to you. Situations that you face are the result of what you are doing as in 'the games you play.'

**Ballet:** Dreaming of watching the type of effortless and graceful movement observed in ballet can be a way of looking for similar qualities in your expression. Being in the ballet shows that you are feeling confident expressing yourself with balance and grace. Dancing in a dream is usually a powerful confirmation of feeling empowered and fulfilled.

**Balloon:** The balloon incorporates the idea of roundness or wholeness and something that rises. It can symbolize how you may need to achieve a lightness in being in order to remain balanced. It can also symbolize your mood or feelings about the present - where its color or behavior can portray how you are feeling - either rising above or feeling like you are going 'down.' The idea of inflation is also at play - so examine if your expectations in a situation are reasonable. You may be having an inflated sense of ego - or the dream can be suggesting you are full of 'hot air.' A hot air balloon ride can portray your attempt to rise above your current situation - and may also suggest that you do not have your 'feet on the ground.' Where we generally dream of planes when we are exploring ambitions - the balloon appears more as an vehicle that allows for a wider view or can represent escapism

**Banana:** Being 'yellow' and a monkey's favorite food, the banana is a playful way that the psyche portrays sexual thoughts. As a symbol of nourishment, it suggests how you need only peel away your outer covering (clothes) to get at the fruit within. Most food symbols portray the idea of how you are seeking more fulfillment (nourishment) in what you are doing. The banana combines the color yellow (jealousy) with a phallic shape that can represent power or potency. A rotten banana can represent neglecting sexuality - or feeling a lack of reward from all of your efforts. See Fruit under **Food.**

**Bandit:** Since all characters in a dream are portraying you or the condition of your 'inner landscape,' meeting a thief in a dream setting can be a message about self sabotaging behavior. Some part of you may be undernourished or 'down and out' and is challenging you to acknowledge the deeper needs associated with what this character is stealing. For example, being held up at gunpoint can be a message that two parts of your current identity may be at odds. Just as the dream threatens the valuable things that you protect, this type of dream can be a call to explore your priorities. See also **Trickster** and **Burglar.**

**Bank:** A dream that takes place in a bank setting can be exploring the idea of self value and also financial insecurities. Asking to withdraw money embodies how you are exploring your value and reserves from the standpoint of attributes. Since the bank protects valuables or savings, it can also be associated with unexplored potential. If a bank robbery is taking place, the meaning suggests that you are trading a valuable part of your nature for something unfulfilling, which may be leaving you feeling depleted or robbed of energy.

**Banquet:** Any social gathering that revolves around food, suggests how you are nourished in your interactions with others. In the banquet dream, you get a smorgasbord of interesting symbols with the audience or critic, the food or how you are nourished, and the social etiquette that is always squaring off with your sense of uniqueness. See **Food.**

**Baptism:** Getting baptized in a dream can be symbolic of a deep awakening or connection with your Higher Self. Water can represent feelings so this can be a symbolic way of being told to examine your feelings. Being reborn from 'holy water' can portray your commitment to move from a place that is unfulfilling toward something that will fulfill you. You are participating in a ritual that celebrates water's 'healing' properties. This can be a message about the power of feelings if you can open to them.

**Bar:** The bar can have different associations depending upon your age. When you are younger and spending more time in bars, the dream can be a way of exploring social exchanges and a desire to be more free to express yourself. Similar to alcohol, dreaming of a bar can suggest a dependency on alcohol that you are not facing. This is a meeting place where everyone uses intoxication as a way of giving free reign to emotions. The bartender in a dream can be representing qualities of escapism symbolized by the character. As the person who serves you intoxicating beverages - consider the other symbolism to explore whether you are able to express your true feelings. See **Alcohol.**

**Barber or Beautician:** The neighborhood character who cuts hair is representing the part of you that grooms your ideas. The barber or beautician in you may be be more interested in conforming to make an acceptable appearance, not necessarily presenting your real face. Being groomed portrays a change in attitude that will allow you to continue growing. At the same time, cutting hair portrays shedding old ideas. Grooming eyebrows can suggest changing your perspective or way of expressing yourself. Since hair grows over time, it can represent wisdom. A dream that focuses on an unusual hairdo can be exploring expressing yourself more creatively or more fearlessly. See **Hair.**

**Barefoot:** A dream that focuses on the feet is a way of exploring your life direction and the sense of taking a path that will allow you to express your real attributes and strengths. Being barefoot symbolizes returning to your authentic nature in making a type of change. If you are looking for shoes - you may be searching for meaningful work. See also **Feet** and **Shoes.**

**Barn**: Dreaming of being in a barn can be a way of exploring the side of you that is non conforming and more passion driven. Houses and buildings are a symbolic representation of areas of the psyche and doing something in a barn shows movement that might be called wild. In a sense you are allowing free reign to explore your more natural urges. See **Houses and Buildings** and **Animals.**

**Barometer:** Dreaming of any type of gauge can personify self limiting behavior. A barometer measures pressure and can symbolize a grudge that needs to be released. A thermometer in a dream can be a symbolic representation of not acknowledging how you feel or how your real feelings are leading you to be reactive. You take your temperature as a way of checking in with your feelings. Gauges can also be a representation of how you measure your accomplishments in terms of life stages. If the barometer or gauge is faulty than the message would be that your assumptions are not correct. You may have categorized or dismissed a situation that is causing the buildup of resentment.

**Bartender:** When a bartender appears as a character in your dream, examine the situation that unfolds to see if you are 'escaping' or not taking responsibility for something related to the dream. Since everyone in a dream is personifying aspects of you, the bartender can represent the side of you that enables a type of dysfunctional escapism. Food and drinking in a dream symbolize fulfillment and if you are drinking alcoholic beverages, you are sedating your awareness. See also **Alcohol**.

**Baseball:** Dreaming of sports can symbolize feelings that your environment has become competitive. If it is a game that centers around catching and throwing a ball, it can represent the idea of balance. There may be two sides of you that require balance and integration. Examine the team members or characters. What adjective would you use to describe them? This part of you may need to be understood and integrated. A dream that focuses just on a ball can be suggesting wholeness or the circular aspect of life as in how all things come back to you. Situations that you face are the result of what you are doing as in 'the games you play.'

**Basement:** Since houses represent our inner architecture, the basement is associated with ideas that are stored 'below the surface' as in repression. Whatever is happening in the basement needs to be explored as a possible issue from the past that has been left (stored) and is unresolved. See **Houses and Buildings**.

**Basket:** As a symbol that allows us to carry and store items, the basket can hold the key to what you are carrying that may need to be released. Most baskets are woven - symbolizing the intricacies of our insecurities. Examine what is in the basket as a symbol to see what you may be carrying with you. Is this a good or bad thing? The dream is suggesting that you give it consideration. If it is a metal basket, it can personify strong defense mechanisms. A basket woven of natural fibers can have the opposite meaning - coaching you to acknowledge some aspect of yourself that you are not giving enough consideration. Throwing something into a basket can represent success or your desire to hit the mark.

**Bath:** The bathroom is a room where you 'come clean' when you feel dirty, and is often the setting of a dream when you need to 'release' something you are holding, reflecting your inability to make a necessary change. When you reveal your intimate side in a situation, you may find your dreams taking place in the bathroom. Of all the rooms you dream about, the bathroom shows your desire to see yourself honestly, without the need to cover up your feelings. During difficult transitions, the bathroom often becomes a symbol of the need to 'get naked' or face the truth. Sometimes urinating when the walls are missing, coincides with entering social situations where you felt forced to reveal yourself to others. See **Houses and Buildings** and also, the **Trickster**.

**Bathing Suit:** Clothing in a dream can signify the persona or the mask you wear as your identity undergoes transformation. When the dream focuses on a bathing suit, it can symbolize your willingness to 'dive deep' into the waters of the unconscious which often occurs when you are going through therapy. Being on vacation and forgetting your bathing suit can be a message about the need to stop covering or protecting something. The bathing suit can signify your unwillingness to reveal yourself. See also **Clothing, Persona** and the **Unconscious**.

**Bathrobe:** Tying together the idea of bath as a place where you are honest with yourself or 'come clean,' and clothing which is your identity or the mask you wear for acceptance, to dream of being in a bathrobe can show the steps you are taking in becoming more intimate or self-actualized. You may feel that you need more privacy to focus on who you really are. Your current identity is changing in a way that is allowing you to become more authentic and fulfilled. See **Bath** and **Clothing.**

**Battlefield:** The conflict created by the many transforming sides of your changing identity over time will often lead to dreaming of a battlefield or this 'setting of psychic battle and integration.' See also **Army**, **War,** and Weapons and Utensils.

**Bay:** This harbor for ships suggests a safe haven or port after a troubling period of traveling over the seas of the unknown. You may be wandering through a ship that is anchored there, exploring the various bed (sex) rooms or chow (nourishment) halls, as a way of exploring these ideas in light of your emotions (water.) The lights in the bay or lighthouse can signify searching for direction or a place to call home. Shaped like the moon, this is also a feminine symbol suggesting heightened intuition. Seeing the lights allows awareness to find its way in the dark as you travel toward the shore of the unconscious. See also **Water**.

**Beach:** Generally a landscape viewed in the daytime, the beach portrays 'consciousness' as it meets the shoreline of the unconscious. As a symbol of water, it represents emotion and feelings. What happens on this beach will offer clues as to how you are integrating unconscious information into consciousness.

**Beads:** Dreaming of beads can have religious or spiritual significance as a symbol of seeking peace or calmness. If you are examining beads on a necklace, you are exploring your attributes and strengths. Look at the color and type of stone to see what the bead can reveal about your special qualities. If the beads are plastic or gaudy, the message can be about doing something for show or acceptance. Counting beads can personify menial tasks that are not fulfilling.

**Beak:** Dreaming of a bird's beak ties together the idea of taking precise action to have your needs met and the idea of getting above the mundane so that you can see where you are going from a more broad perspective. If you dream of a bird pecking at something, you may feel frustration, but you will break through. Look at the qualities that make the beak stand out for insight or clues about how to transform difficulty. See also **Birds**.

**Bear:** A bear often appears in dreams when you are going through a period of feeling overly protective or defensive. Since its appearance can represent you, something may be occurring presently that has made you extra sensitive or more self protective. Perhaps your ego has been bruised and it has brought out a type of grouchy or 'over bearing' behavior.

This powerful, maternal and protective animal can also symbolize maternal influences. Dreaming of a bear can be a way of exploring adopted behavior when you are being emotionally over-protective. The bear can symbolize a sudden emotional outburst that appeared to 'come out of the woods' when you are not owning your feelings during the day. The bear is also a complex symbol because of its associations with 'bearing' responsibility, 'bearing' offspring or results, losing one's 'bearings,' or something that is hard to 'bear.' The bear in a dream should also be considered in light of what you hold and what you might need to release. See also **Animals**.

**Beating:** See **Attack and Being Chased** and **Fear**.

**Beautician:** Hair is associated with ideas that grow over time and need to be groomed (cut) as we move through change. The beautician also works on improving our appearance and can represent a desire to be accepted. See also **Barber and Beautician**.

**Bed:** Since furniture suggests the ideas that we rest upon, to dream of something taking place on the bed can have associations with sexual ideas. The bed also symbolizes what we make of experience as in 'make our bed and lie in it.' As a furniture symbol, it has associations with the deepest part of our nature, what is not easily changed about us. The sheets and pillows can symbolize how we hide or cover up this aspect of ourselves. See also **Furniture**.

**Bedroom:** The bedroom is associated with the house, which represents your inner architecture as in thoughts and ideas. Since the bedroom is often a place of intimacy, something occurring in the bedroom or on the bed signifies issues that are very ingrained or habitual, often of a sexual nature. This room represents the most intimate side of your nature and can appear when you are moving to become more intimate. Also see **Houses and Buildings.**

**Bee:** The bee symbolizes the purposefulness of life and a desire to find meaning in what we do. Since they also sting, the bee can symbolize habitual behavior that is actually 'bugging' us or a well intentioned approach that may be holding us back from real fulfillment. See **Insects.**

**Beggar:** Meeting the side of you represented as a beggar in your dream offers a message about your current failed approach in having your needs met. This dream suggests that a change is needed that will increase self-worth and authentic fulfillment.

When you are unaware of being 'undernourished' or 'homeless,' the beggar in a dream may appear disturbing to you, challenging you or blocking your way. It is a message about slowing down enough to ask yourself if you are really happy. Anything that stirs or 'disturbs' us in our dreams is a message about facing the truth about being unfulfilled in your current situation. Your ability to provide for yourself would lead to greater fulfillment if you can recognize what you are doing to undermine it.

**Behind:** See **Placement and Perspective**.

**Bell:** Each time you hear a bell, you are alerted to do something. The ringing of bells can be associated with knowing when it is time to go and it can also symbolize a sense that you are late for something, as in life stages. Hearing a bell can reveal where you should go next if you explore the other symbolism associated with the bell. The bell can be a wake-up call to acknowledge something you are not facing.

**Belongings:** Dreaming of belongings usually coincides with looking for or protecting them. These are things you own that may or may not be important. See **Clothing and Makeup** and also, **Purses, Wallets, Luggage, Jewels and Keys.**

**Below:** See **Placement and Perspective**.

**Bent:** Seeing a bend in the road or in an object suggests a 'kink' in your current understanding about your direction and motivation. Associated in many dreams with an object you would hold in your hand (what is done to have your needs met) or something you would sit on (the ideas you rest upon) the crooked or bent object suggests this area that is not quite right and needs to be 'straightened' out. If the object bends and breaks, it shows how a necessary change can help you let go and move out of difficulty. Rickety or bent structures embody how the future is yet unbuilt and is a common setting in exploring work direction and what you are building. See Rickety Structures under **Houses and Buildings.**

**Beside:** See **Placement and Perspective.**

**Bicycle:** As a type of transportation symbol, the bicycle is symbolic of exploring how you are moving forward. In this case you are feeling that you are propelling yourself by your own effort. You may have slowed down recently to connect more with your path in terms of actualizing your real capabilities.

The idea of balance is also suggested since the bike requires a sense of balance to keep it upright. If there is something odd about the bike, explore the color for information that can help you define your direction. If the wheel is faulty - you may not be recognizing the cause that is leading to the type of events you are experiencing - probably tied to being negative. Handlebars allow you to steer and can have associations with your ability (or not) to change course. A play on the word 'bars' can suggest self restraint or even the idea of drinking and how it is affecting you. See **Vehicles and Places of Transportation**.

**Big:** See **Large and Small**.

**Binoculars, Glasses and Microscopes:** Microscopes and glasses in a dream show how you may be focusing more clearly on little things you dismiss. Getting caught up in the details of life, you can also lose your focus on the horizon, which a telescope can symbolize. A dream of a telescope can be a message about seeing the bigger picture. Increasing and focusing your power of vision, these tools allow you to see what you normally miss. On the other hand, they suggest that you may not be seeing clearly and need to change your perspective. Whether you are seeing the 'forest' or the 'trees,' this dream is a call to adjust your focus to see life from another perspective.

**Birds:** Because birds fly, they are representative of higher thought, inspiration, conscience, hopes and your ability to transcend limitations. The behavior and well-being of birds in a dream will portray your current sense of optimism. Birds associated with a **nest** will often signify issues of independence or dependence. **Parrots** 'mimic' what they have been trained to say, but they are also colorful and exotic creatures that can symbolize untapped abilities and unique qualities yet to be expressed in you.

The **blackbird,** crow or raven can have mythical associations that tie it to the 'Trickster.' They portray aspects of the evolving mind that can 'trick' you into growth, like Freudian slips. Often we dream of the Crow when we are first breaking through a difficult transformation. It calls for a sacrifice of the past in order to meet the future. In some situations, becoming crafty is a necessity, unlike the **ostrich**, which is a symbol of keeping your head below the ground or not facing something.

Like the **bluebird** of happiness, it is associated with hope, while a group of birds can suggest migratory behavior or following the crowd while still following instincts. Seeing **birds in flight** suggests following your drummer and to only believe in your success to make it happen. **Ducks** and **waterfowl** remain at the surface of the great sea, representing the unconscious stirring, as a way of suggesting movement. You can be 'chicken,' or 'cuckoo' and sometimes act predatorily like the **hawk** and **eagle**, suggesting the ability to 'see' clearly the things below, which remain hidden. The **owl** is a symbol of the patience that comes from intelligence and experience. The **canary** is said to know of danger before it is obvious.

Reptiles use shade and the warmth of the sun to regulate body temperature. As some dinosaurs evolved into birds, **feathers** became an evolved way of trapping warmth and cooling the body. Beyond their association with survival, feathers can symbolize the ability to rise above beliefs or move toward evolution in this way. Finding a feather describes insight related to the type of bird or color of the feather. Representing accomplishment, you can 'have a feather in your cap.' The elaborate feathers of a **peacock** can symbolize your fearlessness in demonstrating new abilities or expressing your beauty. A **rooster** crows and can represent the need to speak your mind - or it can offer a wake-up call to do something differently. Their association with being virile can make roosters and cocks a sexual symbol.

The **quail** and **pheasant** are unusual in that they only fly short distances and live in the brush. They can symbolize aspirations that are grounded in both the positive and negative sense. The quail has an interesting top feather and can symbolize the desire to have 'a feather in one's cap.' The pheasant has unusually long tail feathers - and like the peacock, can symbolize the idea of one's exotic beauty. These **game birds** can also be associated with feeling preyed upon.

**Farmyard birds** have different associations. You can be 'chicken' or not acknowledging fear in some area or need to talk '**turkey**' or get at the truth. If someone were to call you a turkey, it would signify copping out. Dreaming of a turkey may be a way of exploring this quality. These birds' association with food give them a meaning more in line with how we might experience self esteem or inner nourishment. Since neither bird really flies, dreaming of them explores the more grounded ideas of sustenance.

**Biting:** You can 'take a bite out of something' and chew on it awhile, suggesting how you digest experience. Like a vampire, a person biting you can drain you of your life force or exuberance, where some side of you may be draining another aspect. An animal will bite you and 'draw blood' as a way of peeling the layers that hide your emotions. An insect bites you when something is 'bugging' you. They are small, but their venom can be deadly. Often an insect bite will paralyze you and so, a decision needs to be made to move beyond what is eating at you. Finally, a bite is pain associated with the mouth and can suggest painful communication that will open the way for intimacy. See also **Teeth**, **Food** and **Tasting**.

**Black:** See also **Colors**.

**Blame:** Being blamed for something you did not do in a dream is a message about behavior that you are not recognizing that may be undermining your success. Explore what you are being blamed for to objectively see if this is something that might provide a key to a breakthrough. This type of dream presents the psyche's amazing power to break through by leaving you puzzled. At first you will awaken sensing that you were blamed for something completely bizarre, which you would never do in real life. The point of the dream is to make a suggestion through any symbolism that can break through.

Sometimes breaking the symbolism down into pieces will show you how being 'blamed' is the same as your psyche saying you need to do it. Example: being blamed for stealing a cake is a suggestion about having your just desserts or finding more reward in life; being blamed for leaving a child alone in a park is coaching you toward a type of rebirth that will lead to more independence.

**Blanket:** A blanket relates to the need for comfort and security. The idea of 'keeping warm' might have a message about feeling a type of 'coolness' in your current atmosphere. During times of difficulty, you may search for a blanket in a dream as a way of returning to your roots to re-establish a sense of security. In this case, family values can go along way in providing the warmth you seek. See also **Quilt**.

**Blind:** To dream of 'not seeing' is the same as 'not seeing' meaning you have shut your eyes to whatever symbolism the dream is exploring, although you are becoming aware of this tendency. To dream of another person who is blind suggests you are not even aware of the part of you that is not seeing clearly. Observing an animal without eyes can represent 'being blind' to the power of your emotions. See Eye under **Anatomy and Body Parts**.

**Blizzard:** This cold and wintry weather makes going anywhere difficult. Being lost in the swirling manifestation of ice and snow suggest how coldness may be keeping you from either participating in or seeing the beauty of life. See also **Snow**.

**Blood:** Dreaming of blood often seem frightening, but it is actually a good dream about opening to your power to feel. Red is a color associated with getting our attention and blood appears in dreams when we need a wake up call to interact with life more deeply. When you see blood on yourself in a dream, it is an image of your free flowing life force breaking through emotional restraints as feelings coming to the surface. At the same time, it can sometimes signify pain associated with feelings. The theme of the dream will tell you which is taking place.

To see blood on someone or something else reflects how you have disassociated from your feelings, objectively exploring emotion in an abstract way. Blood can represent the blood line of family, or sometimes work, for those who work in the healthcare profession. See blood under **Anatomy and Body Parts**.

**Blue:** Blue is a color that can represent aspirations and freedom. It can serve as a cryptic way of having you explore the idea of being 'blue.' Wearing blue clothing can tie your work to the idea of service - maybe becoming more giving of yourself so you can identify your gifts. A person becomes blue when they are not breathing and so, blue can have a message about stopping to relax. smell the roses and enjoy the ride. Its association with the sky makes it a color related to expansive ideas. See also **Colors.**

**Boat:** Traveling by boat brings forward the idea of 'emotional passages.' Water represents your current feelings and how the water is portrayed will suggest the condition of your emotions. If the water is turbid, there may be past hurts that need to be processed and released. Choppy water can portray emotional difficulty as you move through changes. Often the passage will become calm after a difficult transition, when you are feeling more peaceful. If the boat is in peril, you may feel like your emotions have become overwhelming.

Boats, buses and trains, in which you are a 'passenger,' suggest how you are following a course that is not self-directed and not easily changed. Travel over water is indicative of emotions and how the 'flow of events' or 'current' is leading you forward into the future, and often represent uncertainty and a lack of trust. See also **Vehicles and Places of Transportation** and **Water.**

**Body:** See **Anatomy and Body Parts**.

**Bomb:** Dreaming of bombs can symbolize the 'explosion' of repressed feelings that are coming to the surface. Oftentimes associated with unacknowledged anger, being in a setting that is being bombed can symbolize recognizing how fear or anger are sabotaging you. In a sense, your inner landscape is undergoing transformation so anger that is festering can be released. See also **Atomic Bomb**.

**Bones:** Since bones support the body, they show what remains about you when all else disintegrates. Dreaming about bones can portray the essence of who you are or the foundation of your character. To unearth bones suggests nitpicking, fussy or overly critical behavior when you are focused only on the negative as in 'having a bone to pick' with others. Since a bone is also associated with the idea of 'throw me a bone' an unusual dream about bones can portray the key to your fulfillment. See **Anatomy and Body Parts**.

**Book:** When you open a book, you are game for exploring new ways of thinking and sharing your ideas like being 'an open book.' To lose a book is the same as 'losing' an outworn perspective, while searching for a book signifies exploring a 'new way' to understand something. The type of book and its condition will offer additional clues to your current ideas and how you are moving to change them.

**Boots:** Like shoes, boots offer a message about getting more grounded, natural, and earthy in the steps you are taking to actualize your aspirations. The boot can also be a symbol of becoming more motivated as in 'booting up' or starting something. Looking for boots can symbolize planning for a difficult transition. Getting 'the boot' is also something to consider in this imagery as a fear of an impending change. Offering more protection than shoes or sandals, boots can be associated with increased discipline and self-protection. Rain boots would carry the symbolism into the area of protecting yourself from wallowing in your feelings (water and mud). See **Shoes** and **Clothing and Makeup**.

**Border or Boundary**: Dreaming of moving within boundaries can represent confinement. Exploring an area that would be called a border represents overcoming limitations. To see the edges of something offers a message about a turning point. This dream can be associated with embarking on a new direction or letting go of the past.

**Boss:**    Other people in our dreams are portraying us in some way. The boss often embodies your higher self as you explore the idea of self esteem that you have attributed to them. Sometimes they can personify aspects of your parents as you work to become more individualized, empowered and less critical of yourself. If you feel your boss is critical of you, they are appearing in your dream as a personification of your own self criticism. You may dream of a type of sexual encounter with a boss as a way of exploring the integration of your own power. See also **People.**

**Bottle:** Looking at bottles in a dream can represent 'bottling up' your emotions. Containers that hold liquids often refer to the flow of our feelings. A waterjug can represent the pursuit of fulfillment, while many drinking vessels embody the pursuit of gratification. You can dream of a bottle as something containing childish urges in the sense of a 'baby's bottle.' If the bottle breaks, your usual ways of finding pleasure will no longer do. The bottle is sometimes associated with feminine genitals and sexuality.

**Bottom:** See **Placement and Perspective**.

**Bow:** The bow, as an instrument used to propel an arrow can symbolize drive. While the arrow can represent goals or your desire to go after what you want, the bow has associations with how you go about it. The bow can be functional or dysfunctional in relation to whether or not you are passionate about what you are doing. It can also portray energy levels and discipline. To bow in a dream can show concession or the need to be more flexible in a situation. The message can also be that you need to 'bow out' or give in. See also **Arrow** and **Quiver.**

**Box:** The box is something that you can store things in, and can be associated with the idea of 'baggage.' It can also symbolize the type of packaging that gifts come in. Opening a box can represent the unknown and can offer a message about opening up to either giving or receiving. The box can personify you in terms of being 'boxed in,' feeling enclosed or how you can turn within to discover the gifts that come through insight or inspiration. In some cases the box is also associated with the womb, female genitals or ideas associated with mother.

**Boy:** The boy can portray innocence in applying traits that would be considered masculine. For example, assertiveness, aggressiveness and the masculine drive to achieve. A woman dreaming of a boy may be awakening to this potential within herself. A man dreaming of a boy can be exploring aspects of actual childhood. See The Unknown Child under **Archetypes and Universal Characters**.

**Brain:** Of all symbols you may dream about, the brain perhaps is the most literal. Since it houses your ideas, seeing a brain in a dream allows you to recognize how you may be adopting ideas that are not your own. If the brain is bloody, you may need to allow for the flow of feelings to balance your intellect. The brain can also symbolize consciousness and if it is floating or sinking in water, can represent allowing for input from the unconscious. Explore the other symbols and setting to understand how your ideas are being objectified so that they can embrace more of who you are.

**Branch:** To dream of a branch of a tree can represent the need to split off in some way from your family dynamics. A branching river can symbolize a new way of feeling that will allow for more fulfillment. If you observe new blossoms on a branch then you are exploring the potential that can come from making necessary changes when you let go of the past. Trees have associations with the deepest part of your nature, often adopted from your upbringing. The branch shows the part of you that is unique from your family. It symbolizes unrecognized capabilities. See also **Trees**.

**Bread:** Dreaming of bread can be symbolic of the body or the need to pay more attention to physical needs. A person is sometimes called a 'bread winner' and so bread can also be symbolic of financial needs and the ability to provide for yourself. Moldy bread could mean that an old role is outworn or that success can be tied to doing something new and more fulfilling. Bread soaked in water can symbolize tapping inspiration and feelings in your work. See **Food**.

**Break:** When something breaks in a dream, it suggests the 'breaking point' where something can be released. Broken bottles often release liquid as a symbol of releasing feelings. Broken heirlooms show how you are breaking from family values. Things that open up and are associated with 'breaking' show how opening up is not easy and the dream is allowing you to explore it. As the idea of 'breaking with the past' or having someone 'break the news' this is a symbol associated with moving through difficulty and exploring it objectively to become more empowered. When break is associated with 'taking a break' see **Vacation.**

**Breakfast:** Portrayed as the 'most important meal of the day,' the food that nourishes you or 'gets you going' is often suggesting the root of your motivation or the 'inner fuel' needed to achieve your aspirations. See **Food.**

**Breasts:** Dreaming of breasts represent the exploration of self-nurturing ideas and behavior. Their roundness combined with their maternal associations can symbolize the circle of cause and effect in how feelings lead us to create situations. In this case your idea of love may be influenced by what you observed in your mother's relationship to the father. You may be drawn to relationships that have a dynamic of your relationship with the mother. Breasts can also signify the power of the self in your pursuit of fulfillment. They can offer a message about turning inward in your pursuit of success rather than focusing on outward situations. Dreaming of breasts can symbolize a desire for love that can only be achieved through unconditional love
and self acceptance. See **Anatomy and Body Parts**.

**Breath:** In mythology, the breath is a divine gift. It keeps you connected to life until you 'take your last breath' and can symbolize your spiritual connection to life. A dream that focuses on breathing can suggest the need to 'get a breath of fresh air' or step away from the situation to see it objectively. Colored breath will be associated with the emotion that the color suggests, as a way of taking it in and allowing it to sustain you. See also **Colors**.

**Bride:** The bride is dressed in white, suggesting purity or a threshold of spiritual awareness. When a woman marries, often her name and much of her identity will change too. A woman dreaming of a wedding is exploring the integration of the sides of her nature that various characters may represent. For the male, the bride can represent integrating sensitivity and intuition or other 'feminine' traits. See also **Wedding**.

**Bridge:** This is a structure erected to 'gain access' across two separate places. It suggests 'bridging the gap' or finding the common thread between two separate ideas that appear to be conflicting, but are actually connected.

**Bubble:** Bubbling can be a cryptic symbol of sexual feelings coming to the surface. The bubble is a round symbol that can suggest an idea of something fragile that might burst, since longevity is not its strong point. As it rises upward, it can symbolize hope and aspirations or ascending in an effort to rise above something by releasing it. Something oozing would suggest repressed feelings that are festering.

**Bud:** During spring, new life pushes forward, although it remains challenged by an unstable climate, signifying perseverance. Buds on a tree show new life growing aside from your family or childhood dynamics. Buds symbolize ideas or new direction emerging that still requires cultivation and care. Observing the budding of something in the ground reflects something growing that requires strong roots to weather the storms. You have planted something that will soon bear fruit.

**Build:** The idea of how attitudes are constructed can be portrayed by building something in a dream. Building is also a way of understanding objectively how you are actively creating your future. The symbol that is being built can provide insight into the area of your life that you are exploring in a 'constructive' way. When you dream of rebuilding or renovating something, you are exploring making changes to your 'internal structure' that will better reflect your needs and desires.

**Buildings:** Where houses represent your inner architecture or personal dynamics, dreaming of buildings has more of an association with work, goals and the career path. Moving through a city of large buildings can symbolize your desire to receive acknowledgment. You interact in a public marketplace and shops when your are exploring self worth related to your career. The dreams that take place in an office setting can portray your feelings about work.

Buildings sometimes appear as rickety structures, representing how you grow to meet a future that has not yet been erected or completed. Buildings can be places in which you are lost or searching for something, as in the case of searching for a new identity when changing jobs.

By traveling to a specific floor or level of consciousness, you can also find yourself outside of your work building or on the roof as you take an objective view of leaving a job because the ceiling isn't high enough. Stairs going up can symbolize exploring aspirations, while stairs going down symbolize retracing steps or understanding the root of your motivation. The floor of a structure can be indicative of levels of awareness or may be associated with the meaning of the number involved: See **Numbers.** You stand on the ground floor of awareness and travel upward to achieve your ideals, or downward to find those things that you keep hidden below. Elevators and escalators in a building can also symbolize aspirations or how your upward or downward journey feels orchestrated beyond your control.

If the building is associated with food, you are exploring more fulfilling work. If the building is a factory, the message can be about learning new skills that can make you more effective. A utility building can have associations of how your inner dynamics or beliefs are operating. A library can reveal the ideas you 'store.' The church relates to spiritual ideas, while the school relates to learning something new. A warehouse can have a message about the need to sort through outworn ideas that are being stored. Remember that the building is personifying you.

The roof of a structure shows limitations. As a setting of activity, something taking place on a roof can portray your desire to break through barriers in achieving your ambitions. When the 'sky is the limit' the ceiling can block your ambitions, suggesting how self-defeating ideas may be blocking your ability to discover success. See also **Houses and Buildings**.

**Bull:**  Since bulls are said to 'see red' they can be a symbol of repressed anger and the bull headed attitudes that keep you from self-actualization or feelings of self-worth. Often representing characteristics adopted from the father, the bull can appear in dreams when you are coming to terms with the source of your repressed anger. As territorial creatures, the bull can symbolize your feelings about Self value and what you hold and protect. The Bull's association with the astrological sign Taurus as an Archetype can represent areas of life associated with security, the senses and the value you place on experience. Bulls have mythological significance in the area of controlling passions in pursuit of a more spiritual awareness. Also see **Animals**.

**Bullet:**  This symbol has a direct trajectory that allows it to hit its mark or penetrate through hard surfaces. Feeling a bullet entering your body is representative of the pain that comes from being forced to 'open' up. This symbolism can also suggest that you are being overly defensive or sensitive in receiving constructive criticism. See **Blood** and **Anatomy and Body Parts.**

**Burden:** The sense of having a burden can coincide with knowing you have to be somewhere 'but…' Whatever symbol arises that you are forced to hold on to or protect, while you miss something else, will offer clues as to how the past is adversely impacting your future.

**Burglar:** The Burglar represents one aspect of you that may be undermining another, as in working too hard and not being open to relationships, and so you dream of having your ring stolen. You may dream of having belongings stolen like a purse or wallet when your identity or job status is changing. Also see Intruder under **Archetypes and Universal Characters.**

**Burial:** The ceremony or ritual performed when someone passes can signify releasing outworn sides of yourself as you move through a transition. Dreams of visiting a crypt, tomb or being at a funeral or cemetery represents the passing of a side of you that you have outgrown. On the other hand, the burial can also be suggesting that you have buried an aspect of yourself that is being explored and resurrected. The person being buried, your feelings about the situation and the characters who attend will offer clues as to this common dream of repression and the necessary transformation that is unfolding. See also **Corpse.**

**Burning:** Something can be burning because of a natural disaster or accident, where the flames (often passion or anger) burn out of control to destroy a structure (something that is holding you back from real fulfillment-like fear.) Something burning and then breaking in a dream suggests how new life emerges sometimes through what appears painful, destructive or bad. This is actually a dream that shows constructive growth. Burning in dreams is often associated with the Phoenix that rises from the ashes of the past. If you are dreaming about flames, it is usually a message that you are not allowing the power of your passion to be released. See also **Natural Disasters**.

**Burying:** Since you are dreaming of burying something or of something buried, you are not seeing how you have buried or repressed an idea, perhaps you do not want to face. See **Digging** and **Burial.**

**Bus:** The bus, as a transportation symbol, can represent your sense of direction when you are unwittingly following the crowd or trying to fit in. Looking for a seat on the bus can symbolize searching for your rightful place among others. Moving to the back of the bus can represent feeling unworthy. As you move to the front, you are becoming more empowered and self directed.

Being on a bus is a common symbol of trying to conform or follow others as you explore direction from the sense of what is required of you. As you adopt new ways of expressing yourself in situations where you are being forced to conform, you are going somewhere, although you remain a passenger to the flow of events. See Vehicles and Places of Transportation.

**Butt:** Dreaming of the backside can be a message about looking to see what is 'behind' an issue, or what is at the root of it. Dreaming of a butt focuses the dreams message on the idea of elimination or endings. See also **Anus.**

**Buying:** Whenever you are buying something in a dream, you are 'shopping' or exploring the idea of what is valuable to you - along with the idea of self-value. If it is a type of clothing, the message can be tied to exploring your identity. Jewelry can represent the things you do to impress others, while furniture represents the ideas that you 'rest upon.' A car would be changes that are being made to your motivation.

Purchasing or buying can be a word play on 'buying into something.' What you get 'in exchange for payment' can show how something valuable must be traded (sacrificed) to achieve something more necessary to your sense of well being. See **Marketplace** and Shopping Center under **Houses and Buildings**.

# C

A dream that focuses on the letter "C" can be guiding you to 'see' or look more closely at something. It can suggest your fear of failing or the idea that you are not giving a situation the attention and focus it deserves. Associated with ideas like car, carrot, catch and charge, this is a letter that can also symbolize getting motivated.

**Cab:** Taking a taxi is a less intimate way of "hitching a ride" forward, when autonomy is being explored. This is not the case of being "driven" by a spouse, family member or acquaintance (suggesting their influences on your direction,) but a stranger or unknown aspect of you. The cab driver should be given consideration as to this part of your nature that is driving you. Taking a taxi that is yellow can signify a pause or taking time out as you look for new direction or assistance from others.

**Café:** As a meeting place to explore less formal characteristics about yourself than a banquet, the café allows you approach the idea of nourishment as a place of a "quick exchange" in a social setting. Getting food on the run shows the demands of social pressures that undermine fulfillment. Observe any characteristics of the waiter for clues in increasing your sense of fulfillment. See **Banquet, Food** and Restaurants under **Houses and Buildings.**

**Cage:** Unlike a cell for prison inmates, cages are associated with animals. Being caged is the same as recognizing how your emotional and spontaneous nature is being stifled. You may get "cagey" if you feel the need to break free from this unnatural restraint. See Cell under **Homonyms.**

**Cake:** Cake symbolizes a desire for reward, perhaps when embarking in a new direction. Any type of food represents nourishment from a more broad perspective. Dessert items have associations with ideas like 'icing on the cake' or 'having your just dessert' as a symbol of reaching for more in life. Food dreams show our attempts to find nourishment from what we do. See **Food.**

**Calendar:** When a calendar appears in a dream it can be a reminder that an event or deadline is coming up, which you'd rather not face. The passing of time as a sense of urgency can also appear as pages in a calendar.

**Calf:** This is the youthful version of the cow and bull and can represent how you suckled or adopted characteristics from your parents. See Cow and Bull under **Animals.**

**Camera:** The camera is the classic symbol of moving toward an objective perspective. As you explore different ways of "focusing" to "capture" an image, it is memorialized in a photograph. Seeing a *photograph* is the sense of not completely owning up to something, and holding it at arms length, while you study it objectively. Something that remains "just outside" of consciousness is coming into "focus." The other symbols in the dream can provide additional insight into clues about what this is. See **Photograph** and **Binoculars, Glasses and Microscopes.**

**Canal:** This river pathway portrays something that cuts through mountains (concrete ideas) to take water (emotions) from a reservoir or reserve (unconscious) into areas where it is most needed. Without this type of "irrigation," the plants upriver would perish, suggesting opening to the opportunity for new growth within you. As a canal that allows for transportation, it becomes a symbol of how your emotions are carrying you forward. See Ships in **Vehicles and Places of Transportation**.

**Cancer:** When cells disconnect from "signals from the host" to become destructive rather than building healthy tissues, we call it cancer. This is an objective way of exploring self-destructive tendencies that may lead to a lack of balance. Some part of you is out of harmony with the flow of events and your nature. See **Healing.**

**Candle:** You may light a candle in the darkness to gain greater vision into what appears dark as a symbol of enlightenment. The candle offers an image of hope and celebration as in the desire for new life, or having a child.

**Candy:** Beyond dessert in the sense of sustenance and "having your cake," candy is often associated with childhood. In the tug of war you play with reality as you are led toward growth, you measure what you want against what life gives back. Dreams of candy often represent the innocent pursuit of something with no consideration as to whether it is nourishing or right for you. See **Food.**

**Cane:** When you are unable to support yourself with your legs, you may use a cane or crutch to hobble forward. When a cane appears in a dream, it is suggesting issues about your ability to carry your weight when moving forward. See Legs under **Anatomy and Body Parts.**

**Canyon:** The canyon is a place where two mountains (conflicting ideas) come together, representing how you are exploring a transition or a pathway forward. Sometimes this dream comes after meeting conflict in another and suggests the middle ground where resolution is possible. If it is associated with descending the canyon can also suggest becoming more down to earth, or grounded in your ideals. See Descending under **Placement and Perspective.**

**Cap:** Like hat, it covers or crowns your beliefs. Generally, a cap is worn for sports so can indicate your ideas about your prowess or health. The cap is also associated with "having a feather in your cap" or getting recognition. See **Clothing and Makeup.**

**Captain and Conductor:** The captain and conductor are experts at navigating a proven course. They are familiar with the destination and so, having a conversation with either of these characters can offer insight as to where current events are leading you. As authority figures, they can represent issues related to your father, who plays a role in helping you to set a course for your success.

**Car:**  The car is a classic symbol of motivation, and reflects whether or not you are feeling autonomous as you move forward in life. If you are driving and the vehicle is out of control, you may be questioning the choices you are making. If you are riding as a passenger, you may not recognize how you are not taking the reins of responsibility for where you are going. You have given power over to the person driving the vehicle and may be needlessly blaming them for failing. If it is a parent driving you, there may be unconscious attitudes or criticisms you have adopted that are holding you back or diminishing your self-esteem.

These types of dreams suggest the condition in which you are currently moving forward. The type of vehicle, and whether or not you are driving, in control or being driven, will portray your present sense of autonomy.  See **Vehicles and Places of Transportation.**

**Carpet:**  The carpet or rug is often a symbol of sweeping issues "under the rug" as you move forward. Patterns in a rug can portray how you are exploring the part you play in creating your circumstances. A flying carpet represents how you would like to rise above current circumstances through fantasy. At some level, you may recognize that your ideals need to be "more grounded."

**Carriage:**  This vehicle of transportation is pulled forward by an animal, suggesting how emotions or drives are at play in your empowerment. See **Vehicles and Places of Transportation.**

**Carrot:**  Dream symbols often demonstrate the psyche's creativity in condensing many ideas in one symbol. Dreaming of a carrot brings forward many ideas: the pursuit of success, procreation because of its association with the rabbit and obvious phallic shape, the color orange as a symbol of standing out in the crowd or being unique, something growing underground in the sense of food that nourishes. The carrot therefore, suggests seeking fulfillment that might require a little digging or returning to our roots and naturalness. See **Food.**

**Cat:**  Cats can portray feminine qualities of your instinctive and sensitive nature and how you avoid 'domestication' as an image of avoiding intimacy. Being manipulative, they can symbolize defense mechanisms that might be holding you back from a fulfilling relationship. They can suggest 'catting' around or unfaithfulness. See **Animals.**

**Caterpillar:**  This insect becomes a butterfly after spinning a cocoon. Suggestive of metamorphosis in its early stages, it is often associated with what is "bugging" you that calls you to transform.  These creatures also eat organic leaves to spin fine threads into silk. Seeing a caterpillar can be a way of digesting difficulty, knowing that success is around the corner.

**Cave:**  The cave is associated with the womb and those parts of your nature that you appeared to be born with. Going within a cave and descending into the earth is symbolic of digging for your roots and getting more "down to earth." The cave also has a strong connection to the mother and may be representing how you are searching for the roots that tie you to her behavior. See **Forest** and **Womb.**

**Ceiling:**  When the "sky is the limit" the ceiling can block your ambitions, suggesting how self-defeating ideas may be blocking your ability to discover success. See **Houses and Buildings.**

**Cell:**  Phones are a symbol of how various aspects of the psyche seek to communicate with you. The person who calls you should be considered in terms of the adjective you would use to describe them - they can be representing a side of you seeking expression. The message that they share with you should also be considered as a message that may be coming from the Higher Self.

To dream that you are in a prison cell can portray feelings of guilt that are often unhealthy. Being arrested and locked away is the action of critical conscience which can sometimes undermine your need for authentic expression. A cell is a small space that doesn't allow for the expression of potential. Even a monk's cell can have associations with how spirituality has become Self limiting.

To dream of a cell as it relates to biology, you are examining the foundation how things grow. Something that you think is insignificant is actually contributing to the situation and may relate to the idea of survival.

**Cellar:** Rooms are associated with areas of our lives. For example, the kitchen is associated with seeking fulfillment and nourishment on a broader scale, while the bedroom can be associated with ingrained ideas (we sleep on) and sex. To dream of a cellar portrays how you are accessing the 'inner room' that lies below the surface. When you are making changes to your belief structures and ideas, the setting will often take you 'underground' as you explore ideas that have not been processed, integrated or released. Often you will sort through boxes or symbols associated with the past as you move toward forgiveness - or let old resentments go. All symbols associated with underground rooms should be explored carefully to understand how they are portraying the past or ideas that need to be re-examined. See also Basement under **Houses and Buildings.**

**Cemetery:** Being in a cemetery or a place where bones are put to rest can represent moving beyond anger, where you may have had "a bone to pick" with another. This is also a place where the outworn side of your nature is buried. See **Burial.**

**Center:** See **Placement and Perspective.**

**Ceremony:** Any formal ritual where characters have gathered represents the consummation and integration taking place within you. Vows and promises are made during a time of transition or when you enter different stages of life. This is a positive image of transformation that is being solidified within you.

**Chain:** Suggesting cause and effect, the chain can be a symbol of either bondage or strength. The links in the chain can signify the circle of life and your connection to it. How the chain is portrayed will provide clues as to which of these issues are being strengthened or broken.

**Chair:** The chair can symbolize ideas from the past in which you take comfort. A broken chair suggests outworn ideas, while a throne or new chair can symbolize achievement and new perspectives. To see chairs in a circle can represent exploring wholeness in terms of your ideas. It can symbolize how thoughts are creating experience. See **Furniture.**

**Chased:** See **Attack or Being Chased.**

**Cheating:** A very common dream scenario involves dreaming that your partner is intimate with someone other than you. Although you may feel that your intuition is telling you something, remember that dreams use other people and their qualities to portray you. Consider the qualities of this interloper and whether or not it might represent an aspect of you that is being explored. As you make changes, you may feel insecure about the effects it will have on your relationship. You may dream of your partner with someone 'new' as a representation of the new you.

Although you may be in a fulfilling relationship, you can dream of intimacy with past partners. At some point in your life - you projected the power for self love upon your mate. It is as if they hold/held the power to make you feel good about yourself. Consciously you may feel that you are functioning independently in a current relationship, but since you dream of what you are not facing, the appearance of an 'old flame' can be activated when you feel uncertain about your value in a current relationship. These past partners embody the idea of self love - they appear as we explore and merge (sexual intimacy) with this potential to love ourselves. This must occur independently from the feedback we are currently receiving. See also **Love**.

**Chest:** As a piece of furniture that protects those things that you cherish, the chest can be a symbol of the things you "hold" and how you sort through them and discard what is no longer necessary. If it is the chest of a body, see **Anatomy and Body Parts.** See also **Furniture**.

**Chew:** You may need to chew on something or "bite through" to see the truth. See also Teeth under **Anatomy and Body Parts** and also, **Bite.**

**Chicken:** This bird has associations with the egg of metamorphosis and transformation. You may also dream of a chicken as a message about being afraid or 'chicken.' A hen can symbolize domestic chores or being 'hen-pecked' or controlled. See **Birds.**

**Child:** A child or baby can represent a new or emerging side of you. See Unknown Child under **Archetypes and Universal Characters.**

**Childhood Home:** Dreaming of visiting the childhood home is a very common dream that allows you to explore and transform the patterning you adopted from the family. Consider the aspects that make the home different from what you remember. These differences are important in recognizing the ways you are different from your family. You are a unique variation of the line you carry forward.

The rooms represent areas of your life that are changing. Since the house represents your 'inner architecture, a symbol of the ideas and aspects of your inner world, visiting the childhood home is a way of re-evaluating some of the belief structures adopted at that point in your life. For example, the front yard may be different, as you test out new ways of expressing your uniqueness in social exchanges aside from what you were taught. Often you will be in the kitchen, since being fulfilled is an important aspect of wellness - and self acceptance often requires that you 'nourish' yourself with the positive reinforcement that could have been missing in childhood.

**Chin:** Dreaming of a chin is associated with perseverance during difficulty. You may have to 'keep your chin up' or 'take it on the chin' to understand how a difficult situation is necessary in helping you to realize what is important and worth fighting for. See **Anatomy and Body Parts.**

**Choke**:  You choke on something because you didn't chew on it in a way that allowed you to digest it correctly. The things that get trapped in the throat are usually representative of emotion as you "get choked up."  Choking someone can show how you are stifling that part of yourself that this person represents.

**Church:** You may visit the church in a dream anytime you are working through ideas that have a religious root or connection to conscience. Taught to simply have faith without reason, the church can symbolize non-rational ideas that no longer serve you in light of who you are becoming. On the other hand, the church can represent the building or *structure* of your spiritual nature. See **Houses and Buildings.**

**Circle:** The circle can have associations with both commitment and the idea of how things are connected. Like the ancient snake that bites its own tail, seeing a circle in a dream can suggest the things in your life that are sacred and remain unchanged, even while you travel through metamorphosis. As an image of returning to the beginning, it can suggest that a cycle is completing so that a new one will soon emerge.

**Circus:** Similar to the **Amusement Park,** the circus is a *transient* type of entertainment, and has more associations with **Animals,** acrobats and clowns. Visiting the circus in a dream can denote how you may cover your feelings and emotions with humor. Like the clown with a teardrop painted upon his face, you may need to peek behind your smile to uncover your feelings. The acrobats take risks and must have a perfect sense of timing. Watching them perform or being an acrobat yourself, means that you are exploring something new, while being acutely aware of its risks. This dream highlights the transient aspect of how you are exploring changing attitudes and trying new things.

**City:** The city is the center of social exchange and suggests a similar hub within you. What goes on in this city will provide clues to your aspirations and need for public recognition. Going to a *foreign city* means that you are exploring social needs that are new or unfamiliar. Life is a constant learning process and as you make changes *all* aspects of who you are change too. Reflect on the nature of a particular city for clues about your current direction. See **Foreign People and Places.**

**Clean:** Like **Bath,** this is a symbol associated with "coming clean" or revealing what lies hidden beneath the layers of repression. Whatever symbol you are cleaning will provide additional insight into that part of your organic or natural essence that might be made shiny or bright. This dream can also help you understand you inner critic that may have labeled something taboo, and therefore led you into a state of conflict or feeling 'dirty.'

**Cliff:**  At the peak of a mountain, the cliff is often associated with danger or not trusting your steps, which may lead to peril. Looking over the cliff, you cannot see clearly, what is below and so, the cliff can represent a threshold or boundary as you move toward something new. Something may be beneath or below you as a way of moving on. See Below under **Placement and Perspective** and also, **Border.**

**Climb:**  You may be attempting to move up in terms of aspirations or to gain a broader perspective. See also Ascending in **Placement and Perspective** and Floors under **Houses and Buildings.**

**Clock:**  Like the **Calendar,** the clock can be associated with a sense of time and urgency, although its focus on a specific hour can bring importance to the number depicted. See **Numbers**. The alarm clock may be giving you a wake up call to acknowledge something.

**Close:**  To dream of closing something signals the need to consciously acknowledge an area of your life that may require closure, so that you can move on. If you are inspecting something up close, see Up Close under **Placement and Perspective.**

**Closet or cupboard:**  Like the **Box, Basement** and **Cellar,** the closet is a place that is often "kept in the dark." Any dream that has a closet as a symbol can be especially focused on the idea of what you are hiding or not facing. What is "kept" in the closet or cupboard and the types of items it normally contains will offer clues as to the issue: dishes/nourishment and satisfaction; clothes/attitudes; and coats/self-protective issues.

**Clothing** and **Makeup:** These symbols relate to identity and are worn in way that may cover your real self to make an impression. Clothing can represent the attitude or the **Persona,** which becomes the mask you wear to fit in. *Changing clothes* or *trying on new clothes* suggests trying out new attitudes or issues related to exploring new ways of expressing yourself. Being in public in *"under clothes"* or naked occurs during times when you are forced to reveal your "hidden" aspects or become intimate in a way that made you feel uncomfortable. See Trickster under **Archetypes and Universal Characters.** *New* or *beautiful clothes* suggest increased self-esteem or a hunger for recognition, while *dirty clothes* are "outworn" attitudes or feelings associated with your sexual or organic nature that you may have rejected.

*Uniforms* can symbolize characteristics associated with the uniform, such as police or the patrolling side of psyche, or fire, representing "danger" or rising sexuality. Drum major and other band costumes can also be sexual or spiritual. You wear an *apron* when "something is cooking," portraying how you may ward off something that might give you nourishment or fulfillment. When you are given increased responsibility, you may dream of an apron as a symbol of releasing "the strings" that bind you to your parents. *Belts* hold the pants up but can also restrain sexual feelings and urges. *Shoes*, like **Vehicle** symbols, signify that part of you that you rely upon to move forward. Searching for shoes is symbolic of finding the means to provide for yourself in an effort to know success.

A *hat* covers the head and therefore, the thoughts, signifying how you may "cover" or hide your real thoughts. The *type of hat* can be associated with a profession that can describe an area of thought: *Baker's Hat*: nourishment; *Police Hat*: discipline and abiding by the rules or conscience, *Fire Hat:* how your thinking can get you into trouble, or *Helmet:* protective or aggressive tendencies.

A *dress* is associated with the feminine qualities of sensitivity, while *pants* often suggest masculine traits, as in "wearing the pants" or issues related to self-sufficiency. You can *"skirt"* the issue to hide something; *"sock"* something away or see others in *"suits"* as a way of exploring "fitting in" with, or conformity.

The idea of emotions can be associated with "wearing them on the *sleeve"* or issues related to a "hair *shirt,"* which covers them up, while they continue to eat at you. At the same time, you may need to "roll up your sleeves" and dig into an issue at hand. Wearing *gloves* offer protection from touching or exploring anything "dirty," while finding a glove can suggest "throwing down the gauntlet" in the sense of establishing boundaries. *Outerwear* such as a *coat* will symbolize a protective covering used to ward off the "elements" or the difficulties you may face.

*Forgetting an item of clothing or makeup* that becomes important in dreams of taking a trip suggests an inappropriate idea of self that might be holding you back from capitalizing on your authentic nature.

*Applying lipstick* and *rouge* can portray how the psyche is trying to rouse the "sleeping" sexuality of a woman, while suggesting the need for increased sensitivity for a man. Bringing color to the face in this way can be an amusing portrayal of "faking" emotion or affection. *Cosmetics* can also have the association of "covering up" the senses. They can be associated with the truth when you are saying something to hide your real feelings.

**Coffin:** To see a dead person or a coffin is a common way of understanding how some aspect of you is "passing away" or transforming. See **Burial.**

**Coin:** This is a symbol of value and how it appears in the dream will offer clues as to how you may increase your sense of self-esteem. The "character" who gives you a coin, can suggest applying or discarding a "way of being" that might lead to fulfillment. To find a coin suggests clues to self-esteem associated with the other symbolism in the dream.

**Cold:** Feeling cold can signify how you have "cooled off" in your emotions to the point that you might be seeking warmth. See **Frozen.**

**Collision:** See **Accident** and **Vehicles and Places of Transportation.**

**Colors:** If color appears pronounced in a dream, it can have special significance. When a color or colors become the subject or focal point, replace the color with its emotional association or aspect of the self, listed below, for clues to its symbolism. This will shed light on the feeling, which the color represents, and how you can learn more about yourself from the dream.

    *White* is purity, virginity, and the idea of coming clean or being truthful. *Black* can be dirty or represent an intimidating aspect of life that might be blocking your ability to see clearly, perhaps leaving you feeling depressed, as in a "black cloud." *Blue* is intuition or insight as in the sky is "the limit" or limitless in your ability for optimism. Deities are associated with living in the sky and portray your greater wisdom and a sense of following fate. *Brown* is an organic element of your nature that you may need to bring down to earth. *Gold* suggests "all that glitters" and attracts you with its aura of allure.

*Grey* can be responsibility or living by routine because of its association with being drab or servant's clothing. *Silver* can be associated with "the silver lining" that surrounds clouds when the sun is about to break through, suggesting hope or the ability to transcend difficulty. *Green* is associated with healing and growth. *Orange* portrays nourishment and sustenance by balancing conflicting aspirations. Something "stands out", or asks to be acknowledged and separated, like "people" in prison attire, who are kept separate from the population because they are a threat to "society." This is the *consensus,* which holds together the many sides of you. *Purple* will often represent joy, spiritual feelings and enlightenment. *Red* is associated with anger and passion; this is a color that demands your attention or that you "stop" doing something. *Yellow* suggests pausing or waiting, or can be associated with the life giving power of the sun, representing how you shine.

When you see something written in a colored ink, both the message and the color need to be considered. Green writing can pertain to health, while red writing is a call for extra attention.

**Comb:** The comb can be a symbol of vanity, a need for attention or a symbol suggesting that you "comb" through your thoughts to see something from another perspective. If you are combing your hair, you are changing attitudes or expanding your ability to achieve a sense of self-esteem. To see a cock's comb can be a sexual symbol that ties vanity and self-acceptance to your sexuality. This symbol captures both the female and male genitals so can appear in dreams with the same message for either sex. See **Hair** and **Head.**

**Compass:** Using a compass can suggest looking for direction, associated with a sense of exploration and adventure.

**Concert:** Attending a concert can represent bringing continuity and balance to all aspects of your life since the orchestra or band plays in unison. Any type of show, theater or performance usually means that you are exploring objectively how all aspects of your life fit together. Seeing something taking place on a stage shows the first steps in observing this objectively before making the necessary adjustments.

**Cooking:** The psyche is always processing information to allow you to feel real fulfillment. Cooking is a clear image of this process that will ultimately nourish you. *Who* is cooking and *what* is being cooked will offer clues as to the need for developing the traits represented by the cook, or elements associated with the food. See **Food.**

**Corn:** Associated with a time of harvest or Thanksgiving, corn can be a symbol of abundance. You may need to plant the seeds of the past in a way that will allow you to harvest future crops or "potential." This is also a sensory symbol because of its association with "ears" and "teeth." It can suggest heightening clarity in communication with whatever aspects the other symbols represent. See **Food.**

**Corner:** Like **Boundary,** the corner is a turning point in the sense of "turning a corner." Often represented as a crossroad, something "right around the corner" suggests the way in which you approach your aspirations. To understand this motivation, observe the *feelings* associated with what is around the corner. If you are being cornered, the symbolism demonstrates the side of you that is also trapping you in your growth.

**Corpse:** Like **Burial** and **Coffin,** a dead body appearing in your dream can represent either the side of you that is not achieving expression or the need to allow the passing of some aspect. The situation and feelings associated with seeing the corpse will reveal which type of direction this dream is suggesting.

**Corridor:** Like Hallways under **Houses and Buildings,** the corridor is a meeting place that allows you to explore the various emerging sides of your identity. It can suggest how you are moving into the neutral space that allows you to transform. This is a transitional space, which connects rooms or aspects of the psyche.

**Cosmetics:** Cosmetics are used to cover up your natural appearance. Dreams that focus on not being able to find what you use to produce your 'everyday face' can be symbolic of a need to move in a more natural or authentic direction. If you dream of accentuating certain features with heavy makeup - consider the part of the face that is being highlighted. Eyeliner can be a message about clarity of vision or the need to focus, while lipstick can be highlighting communication.

Dreams of blush or rouge can signify the need to allow your natural feelings to come to the surface. Dreams that focus on cosmetics are usually exploring the disparity of one's external appearance and the life of the real person below the **Persona.** See also **Clothing and Makeup.**

**Cover:** If it is a bed cover, it can represent how you "cover" your sexual feelings. If you are taking cover during an air raid, some part of you is feeling insecure about your aspirations. If you are taking cover during a natural disaster, you are fighting against the forces inside of you that recognize that an important transformation is necessary. See Natural Disaster under **Landscape and Scenery.**

**Cow:** Dreaming of a cow is a popular dream symbol. It has associations with the mother and the idea of milk and nourishment. Often people dream of an angry cow breaking through a gate as a symbol of breaking free from a sense of restriction. Since cows are highly domesticated, an unruly cow is often related to breaking free from guilt associated with the mother. The mad cow can symbolize maternal manipulation that is holding you back. See **Milk** and **Animals.**

**Coyote:** A dog is 'faithful' and demonstrates unconditional love as the easy expression of feelings and love in your relationship with others. If you are dreaming of a dog, you are exploring unconditional love and the idea of being domesticated or changed by a relationship. A coyote on the other hand, is wild and uncivilized and can portray the need to have a type of freedom in your relationship that can only come from unconditional love. Wild animals with teeth in myths guard the way to the underworld and can symbolize fear about digging within to discover the roots of your feelings. When an animal bites you, the message is that you need to bring your feelings to surface level. See **Blood** and **Animals.**

**Crab:** All creatures associated with the sea generally portray the "living side" or movement of the unconscious. To dream of a crab can suggest moving back and forth indecisively as you pursue something. This is a highly self-protective creature that can be "weighted down" by its own armor. Dreaming of a crab can be a message about moving beyond insecurity and fear. See **Sealife** and **Water.**

**Crack:**   Similar to the symbolism of **Break,** a crack shows an opening that is not taking place consciously. To see a crack in something suggests a missing aspect or inaccurate way of understanding a situation. If the ground cracks beneath you, it is because you are feeling the ramifications of a flawed way of thinking that is undermining your current *foundation* or beliefs. See Natural Disasters under **Landscape and Scenery.**

**Cream:**   This can be a sexual symbol representing how fluids flow naturally from the body. Also associated with aspirations, cream can be the idea of "milk and honey." Cream rises "to the top" and can be associated with exploring the best of what you might become.

**Credit Card:**   Unlike cash, using credit as a way of getting fulfillment in the moment leaves you with the sense that you have to "pay later." This is the idea of trading what seems like a good idea *right now,* at the cost of something else. The credit card is a classic symbol of how the past can burden how you can remain open to the future. You can be "saddled with debt" or burdened by seeking instant gratification to hide a lack of real fulfillment.

Also associated with security, the subject matter surrounding the credit card can point to clues about self-esteem or feeling more secure in life. Often representing a complex symbol of subconscious processes, a credit card can symbolize feelings of guilt associated with the parents, which undermine self-esteem.

**Crippled:**   Generally, the legs are impacted in a dream of being crippled or seeing a crippled person. An unfortunate set of circumstances may have left you feeling victimized, questioning your power to carry your own weight. If the hands are crippled, it is a message about the ability to take what you feel you need. Dreaming of being crippled often suggests that the power to heal can be activated by exploring the other symbolism associated with the dream.

**Crocodile:** This reptile lives below the surface of water symbolizing what is unknown and stirring in the unconscious. Something that is being repressed is also threatening you. See Alligators and Crocodiles under **Reptiles.**

**Cross:** An obvious religious symbol, the cross can also be a burden in the sense of the "cross you bare." As the symbol of "X" turned sideways, it may not be apparent how beliefs may be blocking your natural drives. Associated with sacrifice and resurrection, seeing a cross can symbolize how you are either sacrificing a part of your nature or must sacrifice something equally valuable, in an effort to achieve a sense of fulfillment.

**Crossing:** Movement described as a type of crossing suggests perseverance into the unknown without direction. Like the pioneers who explored uncharted territories over land and sea, the landscape you are crossing often provides clues to the part of you that is undergoing exploration. Crossing associated with writing can portray getting something right in the sense of "dotting the i's and crossing the t's." Crossing the arms or legs can suggest a sense of blocking the heart or sexual feelings. See **Landscape and Scenery.**

**Crossroad:** Representing a choice or a place where the past is abandoned, the crossroad combines the idea of traveling forward with the idea of making a choice. See **Landscape and Scenery.**

**Crow:** This bird is a common Archetype or thematic symbol when one must sacrifice the past in order to meet the future. Birds usually represent higher thought and spiritual desires. This type of dream commonly coincides with intensive therapy or when you are going through transformation of a spiritual nature. See **Birds** , Trickster under **Archetypes and Characters,** and Black under **Colors.**

**Crowd:** Unlike **Audience,** where you have a sense of being judged by the inner critic, having a dream about a crowd is often portrayed with the idea of being faceless or unrecognized. The crowd can be moving in a direction that is unclear to you and yet, you are following them, as a way of exploring peer pressure and autonomy. See **People.**

**Crutch:** You may dream of being **Crippled** or using a crutch when you feel disempowered in a situation. As an instrument that you "lean upon," or "fall back on" it is similar to an excuse or reason for why your forward movement is impeded. The crutch can signify the part *you* play in not being empowered. Seeing a crutch can be helpful if you look at it like the word "but" against the other symbolism. It negates or undermines the power of what precedes it: "I want to save for retirement, but....I know I should take care of my body, but..." Using a crutch or seeing someone on a crutch, is a way of exploring the power of disempowering thoughts against the idea of "just do it." It reveals how you negate your power in daily life.

Like the **Cane,** you may question your ability to move forward, although the crutch is something you lean upon to avoid personal responsibility. The part the crutch plays in the dream will suggest how disempowering thoughts are actually serving you in another way.

**Crying:** Since dreams usually reveal the exact opposite of what you believe to be true about yourself, dreams of crying or seeing someone crying is showing the emotion of sadness in its unexpressed condition. The dream symbolism may be such that it would not normally bring you to tears, and yet, you awaken somewhat sad or perplexed. This is the psyche's way of exploring unrecognized feelings or pain. Another character crying portrays unacknowledged suffering in terms of the characteristics that you associate with them.

**Cup:** If you cup your ears you will hear better and if you cup your hand you will catch the things that may slip through your fingers. Therefore, the cup is often associated with the things you hold to be important. The cup holds liquid refreshments that associate it with feelings or the intuitive flow of information. Dreaming of a cup can portray holding or trying to capture these things in an effort to gain insight about sustenance. A broken cup portrays your inability to contain or achieve fulfillment.

**Cupboard:** See **Closet and Cupboard.**

**Curtains:** The coverings that go over windows can offer a message about your ability to see clearly where you stand in social situations, As an element that can block or "shut out" the light, it is associated with hiding your authenticity.

**Cutting:** Symbols or instruments that cut describe your desire to "cut the strings" that bind you as the idea of letting go. If cutting something draws **blood,** the message is often related to exploring feelings. Unlike **Break,** the idea of letting go is being done in a more conscious way. See **Seamstress and Tailor.**

**Cyclone:** See **Landscape and Scenery.**

# D

Dreaming of the letter "D" shows a sense of failure or not measuring up to others in some way. This letter has associations with words like dark, death, depression and difficulty and might be a cryptic way of exploring a lack of fulfillment or ignoring how you are not happy. Its message is to 'dig' a little 'deeper' into something you may be 'dismissing' so you can make an adjustment. Tilted just a bit - and the letter "D" becomes a smile.

**Dagger:** A dagger, knife or other instrument that threatens to break the surface (of awareness) to cause pain or injury can symbolize fears of intimacy or the inability to allow for the expression of feeling. This type of weapon can also have sexual associations where the inability to control passion or lust can feel self threatening. See **Weapons and Utensils.**

**Dam:** An unnatural structure erected to hold back water portrays the symbolic blocking or "holding back" of emotions. The condition of the dam and the details surrounding this imagery can suggest whether the emotions demand release; the clues to what is blocking their expression, or the flood that may ensue should the dam break. See **Water** and Natural Disasters under **Landscape and Scenery.**

**Dancing:** Dancing in a dream often occurs when you are exploring or integrating the aspects of yourself that are portrayed by your dancing partner. A woman dancing with a man might be "learning how to move in step" with her animus or assertive and aggressive nature. A man dancing with a woman is exploring the idea of moving in step with his anima as he moves toward sensitivity. Dancing with a frightening character can symbolize the integration of the **Shadow** or organic side of the self that appears beyond one's control. See **Animals, Anima, Animus** and **Shadow.**

**Danger:** Dreaming offers a safe environment to explore difficult ideas. Even **Nightmares** are a positive sign that something powerful is stirring within you. The more frightening the dream, the more urgency the psyche feels in trying to bring awareness of conflict out into the open where it can be resolved. The idea of something appearing dangerous in a dream arises because of a transformative event that may have led to an 'uncomfortable shift' within you. Explore the symbol associated with the danger such as: **Accident**, Rickety Structures in **Houses and Buildings**, **Attack or Being Chased**, Intruder and The Shadow under **Archetypes and Universal Characters** and also, **Natural Disasters.**

**Dark:** To dream of being in the dark shows that you are 'in the dark' about the symbolism being explored in the dream. Something has yet to come into conscious awareness. If the same dream moves from night to day, it shows the issue moving into conscious awareness. See Dark under **Placement and Perspective** and **Landscape and Scenery.**

**Day and Night:** Daytime represents consciousness, or what you are aware of, while a dream in a night setting often suggests issues that you are not consciously facing. Explore the other symbolism as clues to what may need to be acknowledged and integrated. See **Placement and Perspective.**

**Dead People:** Seeing a dead body appearing in your dream can represent two things: Either a side of you is not achieving expression or you may need to allow some aspect of a past way of being to 'pass on.' You can be 'haunted' by the idea that a side of you is not being expressed. Since you don't acknowledge this - it haunts you. See also **Shadow, Death** and **Corpse.**

**Death:** The idea of death is a complex symbol with many meanings. If you dream that your life is being threatened, the dream is exploring how you are letting go of a side of you that is no longer appropriate or that you must let 'pass on.' If you are committing suicide, it can symbolize self destructive tendencies or your willingness to allow some part of you to 'pass on.' If you are witnessing someone else being killed, you are not owning this transformative process that is required of you. Ask yourself how the death of this 'other person' might represent a side of you that needs to undergo some type of change or metamorphosis. Since all people in dreams represent sides of you, think of the adjective you would use to describe the person who has died and how it represents you. Many people dream of seeing a loved one who has died and comes back to visit, as a way of taking baby steps in the acceptance of this loss. Often, they will see the person who has passed on a television show or in some other media form as the idea of accepting the death makes its way into consciousness. See also **Advertisement, Murder,** and **Attack and Being Chased**.

**Decay:** Something may be rotting as the image of the potential for "new life" that is festering because it is not receiving proper care. You may need to prune away old growth to allow something new to grow in its place. New doors may be opening, while you remain focused on only loss. Somewhere within, you are recognizing that some part of you requires care. See **Food** and **Corpse.**

**Deep:** To dream of deep water in which you cannot clearly see the bottom shows both the unknown potential within you and your fear of activating this power. A deep hole can symbolize feelings of being in a rut at the same time that it can suggest feelings associated with the mother. Whenever the idea of 'deep' appears in a dream, it is a good exercise to meditate on the imagery and actively explore what 'lies below the surface.' This type of dream is often associated with the activation of unconscious information as it seeks to have expression. See **Water** and **Placement and Perspective.**

**Deer:** A deer is associated with gentleness and the idea of the soul. It can be a message about what is 'dear' in life and the need to find it. See **Animals.**

**Defecate or Excrement:** In the same sense that we "chew on," "digest" and then, "eliminate" past experience and perspectives, seeing excrement can symbolize how something originally nourishing, may need to pass. To defecate in public can be a symbol of the embarrassment associated with exposing your most organic and natural aspects. The negativity or repulsion that is often associated with seeing excrement shows how the unconscious has rejected what you are holding on to, in a way that moves you to release it. Associated with another character or animal can suggest the side of you is being eliminated, such as feelings or the characteristics you associate with this person. See **Animals** and **Archetypes and Universal Characters.**

**Defend:** The symbolism that you feel the need to defend can offer insight into the area of your life that you are currently protecting, sometimes in an unhealthy way. Territory can suggest what you have built or "earned" as in your public identity, career, family or position in life. The idea of protecting something can either suggest recognizing its importance in your life, or seeing how protecting it has trapped you in your growth. See **Weapons and Utensils, Houses and Buildings,** and **Purses, Wallets, Luggage, Jewels and Keys.**

**Defense Mechanisms:** Habitual behavior or the "trained" mental and emotional responses that protect the psyche are called defense mechanisms. In your early years, you are like a sponge, "absorbing" incoming information to understand the person that you are becoming. Sometimes the feedback you received was positive and at other times, it may have been negative. Just like the other natural mechanisms in your body, the psyche has a way of protecting itself from pain by employing defense mechanisms. It can block any incoming information that causes you to feel "uneasy."

At some point in your life, a type of subconscious "net" begins to both trap beliefs within the subconscious, while rejecting anything that goes against what *you have been trained* to believe about yourself. A defense mechanism can be as simple as the psyche's ability to block emerging or transformative ideas. It can be as complex as how it attempts to work through difficult or repressed emotions by *leading you to confront repressed emotions through difficult experiences that hold a certain fascination for you.* In this case, you tend to attract the situations that you need, while these are the very situations that you would also prefer to avoid. The more you avoid this transformative aspect of the psyche, the more this symbolism will become the subject matter of your dreams and perhaps, daily experience.

You spend two-thirds of your life building belief structures that are "disassembled" during the one-third of your life that you spend dreaming. The human body was designed to receive and release energy, while it also has the ability to store and transform it. See Defense Mechanisms under **Biology of Dreaming.**

**Deformed:** Generally, this will portray a living thing, although any symbol that is deformed, or constructed in an "unusual" way, offers clues to that part of your nature that is undeveloped, or behaving unnaturally. See **Anatomy and Body Parts, Animals, Reptiles, Houses and Buildings** and **Landscape and Scenery.**

**Delivery Truck:** A delivery truck ties together the idea of moving forward with carrying baggage. Special delivery can signify being given insight about how thoughts become manifestation. Any package that is delivered can provide clues to what you are carrying around in thought and action that contribute to your experiences. You may dream of a moving van when you are having difficulty letting go of past resentments.

**Demolish:** Just as you "construct" belief structures, you also have the power to tear them down. If you are dreaming of demolishing something, chances are you are protecting something that is no longer necessary. Your feelings and the symbolism surrounding what is being demolished can portray how something may require protection against the "side of you that would tear it down"; i.e.: self-criticism. On the other hand, it may be an outworn aspect that needs to be torn down. See **Build** and **Defend.**

**Demons:** Similar to dreaming of **Aliens**, you are disowning some aspect of yourself that you have associated with being "evil," or you are having a difficult time "identifying" with. As you grow, you repress natural and instinctive traits, like aggression, neediness or pain if you believed it was *not good* in the face of social restraints. Evil is simply the opposite of the good or unacknowledged power within you. As this energy seeks expression, it can appear threatening or repulsive in proportion to how tightly you block its expression in daily life. See **Evil** and Shadow under **Archetypes and Universal Characters.**

**Dentist:** The character that pulls or fixes your teeth is associated with the side of you that cares for "what happens with the mouth," like expression. If **pain** or **blood** is involved, the dream is exploring the idea of painful communication, where "pulling teeth" symbolizes your frustration and inability to change your expression. Associated with **Teeth,** it can also represent enlightenment. See the Wise Man and Wise Woman under **Archetypes and Universal Characters.**

**Departing:** To dream of leaving is a common theme associated with **Vehicles and Places of Transportation,** in which you are hurrying or late. The time of departure can have symbolic meaning, portraying the sense of where you stand in relation to the stages of your life. Generally, if you are dreaming about the need to depart, you may be stuck in a transformational stage and need to "let go." The other symbolism of the dream will shed light on what part of you is departing, embarking or coming forward. See Time of Day under **Placement and Perspective. Arriving and Leaving** and **Numbers.**

**Descending:** See **Position and Placement;** and also, Floors under **Houses and Buildings.**

**Desert:** The environment portrayed in a dreamscape can personify the condition of your 'inner landscape.' If you dream of being in a desert, you may be feeling undernourished or unfulfilled. The barren landscape can be a message that coaches you to make changes that will lead to abundance and growth. A desert can also be associated with religious ideas as you explore your spirituality and how it might become more fulfilling or enrich your daily life. See **Landscape and Scenery.**

**Desk:** Representing your "work space," the desk is often associated with finding something unusual, looking for something, or writing as a way of exploring potential and your idea of authority through communication. See **Book;** Black, Red or Yellow writing under **Colors;** Lighting under **Placement and Perspective,** and Room under **Houses and Buildings** to uncover additional meaning.

**Devil:** The devil is a common Archetype explored in dreaming. One can have unconscious associations with the devil because it can represent a type of power within that is unexpressed and appears frightening.

The devil can wear the mask of the critical tapes of conscience that would prefer we *do right* and not rock the boat of evolution. Joseph Campbell explored the idea of "thou shalt" in his study of myths. Like dreaming, the hero undergoing initiation will first discover the clues that will reveal one's true identity. Like any good story, just when it seems the hero is home free, the monster appears to scare the hero back into a fearful world of seeking only acceptance.

In dreams, we are the hero who must slay the dragon as a powerful symbol of claiming its power. Dreams are like the mythical tales of mortals who confront frightening giants and beasts to succeed - only by doing so are we worthy of our destiny. By confronting one's deepest fears, we discover the magical elixir that releases us from our shackles and misunderstandings. In fact, it is common when one is going through a type of transformation that includes honesty and self-examination that these type of Shadow dreams come forward. Confronting fear and transforming it into self-actualization is a necessary part of the hero's journey of individuation. See **Shadow, Evil** and **Demons.**

**Diamond:** This "precious stone" often emerges in dreams where you "discover" it as the answer to all the difficulties that you may face. As the most valuable aspect of your nature, the associated symbolism will reveal its current "well-being" and how "uncovering it" can help you through difficulty. See **Purses, Wallets, Luggage, Jewels and Keys.**

**Dice:** As a symbol that suggests the random turning of events, dreaming of dice can portray the idea of gambling, or the uncertainty that you feel about the choices you are making. See **Numbers.**

**Dig:** In daily life, you dig to uncover the roots of something. You may dig for the truth or dig to bury an aspect, which you'd rather not face. This symbol goes deeper than just searching for something. It suggests that you know where it is and need only discover the roots to bring it back to life. On the other hand, digging can suggest the need to remove it completely, by destroying its roots. See **Burial.**

**Dinner:** Like **Banquet,** you are exploring nourishment in a social setting, sometimes associated with family dynamics. Its connection to "the later part of the day" brings a sense of impending darkness or "issues you'd rather sleep on," as opposed to the nourishment of **Breakfast** that sustains and motivates you. See **Food.**

**Dinosaur:** Reptiles can personify areas of the brain that act instinctually or autonomously. Stress or the flight or fight response can take the form of a reptile, and sexual impulses too, can be personified by these creatures. If a dinosaur threatens you in a dream, consider whether you are existing in a prolonged anxiety condition that may not be healthy. At the same time, not allowing for the free reign of sexual feelings can make these feelings overwhelm you in the dream state. There is a part of all of us that is as old as time and not easily controlled. Dreams of dinosaurs can show the activation or life of these instinctive responses. If you are finding only the bones of dinosaurs, the message can revolve around old issues, wounds or a healing that needs to take place. See **Reptiles.**

**Dirty:** This is a symbol often associated with sexuality and intimacy. Something only becomes "dirty" because it is "unclean" or taboo. Whatever symbol is recognized as being dirty will suggest *that part of you* that has been overlooked or neglected. Dirty can also be associated with attempts at transformation. When you are moving away from a past way of being that was adopted through conformity, your new persona, costume or clothes can appear dirty, yet dirty symbolizes a more earthy and organic side of you that is emerging. This is also the case when you dream that your house or inner architecture is dirty. Whether it is sexual or organic, the idea of dirty is a positive symbol about growth. See **Bath** and **Clean.**

**Ditch:** As a waterway, the ditch can portray how emotions are wearing away at your foundation. It can also suggest a place where you "ditch" something and allow it to be covered or buried through the accumulating passage of time. Sometimes it suggests a "last ditch effort," where you may be forced to approach the ditch to *dis-cover* or "uncover" the truth of something. The ditch symbolizes how you have buried something that "collects floating debris" in the same way that projection overlays the past upon the present. See **Abyss, River, Water** and **Ravine.**

**Diving:** A symbol associated with "going beneath the water," or "diving toward the earth" can reveal how your aspirations and sense of achievement remains connected to that part of you that stays submerged below the surface. You may have a sense of "being brought back to earth" if your ambitions are not fulfilling. At the same time, diving is a classic image of going *deep* to retrieve the treasure of untapped potential. See **Water;** Plane under **Accident,** Boat under **Vehicles and Places of Transportation** and Deep under **Placement and Perspective.**

**Doctor:** The doctor is the character that heals us. As a part of the psyche revealed by characters in our dreams, when this character appears you are working to heal something or moving toward integration as a type of 'operation' takes place. Your well being may require the symbolic removal (surgery) of another aspect that no longer serves you. See Hospital under **Houses and Buildings.**

**Dog:** A dog is a faithful companion and demonstrates unconditional love as the easy expression of feelings and love of this type in your relationship with others. If you are dreaming of a dog, you are exploring unconditional love and the idea of being domesticated or changed by a relationship. See **Coyote** and **Animals.**

**Dolphin:** This playful mammal interacts with humans and could be classified as "the dog of the sea." Like *dogs,* who are "faithful" and represent the easy expression of feelings and love in your relationship *to others,* dreaming of a dolphin suggests this loving connection taking place *within you* as you move to access the depths of the **Unconscious.** See **Sealife,** and **Water.**

**Donkey:** Beasts of burden suggest being saddled to responsibility, while the 'animal-ness' of these creatures suggest that it is not the right representation of who you are. The donkey is stubborn and can portray how you fail to see how you are yoked to responsibility that is not really yours. At the same time, the donkey can appear in a dream when the psyche is poking fun at obsessive or hard headed behavior. See also **Animals.**

**Door:** Doors represent both barriers and the idea of exploring potential. You may dream of a familiar house with a door leading to a room you didn't even know existed. Since the house represents your 'inner architecture,' the door can symbolize opportunities, unacknowledged potential or strengths that you are not considering. The door captures the idea of the way you hold yourself back from new experiences and also, the pathway to new experiences. The door can also be a sexual symbol if this area of your life is currently being held back.

     The front door is associated with how you reveal yourself in social situations. Dreaming of the front door represents a type of 'coming out' or a change in the way you appear to others. The backdoor leads to the area of the mind that is kept more private, and a dream associated with the backdoor can symbolize blockages or opportunities that you are not facing head on. Side doors capture the idea of influences, or the middle way between two tough choices. Associated with peripheral vision, the side door embodies ideas that encompass more of life than you are currently 'allowing in.' The coming and going through side doors can signify a type of hiding. Any characters associated with door openings should be explored. Consider the adjective that best describes the person and explore how they represent aspects of you that are currently 'coming or going' as in being adopted or released. See Door under **Houses and Buildings**.

**Dragon:** The dragon is an ancient Archetype found in stories where the hero is challenged to a type of metamorphosis. In mythical stories of virtually every culture - the dragon embodies the power to go 'below the surface' and rise above the earth with 'expanded awareness.' This is a powerful dream that captures the transformative journey that will allow you to tap your fullest potential. Although the dragon may be frightening - symbolically it represents your power for rebirth. At the same time, the fire breathing dragon can personify anger or defensiveness to cover your insecurities. A parent may have demonstrated a fiery temper, while you were not comfortable expressing anger because it was viewed as something bad. Later, you may dream of the dragon as a representation of unprocessed anger. In any case, the dragon symbolizes the awakening of full and free expression that leads to empowerment. See also **Reptiles.**

**Drapes:** Since drapes cover the windows, there is a sense of not being willing to see something or putting on pretenses, rather than expressing who you really are. See also **Curtains.**

**Dress:** Clothing in a dream can symbolize aspects of the **Persona**. The various articles of clothing will have different meanings. The dress is the most feminine of these symbols and can portray sensitivity or the aspects of the persona influenced by the mother. If the dress appears in a positive way - the message leans more toward acknowledgement, arrival or making your debut. If the dress appears in a negative way - you may have insecurities about how others view you. For a man to dream of a dress, the dream may be using this symbol as a representation of the activation of the **Anima**. For the woman, the message relates more to her identity. See **Clothing and Makeup.**

**Drink:** Drinking fluids suggests fulfillment or a necessary change related to emotional needs. See **Food, Alcohol, Water** and **Cup.**

**Drive:** Dreaming of driving has associations with what motivates you. If you are driving, you may be in control of your sense of direction but if the vehicle is out of control, you may feel insecure about changes you are making. The person driving you needs to be considered in terms of how they may be dominating you or more in control of your sense of destiny. See Driving under **Vehicles and Places of Transportation.**

**Drowning:** Like other **Water** dreams, your movement in water signifies how you are approaching change and how you feel about the changes. To dream of the need for survival in water, shows the enormous impact of your emotions, and how you are fighting to keep your head (thoughts) above water (your feelings). Drowning dreams are a wakeup call to integrate your feelings and express them so that you can master them.

**Drugs:** Similar to **Alcohol,** dreaming about drugs can be indicative of not facing the idea of substance abuse. Since they alter perception, taking drugs or being given a drug can be a message about changing how you view experience. If the drug is associated with healing, the other symbolism can provide additional insight into a lack of wellness or dis-ease. Receiving *an injection by a needle* has the additional association of pain and **blood,** which suggests difficult feelings that once integrated or "injected" into consciousness will have the power to heal.

**Drum:** The idea of "beating a drum" can symbolize a cause or something that has become a major focal point to the exclusion of other equally important issues. The drum can also represent the heart, bringing to light the things that you are passionate about. Drums are also sexual symbols and can relate to organic or earthy processes that are being activated.

**Drunk:** Being intoxicated in a dream can symbolize how you are exploring the idea of being uninhibited, See **Alcohol.**

# E

The letter "E" in a dream can be a symbol of harmony, ease or the idea of using the senses more as you take in experience. This letter can also suggest elimination and is related to extra sensory, energy and the less tangible side of life.

**Eagle:** The eagle is associated with keen vision and the ability to 'soar.' This powerful bird of prey can appear in dreams when you are feeling the need to expand your horizons or explore life in a more all-encompassing way. If there is something frightening about the eagle, you may feel that your desire for success and power is 'preying' upon your sense of fulfillment. Birds often appear in dreams when we are exploring critical conscience or ideas related to spiritual fulfillment. See **Birds.**

**Ear:** The focus on a ear in a dream can be associated with peripheral perception from the standpoint that you are aware of something that has yet to make itself clear to you. It can also suggest the need to be more attentive or to start listening more. Seeing an ear is an objective way of *seeing* how you fail to *listen*. Something is being said that you are not hearing. Explore the other imagery to shed light on what it is. See **Anatomy and Body Parts.**

**Earn:** When what you earn becomes the subject of a dream, you are exploring the idea of self-worth. Even receiving change from a clerk in a store can be a message of this type. Often the numbers are significant in understanding how self worth can be increased.

Representing what you receive in return for your efforts, this type of dream can offer a message about balance and finding value in what you do. The sense of bartering or trading shows this desire for balance, yet being 'paid' can represent fulfillment or finding work that really fulfills you.

Arguments about the amount of money due on a bill can symbolize issues related to the number discussed. In a sense, one side of you (waiter/what you do to gratify and nourish yourself, or builder/what is constructing your mindset, or tailor/what is constructing your identity) isn't adding up to everything your worth. Arguing over the bill can be symbolic of giving importance to one area at the expense of another. Also see Urn under **Homonyms.**

**Earring:** Since earrings 'adorn' the ear, dreaming of this type of jewelry can symbolize the need to hear and believe the positive reinforcement you are receiving. Additionally, you may be hearing only what you want to hear and are ignoring or covering the negative influence of another. Since the ear relates to listening and the jewelry enhances it, this type of dream can focus you to listen closely to what you hear. Finding, losing or giving an earring shows the power of words and your relationship to them.

**Earth:** Your relationship to the "earth" in a dream can show if you feel your "feet are on the ground." Perhaps you feel that your "foundation is giving way," since any shifting of what appears to be "solid ground" disrupts your foundation or beliefs. Working with the earth to grow something or digging beneath it suggests work that you are doing to uncover your "earthy" or organic and natural aspects. See **Dig, Natural Disasters** and **Landscape and Scenery.**

**Earthquake:** In life, you can have the feeling that once a foundation (usually beliefs) is in place - it should not be changed. You may have the sense that changes need to happen - but are afraid to allow any type of 'inner shifting' to occur. When you dream of an earthquake - the dream is bringing about this foundational change. Unlike a landslide that shows an inconsistency in thinking that undermines the foundation, or a flood that embodies how emotions eventually wear away at the foundation - the earthquake relates more to a tendency to block change - or a tendency to hold your ground. Dreams provide a safe environment to explore change. When you dream of an earthquake - the message is to loosen up your rigid outlook and move with the changes so that a foundation more appropriate to your needs of the present can be established. See Natural Disasters under **Landscape and Scenery.**

ent times, the East has been associated with new start or "new day" since the sun always rises from the East. **Houses and Buildings** that focus on the East, suggest some new aspect emerging as your sense of identity is given definition. Dreams of **Anatomy and Body Parts** associated with the idea of the East can represent the left side of the body. Finally, the East is revered as a spiritual symbol and may represent changes in your spiritual outlook.

**Eat:** Dreams about eating portray "ingesting" something and usually involve **Food.** The type of symbolic nourishment you are "hungry for" will be revealed by the food's symbolism. If you are eating something other than food, the dream may be portraying the idea of "hunger" through this symbolism as "food for thought" while you "digest" new experiences.

**Eating Utensils:** Kitchen utensils are associated with changes you are making. You use them to take what you need in order to find nourishment and self worth. Like food, the symbolism is exploring fulfillment. The difference between a fork and a spoon is their shape. A spoon suggests what you need to hold onto in order to feel satisfied, while the fork is more symbolic of taking a stab at something, or making a change in direction that will help you provide for yourself. The fork can also symbolize choices or a crossroad, as in a 'fork in the road.' The knife can symbolize ideas that are painful or the cutting away of something. You may have to face the truth or eliminate outworn behavior. Since it is used as a weapon, it can symbolize allowing feelings to rise to the surface. A spatula is associated with turning something over or seeing another side of the situation. See **Food** and **Cooking.**

**Eclipse:** Seeing an eclipse of the sun and moon can symbolize the harmonious alignment of feelings (moon) and assertiveness or power (sun.) If the landscape suddenly becomes dark because of the eclipse, you may be testing your idea of power against external powers that feel beyond your control. The onset of sudden darkness is also symbolic of recognizing how there may be issues that are still outside of your awareness. How the eclipse makes you feel becomes important in understanding the message of the dream. It can suggest a turning point and remind you to take stock of the magic and miracles that unfold around you.

**Egg:** The egg has many associations and is a universal symbol of renewal. Many ancient cultures decorated eggs to celebrate the onset of spring. Since new life is gestating inside of the egg, it can be associated with the birth of some aspect of you. See **Circle** and The Unknown Child under **Archetypes and Characters.**

**Egypt:** Dreaming of ancient Egypt can signify the symbolic 'archeological digging' of the deeper layers of the psyche. Its association with magic and resurrection offers a landscape of initiation and metamorphosis. To see a mummy can symbolize being wrapped up in one aspect of life at the expense of another. It can also relate to the idea of 'mommy' and whether or not you were encouraged in the free expression of feelings and affection. Often you will visit this type of setting when you are going through a difficult transformation, or when you are embarking on a spiritual path.

**Eight:** Eight can symbolize wholeness and the infinite aspect of life. In numerology, eight is considered to be a powerful number of creativity and leadership. Eight on a clock can symbolize a threshold where consciousness and the unconscious exchange places, signifying a type of transition in awareness. Eight can symbolize both awakenings and deeper levels of activating power. To see the number 8 written out can be showing you that two things are connected and you might explore how they are inter-related. The eighth floor can symbolize arrival and a sense of accomplishment. See **Numbers** and eight/ate under **Homonyms**.

**Ejaculation:** If you are dreaming of this type of sexual release - you may need to examine whether you are finding outlets for the release of your energy and passion. Semen can represent new life from the sense of rebirth. It can symbolize the release of power in a way that has previously felt trapped. We generally dream of what we are repressing - so dreaming of ejaculation can be a sign that you are not expressing your urges.

**Electricity:** Dreams of electricity often depict faulty wiring that leads to "unreliable" lighting, affecting your ability to see clearly. Its association with "charge" can portray "emotionally charged" encounters, or the type of conflict that can activate growth within you. As a source of energy, the well-being of the electrical circuits can reveal your current feelings about how things are "flowing" within you. **In Houses and Buildings,** electrical dreams can also be associated with neurological issues or being somewhat aware of the changing brain patterns that occur naturally during sleep. See **Sleep Paralysis.**

**Elephant:** As a powerful mammal, the elephant can signify feelings that are below the surface, yet have the power to trample over you. It is said that elephants 'never forget' and can be associated with long held emotions that need to be processed and released. See **Animals.**

**Elevator:** There are several ways to move between **Floors**, which represent the various areas of the psyche. *Upper floors* are aspirations, while *lower floors* can symbolize fear, or the subconscious attitudes that affect your ability to move "forward." The elevator "transports you" without any sense of control. Rather than taking actual "footsteps," you "hit a button" and trust that you will arrive at your destination.

Often associated with anxiety, you are forced to rely on a "mechanical vehicle," to get you where you want to go. In this way, the elevator can suggest patterns of emotions or programmed responses that influence your motivation and therefore, your ability to achieve success. At the same time, you "remain in a **Box**," where "doors" open automatically, and so, the elevator can offer a message about transcending these mental "programming" restraints. The ride can be smooth and reliable or something confusing and chaotic in proportion to the "circuitry" existing between aspiration and arrival. The other symbolism surrounding the elevator can offer clues on how your approach is working, or how you are integrating the idea of success and motivation. See **Vehicles and Places of Transportation** and **Arriving and Leaving.**

**Eleven:** Eleven is a number composed of one listed twice. It can symbolize an inability to bring two things together (as in the idea of two or relationships.) The eleventh hour suggests a sense of doing something against a deadline. Often you will explore the idea of balance and integration in the number eleven. See **Numbers.**

**Embarrassed:** Since dreams are exploring insecurities so that you can transcend them, often you will dream of doing something that leads to embarrassment. Dreams push you out of your comfort zone so that you can be who you are - independent of what others think of you. In new situations when you are revealing yourself to others, you may dream of being underdressed, in your underwear or going to the bathroom in front of others. Feeling like your dress isn't appropriate is the same as feeling that who you are doesn't quite 'fit in.' Evert aspect of nature is unique and human beings are no different. Even among family members - you are a unique variation of your the line you carry forward. The dream is showing you that you are indeed, different and should cherish what makes you unique.

**Emerald:** This "green" stone has associations with healing and the idea of your "precious" connection to your natural existence and life. See **Colors, Stones** and **Purses, Wallets, Luggage, Jewels and Keys.**

**Emergency Room:** You may have a series of dreams where a portion includes a visit to the emergency room, doctor's office or other crisis setting. Generally the prior dreams will be describing a situation you are working through and going to the emergency room is a message about seeking help. Our memories associate this symbol with the idea of a last resort or a life and death situation. This type of dream should be considered as the idea that you are not getting the message, or are not achieving the breakthrough. Surgery can suggest the 'cutting away' of unhealthy beliefs and often there is some type of pain involved in healing. Your defenses may be ingrained to the point that a necessary change is not being heeded. See also **911.**

**Empty:** The idea that something is "empty" in a dream suggests that you have a sense of fulfillment that may not be real. Whatever symbol is associated with being empty can provide further clues to the area of life that may be more appropriately recognized as being unfulfilling. The action of emptying something has associations with releasing or discarding the unnecessary.

117

**Enclosed:** Something that is enclosed, like a courtyard or corral, can have associations with feeling trapped. At the same time, the idea of being enclosed can suggest a circle or the cycle of life. This portrays how feeling trapped can be traced to dynamics within you that continuously creates opportunities for you to escape. When you are experiencing constant rejection, you might explore its root as your fear of intimacy. Feeling trapped goes hand in hand with ideas of being a victim, when in actuality you are the perpetrator of a perpetual cycle.

**Encyclopedia:** Not usually a type of book that is read for pleasure, dreaming of an encyclopedia can reveal a type of disconnection between thought and real experience. You may be moving forward in life classifying things into neat categories, while you miss the opportunity for real discovery. See **Books.**

**End:** As a sense of finality, exit or route of escape explored in a dream, the idea of "searching for closure or a way out" suggests feeling that there is no end in sight. The dreamscape offers a more holistic perspective, where one thing simply merges into something else. At the same time, the unconscious demonstrates a type of perception that also transcends your normal distinctions. If the end and a lack of resolution becomes a major focal point that stirs feelings of anxiety within you, perhaps you are learning to release a way of perceiving that only limits you. Anytime a door closes, another one opens and all endings hold the seeds of a new beginning. See End of the World under **Apocalypse** and **Landscape and Scenery.**

**Enemy:** Dreams offer us inspiration about relationships and living. All the people that appear in our dreams represent an aspect of who we are/were or might be. These characters can personify emerging or unknown aspects or areas of the self undergoing exploration. Dreams seem to say that the same process might be happening in our daily existence. What if all the people on our path are meant to teach us something about ourselves?

This is what is occurring in the dreamscape. There are no enemies and none of us are victims. We simply bring our baggage (good and bad) into situations to identify what parts of us should be strengthened - and what parts of us are unproductive and may need to be discarded. When a dream presents a character that threatens you or is at odds with what you are trying to do - examine how this character might represent your own unconscious tendencies. The enemy tests your vision, sincerity and sense of direction. You are the hero on a journey to activate your potential and discover your destiny. Just as the characters that test the hero of our ancient myths activate Self Awareness - the 'enemies' that appear in dreams and on your path are serving the same purpose. See **Evil** and Shadow under **Archetypes and Universal Characters.**

**Enter:** The idea of entering a structure shows inner movement toward exploring new aspects or potential. The entrance of a building symbolizes our inner ideas and the threshold of conformity separating what society expects of us. We enter a house to explore our 'inner architecture' and may enter strange rooms as a portrayal of untapped potential. We can enter a building to explore our potential more from the aspect of work or sense of self-worth. See **Cave, Houses and Buildings** and **Arriving and Leaving.**

**Erupt:** See Volcano under **Landscape and Scenery** and **Atomic Bomb.**

**Escape:** You can dream of trying to find a way out of some situation as the representation of how you are attempting to make a similar change in daily life. Feeling trapped can signify your own self limiting ideas - and seeking an escape can portray how you are moving to broaden your options. The dream is exploring the limitations you place on yourself where buildings can portray work; houses can portray ideas; and escaping in a vehicle through streets can symbolize needed changes in motivation or a new sense of direction so that you can find fulfillment. Escaping through doors can represent being open to opportunity, while escaping through windows symbolize a change in perspective or how you see the world. Since everything in a dream is embodying your inner world - you need only open the things you close so that you can move freely. See **Attack and Being Chased.**

**Evening:** The idea of evening is slightly different from night. It suggests subtle awareness, in that some light remains before the symbolism makes it way into the darker realms, where it can be repressed, or forgotten. Sometimes evening can represent time restraints or the idea that you are in your twilight years. See **Day and Night** and Dark under **Placement and Perspective.**

**Event:** A dream that focuses on a special event is bringing high focus to an area of your life. If it is a concert, you are exploring the expression of passion or the need to balance your life so you achieve harmony. If it is a performance, you may be viewing a type of change objectively or exploring how you may be acting. A fundraiser can symbolize the need to develop more self esteem. A sporting event can be exploring your sense of competition or your need for acknowledgement. If a spiritual leader is speaking at an event - it can be the activation of your Higher Self as you learn to trust its guidance. The theme surrounding the event can shed let on the area of your life that you are being drawn to 'witness.'

**Evil:** Human beings receive both physical and mental nourishment. As you grow, you are trained to express behavior that is 'correct and good.' Your more natural way of expressing yourself in behaviors that may have been classified as bad, can become repressed within the unconscious. Maybe you were exuberant when your family was not. This part of your nature does not go way, but continues to seek expression. Dreaming is a way for the psyche to express and integrate unprocessed qualities that you believe are not acceptable.

Nightmares or dreaming of something evil is actually the personification of your own misplaced power. They are a sign that something powerful and good (yet unexpressed) is coming to the surface.

Nature abhors a vacuum and energy that is created does not disappear; it simply transforms. Unprocessed ideas can fund a fear of a boogeyman or the enemy 'out there' who simply mirrors how you might confront the things you are hiding in here.

The less this energy finds natural and outward expression, the more powerfully it colors dreams, giving added charge and dimension to your encounters. If you are brave enough to open the door of your fears, you would find your childish and disowned nature, standing on a stool like the Wizard in the story of Oz. The by-product of disowning your natural vitality is how you create the idea of good and evil out there to avoid taking responsibility for what is happening in here.

The ancient stories at the root of western religion personified good and evil as opposing characters. Nature teaches us how opposite forces simply drive life in a state of change. What we might label as bad is the way that something evolves before we can understand its purpose. The ancient Greeks first described evil as the uncivilized passions that were not actively under the control of the will. As these ideas were tossed through the hands of time, and applied to dogma, the image of evil merely gives us permission to become victims.

Today, psychologists agree that evil is something that is committed by people conflicted by inner crisis. While you may believe that there is some mysterious or negative influence working against you, life has been committed to your success since the beginning. Denying or repressing anything only gives it the power to overwhelm you. Because it is repressed, it can become obsessive and compulsively driven. You become drawn to the very situations you fear because the psyche, like any other part of the body, seeks to process any energy that is unhealthy and counter-productive. See **Shadow** and **Nightmares.**

**Excrement:** See **Defecate and Excrement.**

**Exit:** Searching for, or going through an exit is another dream that is exploring the idea of closure and transformation. See **End, Departing** and **Arriving and Leaving.**

**Explosion:** Any explosion signifies the release of repressed anger or emotion of some type. The natural energy released shows the extent of how repressing emotions is not healthy. This type of dream explores the necessity of releasing feelings so you can be renewed and open to a changing world. In a dream, seeing the explosion of an atomic bomb and its threat of 'radio-activity,' can also warn of the psychological manifestation of physical symptoms due to the inability to recognize and process anger. An explosion is a positive sign that the past can be released so something new can grow in its place. See also **Atomic Bomb**.

121

**Eyebrows:** Eyebrows frame your expression and can symbolize your response and behavior. If you are grooming your eyebrows, there is a sense that you are changing your approach and self-image.

**Eyes:** To dream of the eye can portray the need to look at something more closely since eyes represent how you are viewing experience. If your eyes are closed, you are choosing not to face something. To see with your eyes closed portrays escapism. On another level, the eye can symbolize the connection of other imagery to the sense of "I" or the self when it is not being acknowledged. See **Anatomy and Body Parts.**

# F

The letter "F" can have associations with the taboo and also captures the idea of a grade that describes failing miserably. It can be associated with sexual ideas or amusement at the expense of being more disciplined.

**Face:** Seeing a face can be the objective idea of "facing" something. The symbolism associated with the face can suggest issues related to self-esteem or expression. See **Anatomy and Body Parts** and **Clothing and Makeup.**

**Faceless:** To dream of a character without a face can symbolize how you may not be 'keeping face' in a situation. You may have recently had the choice to make amends or do something that would have been embarrassing to earn back respect but chose not to. The faceless character can also be personifying your unknown potential as it exists as an 'open slate.' Finally, the most revealing aspect of a faceless character is the lack of senses. To see someone without a mouth, nose and eyes can be a message that you are not being natural, authentic or receptive in your communication with others or yourself.

**Facial:** Washing the face can symbolize wanting to change your identity or expression in a way that reveals your true self. If you are having a facial that focuses on pimples, your self esteem can be festering below the surface because of old tapes or feelings of being unworthy. In a sense, you are coming clean and allowing old wounds to be healed so your beautiful nature is revealed. The freshness associated with the face can also represent facing a situation from the standpoint of starting over. See also **Anatomy and Body Parts** and **Bath.**

**Facsimile:** The fax machine, like the phone, is a symbol of how communication from your unconscious is attempting to reach you. Since one document or idea is transmitted as an exact copy at the other end, the fax machine can also symbolize how thoughts become manifestation. The message or symbols on the fax should be explored to see what area is being brought to your attention. See also **Phone**.

**Factory:** A dream that takes place in a factory can be exploring 'manufactured' behavior or how you are going through the motions without feeling fulfilled. Since new things are made in a factory, you can be exploring how you might develop new skills or express new potential at work. See also **Houses and Buildings.**

**Fail:** The sense of humiliation that comes with failing in real life is transferred into the dreamscape with intensified emotion. Dreams always offer a playground to explore and process anxiety. However, "new" details or symbolism will be blended into a dream of failing something you are about to do, as a way exploring self-defeating thoughts. In real life, you may hold back your emotions and some incident can "set you off" with more emotion than the situation warranted. In the same way, the psyche takes a similar opportunity, by using "short range" or passing situations to work through "longer range" issues that can lead to wellness and balance.

**Fair:** See **Amusement Park** and **Circus.**

**Fall:** See **Autumn.**

**Falling:** A dream in which you are falling has the exact opposite meaning as the dream where you 'wake up' to discover that you can fly. Where flying suggests an awareness that can transcend self-restraint, falling suggests the anxiety associated with setting unrealistic goals. Another reason that is suggested for the common occurrence of 'falling dreams' is that some part of the psyche is aware of 'falling asleep' or 'sinking' into a state of unconsciousness during dreaming. See **Diving, Accidents,** Airplanes under **Vehicles and Places of Transportation,** and **Flying Dreams** under **Common Themes.**

**Family Members:** Dreams of family members often take place after an experience that has left you wondering about your personal dynamics. Dreams are often portrayed in cycles of three, where one dreamscape morphs into two other settings. The first part of the dream suggests the crisis at hand, while the second part of the dream often includes family members as a way of exploring early dynamics that were inherited, and may need to be released. The third part is usually the most bizarre, offering clues to your transformational process. You wake up and dismiss the peculiar when this is the most relevant part of the dream. The psyche seeks to break through in any way it can. The things you find most difficult to face will appear in symbolism that leaves you puzzled. Family dynamics that you have inherited offer an enormous pallet of symbols for transformation as you move forward to discover your *real* identity.

Natural selection drives divergence in character because the more diversified we are, the better will be our chance for survival. Even family members within a particular species are endowed with variations. This ensures that competition for short supply in a shared environment is minimized. The family can be a source of support, even while their dynamics shape you like water shapes a stone. In the contrast of your differences, they often reveal your deeper color. You simply stand in the present as life's best example of *one* variation of the line you carry forward.

The characters that appear in dreams are always portraying aspects of you. Siblings can personify your competitiveness or aspects that you associate with them, while parents suggest motherly and fatherly traits within you. See **Relatives, People** and **Archetypes and Universal Characters.**

**Famous People:** All people in our dreams represent sides of us. When you dream of famous people you are exploring the side of you that would be associated with the character. What are the adjectives you would use to describe this icon? These same qualities are being explored as emerging aspects of you. See **People** and **Archetypes and Universal Characters.**

**Farm:** Since a farm is a place where animals are domesticated, dreaming of being on a farm is a symbol of getting to the roots of your emotions and behavior. See **Animals.**

**Farmer:** To dream of a farmer explores how you are planting and harvesting your desires. In a sense, you are getting grounded to examine your thought processes. If the dream involves harvesting food, you are investigating how your natural desires and talents can lead to fulfillment. If your association with the farmer in the dream is negative, you may not be taking responsibility for how your thoughts are undermining what you are trying to accomplish. The farmer seems to suggest that you 'reap what you plant."

**Fashion:** You may dream of being a fashion designer as you explore a new way of presenting who you are. The act of producing clothes shows a change in the identity that is being cultivated through Self direction. If you are in a fashion show, you may be trying on different identities to gain acceptance when the real you is being neglected. If you trip or have a mishap, your insecurities about what others think of you are undermining your development and self esteem. The message can be to stop 'dressing the part' and find a way of expressing who you are from the inside - out. Fashion can show trends or covering your real identity with a false persona. Shopping for clothes can portray how you are seeking the type of work or expression that 'suits you.' See also **Clothes**.

**Father:** Generally all people in a dream represent us. The father in a dream signifies what we were taught in terms of aggression and asserting ourselves to become independent. The father portrays that part of us undergoing exploration, and the dream offers a message about its well being through the drama of what takes place with the father. See **Family Members.**

**Faucet:** This fixture allows you to turn the flow of water on and off. To dream of a faucet suggests that you are exploring how you turn emotions on and off. In a new relationship, you may be trying to overcome feelings of jealousy and possessiveness, or are being forced to subdue your real feelings. A situation may be forcing you to control your emotions and the issues surrounding the faucet will describe whether this is healthy.

**Fear:** If you were to boil all negative emotions down, you would find fear at the root in nearly every case. If something is unknown or not classified as good, it tends to go hand in hand with fear. As a self-organizing system, all human beings seek stasis, while life leads you to move beyond your tendency to hold to the familiar. Every plant and animal on the earth has outlasted a struggle for existence that is three and a half billion years old. Driven toward survival, overcoming fear is never second nature.

Fear and anxiety fund a large portion of what we dream. Why? Because we spend all of our lives *trying to control the outcome.* Change is the enemy unless we are the one orchestrating it. Dreams seem to push us beyond our need for control because growth is always easier when we are fearless.

Dreams are a safe environment to explore insecurities and fears. In fact, the vast majority of dreams involve some type of conflict. Dreaming allows difficulties we are facing to be 'acted out' through symbolism. Much inner shifting and growth occurs even while we are not remembering our dreams. When facing crisis, we are told to 'sleep on it.' When we wake up the situation always looks different. This is because much processing goes on in the dream state. Fear too, is diminished in this way.

When you wake up remembering the dream or feel afraid, you carry the strangeness of the dream back into consciousness. Often the bizarre symbols will stay with you as you explore its possible meaning. Dreaming specifically arouses emotion as a wake up call (not necessarily bad) and feeling fear is a strong motivator for change. Even the most frightening dreams are a good sign that something powerful is stirring within and seeking expression. See **Evil**, Nightmare and **Shadow**.

**Feather:** Seeing a feather in a dream can be a message about the need to 'lighten up.' If it is associated with another symbol, it can direct you as a key, pointing out what is required so you 'can fly.' The feather can personify the soul or spirit and the need for a more lightness in being. See Feather under **Birds.**

**Feces:** See **Defecate and Excrement.**

**Feet:** Feet can symbolize the ability to stand on your 'own two feet' or the ability to walk away from difficulty. Strange feet can suggest the path not traveled suggesting an unusual approach or way of carrying yourself forward. Bare feet suggest taking a path that allows for the natural expression of who you are. When a dream focuses on feet, you are exploring a way of going forward that better reflects who you are. See **Shoes** and **Anatomy and Body Parts.**

**Female Genitals:** Regardless of whether you are a man or woman, dreaming of female genitalia embodies connecting with sensitivity, intuition and the idea of rebirth associated with opening to what is kept hidden. For a woman, dreaming of breasts can portray her sense of value and the special qualities that she gives to the world. She may dream of another woman's genitals as she explores her own sexuality and openness, along with the idea that she may be keeping some aspect of herself hidden that is now being examined. For a man, dreaming of breasts can symbolize the desire to be nurtured and cared for. He may dream of the womb/vagina as a symbol of transformation or connecting with his latent sensitivity. See also **Genitals**, **Womb**, **Anima/Animus** and **Anatomy and Body Parts.**

**Fence:** Like the symbol of being **enclosed,** a fence can have associations with feeling trapped. In the case of the fence, it doesn't really keep things out and can be removed or bypassed quite easily. Feeling trapped goes hand in hand with idea of being a victim, when in actuality you are the perpetrator of a perpetual cycle. That you are dreaming of a fence, suggests that you realize that "established boundaries" can be torn down. The fence can portray the idea of "no trespassing" in a new relationship where boundaries are being explored.

**Fender:** Unusual fenders can be a clear symbol of an elaborate defense mechanism that is blocking or protecting your motivation. It is not uncommon to dream of an **accident** that causes a dent in the fender of an automobile. Since the car represents your power to move toward your goals, this is a common dream scenario. Look at the rest of the dream to understand your motivation and issues that may be keeping you from feeling empowered. See also **Vehicles and Places of Transportation.**

**Ferry**:  The ferry combines the idea of public transportation (moving with the crowd toward conformity) with being on a ship (exploring emotions and feelings.) If you are waiting for a ferry, you may be too concerned with the idea of acceptance and are not able to express your real feelings. Since you are waiting, you may be giving the power to be fulfilled and autonomous in life to others, or to the whims of fate. The message might be to stop expecting and take responsibility for how you feel.

The condition of the water in relation to this type of boat ride can portray what is going on below 'the surface,' or how you really feel. Turbid water can represent old hurts that you need to process and release. Choppy or frightening water can represent a sense that you are not feeling in control of your emotions. Not being able to control what the ship is doing is the same thing as not taking responsibility for where you are going in life. The message of the dream might be to explore your feelings and sense of autonomy. If you wake up each day expecting difficulty - you will find it.

If the theme is more of solace and peace - you may have recently overcome a period of crisis and are moving happily with the flow of events. Receiving acknowledgment in the social sphere also manifests as traveling on a ship with others over smooth water.
Explore what takes place on the ferry for additional insight into this emotional crossing. See **Cab** and Ship under **Vehicles and Places of Transportation.**

**Field:**  You can dream of a ball field as a way of exploring the idea of balance or feelings of competitiveness. In a more natural setting, you can be examining the part of your nature that is more natural and open. To dream of wandering into an empty field suggests a type of openness in meeting the future, where ideas can rise as inspiration. Regardless of what you are doing in the field, it is a symbol of expanding your awareness. Lush meadows can symbolize the fertile garden growing within you. You may come out of the forest after a difficult transition and arrive in the field as a representation of your newly expanded awareness. If the field reminds you of something from your childhood - you can be re-exploring your roots and limitations. If the field holds livestock, you can be exploring your spirited (horse) or domesticated (cow/goat) nature.

**Fight:** The idea of fighting with someone or something is slightly different from the fearful dream in which you are running away. In this case you are taking stand to defend some aspect of yourself against another part of you. As a dream of integration, it will reveal whether something is emerging or being discarded. See **Defend** and **Attack.**

**Film and Television:** To dream of something taking place on film, television or as an audience member shows how you are exploring something objectively that you have not yet integrated into consciousness. The character, drama or even the news has taken a format where you are 'entertaining the idea' but it has not yet been accepted. The message is being played, although you could just as easily walk out of the room and it would continue playing. This portrays a type of disconnect from the issue at hand and exploring the other symbolism in the dream will shed light on what it is.

Operas and concerts show how you are exploring harmony between various sides of you so that all can function in 'concert' or unison. When music is involved, the dream is exploring the free expression of emotion. Often the character that accompanies you to the concert can signify a side of you that is currently unexpressed. Many times people will dream of a loved one who has recently passed appearing on television, as their psyche moves toward the first steps in dealing with the loss. Television and movies can be see as displaying reality in a format of 'hyperspace,' ie: transition, or 'one step removed' from what you are prepared to acknowledge or face. It is common to see a loved one who has recently passed on tv as a way of coming to terms with the idea that they are no longer present.

**Find:** Just as fear and anxiety are at the root of many dreams because they are a large part of the emotions we are processing, discovering something seems to be at the center of all we do. When you dream of finding or searching for something, it is because whatever aspect that symbol represents in daily life is not given much consideration. To "find" it in a dream suggests that you must "find" or discover it in daily life.

**Finger:** The finger can be a symbol that is pointing you toward something you are failing to see. A finger on the right hand shows direction, while on the left hand, can symbolize commitment. See **Grasp** and Hand under **Anatomy and Body Parts.**

**Fingernail:** Since fingernails grow and must be groomed, because they are associated with the hand, dreaming of fingernails can symbolize new ways of providing for yourself or taking what you need. Extremely long fingernails can symbolize not letting go, while broken fingernails show how change must take place even while you hold to the past. If your fingernails fall out, there is a sense of learning to let go of what you thought you needed. Fingernails can also be associated with wisdom, although they are still associated with the hand.

**Fire:** Associated with anger, fire is a symbol of how this emotion can "burn" out of control. When fire becomes the subject of a dream, there is a sense of recognizing the destructive power of anger. This emotion is a variation of pain. When you are angry, it is because you are hurting in a way that you are unable to understand or process. Dreaming of fire and the other symbolism surrounding it can be a catharsis or healing vehicle for transcending the pain you feel. Fire is also associated with sexual feelings that are not finding an outlet. See **Ashes.**

**Firefighter:** Representing the character "who puts out fires" the firefighter offers interesting symbolism. Meeting **police** in a dream can be a symbol of restriction, but the firefighter always comes to the rescue during a time crisis. At work, you may be the "firefighter" rushing in to solve everyone's problems as a way of validating your worth. Perhaps there is insecurity surrounding your ability to delegate and as a problem solver, you find a road of many problems. Just as a person with a hammer sees only nails, a person with a fire-extinguishing device will find many fires. As a character representing you, the firefighter may be "putting out your fire" in terms of passion, sexuality and feelings. This character can also portray the defense mechanism at play in controlling anger. In this case, acknowledging anger may be required. See **Fire.**

**Fish:** The creatures that live beneath the sea bring together the theme of instinctual behavior and the idea of repressing emotion (water) as something that stirs "below the surface." Any living thing associated with the sea will generally portray the "living side" or movement of the unconscious in this way. Since ancient times, the *fish* has been associated with the idea of "trapping fate" or a lucky break. You may dream of a fish when everything seems to be "going your way." The different types of fish or creature and its **Color,** can shed light on how you are currently "connecting" with information from the unconscious. "A fish out of water" can also be a symbol of the uncertainty you may feel in integrating your authentic nature with what is expected of you. A *dead* fish often has an odor and may be a symbol that "something doesn't smell right" or the idea that what you are hoping for has passed you by. See **Sealife**.

**Fishing:** This is a classic symbol of trying to "hook" the things that are moving below the surface of awareness. See **Fish** and **Sealife.**

**Five:** Five is often associated with fertility and creativity. Like the five digits of the hand and feet, it can symbolize our path or how we take what we need to be fulfilled in life. See **Numbers.**

**Flame:** Dreaming of a flame can signify taking a closer look at what you are passionate about. Trying to light something in the rain can suggest the sense of something or someone "raining on your parade." See **Candle** and **Fire.**

**Floating:** Many things in life float. When a dandelion seed floats by in the wind, it has combined an intricate design with an ability to use the wind in its pursuit of regeneration. Floating does not always suggest aimlessness. However, when you see a symbol suspended in the air that does not usually float, the message suggests seeing beyond restriction. As you let your defenses down and move toward intimacy with another, you have the sense of "floating on air." Floating or seeing another symbol float is often a good indication that you are letting go of self-restrictive tendencies. See **Flying.**

**Flood:** Water Dreams are very common because water represents your emotions, and how you feel about *the changes* that you face, as you move through life. To dream of *turbulent water* suggests a sense of emotional crisis associated with moving forward. Any time this type of dreams occurs, later, you may dream about being on a similar ship and crossing the water that has become calm. This is representative of the emotional growth that you have achieved. In all of our ancient stories, water is the mysterious reservoir where the hero is to retrieve a treasure. Similarly, raging water often initiates you into a process of self-discovery. *Floods* can undermine the foundation of your beliefs until you are forced to let go. What you thought was solid and what you thought you needed, is washed away in the pursuit of basic survival. Water can also represent health and wellness since it is a symbol of the elixir of life. See **Dam** and Natural Disasters under **Landscape and Scenery.**

**Floor:** Dreaming of a floor can symbolize the foundation you stand upon. The condition of the floor shows whether or not it is stable. By traveling to a specific floor, you can be exploring levels of consciousness, where the upstairs can represent spiritual ideas and aspirations, while the basement has more of an association with what you are holding in the subconscious.

Stairs going up can symbolize examining aspirations, while stairs going down symbolize retracing steps or understanding the root of your motivation. The floor of a structure can be indicative of levels of awareness or may be associated with the meaning of the number involved: See **Numbers.** You stand on the ground floor of awareness and travel upward to achieve your ideals, or downward to find those things that you keep hidden below. Elevators and escalators that lead to different floors can also symbolize aspirations or how your upward or downward journey feels orchestrated beyond your control. See **Houses and Buildings.**

**Flower:** The beauty and delicacy of a flower can reflect the budding, blossoming or fragility of your "beautiful and sensitive" nature. It can sometimes reflect the sexual organs or the pleasure you give or receive.

**Flying:** Dreams of flying occur during exhilarating or empowering points in your life. You may be dreaming and suddenly "wake up inside of the dream" to realize that anything is possible and that you can fly. This is an aspect of the psyche exploring potential and self-imposed limitations. On the other hand, you may "wake up inside the dream" and do something of a routine to start the day. When you really wake up to discover that it was only a dream, it can portray the need for a "wake up" call in some situation. See **Airport and Airplanes**.

**Flying Saucer:** Like the dream of aliens, there is something unfolding that is so "foreign" to you, that you find it hard to identify with. The flying saucer combines this idea with issues of empowerment or forward movement. See **Aliens** and **Vehicles.**

**Fog:** The inability to see your way forward in some situation can be portrayed by fog. As the emerging or transforming and therefore, temporary state of affairs, it can also signify being "cold and wet" or reserved in your feelings.

**Follow:** When you have a clear sense of following the crowd or being led, it can represent how some patterned or conditioned aspect of yourself is currently dominant. If you are dreaming about it, chances are there is a need to follow a path that is not so habitual. Sometimes you will follow a **Wise Guide** in a dream to explore untapped potential. This can be an initiation type dream of discovering the clues that will help you actualize your destiny. Explore the landscapes and symbols associated with following to gain additional insight into the type of potential that is being explored.

**Food:** In daily life, food is obviously the essence of nourishment, and has similar associations in dreams. Your relationship to the food in a dream will reveal what you might need, or are currently giving away, or in search of daily life. Food and its connections to others or events suggests your hunger for success, or your relationship to others. If *eating is disrupting* something you are attempting to do, then you are not finding fulfillment and need to "digest" something to achieve satisfaction.

*Bread* and *water* represent basic needs, where bread can symbolize the body and water, the emotions. The nourishment that is taken in by *"drinking"* is associated with a "thirst" for something describing necessity, or luxury and pleasure, like "lapping it up" and "drinking it in." *Milk* actually takes the idea of nourishment a little deeper because of its associations with mother and childhood.

*Cake* or *desserts* represent enjoyment or escape in the sense of "having your cake and eating it too." *Vegetables* will have associations with their shapes and **colors**, often portraying sexual needs or fullness. *Vegetables that grow beneath the earth*, such as *carrots, potatoes, onions* and *radishes* often suggest how you are gestating or not actively acknowledging what is growing within. *Corn* has a special significance because of its association with teeth and ears, signifying increased sensitivity. The *carrot* is a symbol of ambition, as in going after the "carrot." *Onions* have many layers and can portray the intricate layers that need to be peeled way to discover sustenance. At the same time that onions make you cry and can symbolize the need to allow something painful to surface so that you can move to greener pastures. *Plants that require that you care for them while growing*, suggest that you must prune or nurture your sense of nourishment and fulfillment.

*Fruit on a Tree* presents a type of food, where sustenance is there for you, to be taken from the "Tree of Life." *Apples* can represent consequences, or achievement and effort, as something that grows and falls to the earth. *Apples* and *oranges* can suggest both health associated with their power to heal, although an orange is sometimes odd, since nothing rhymes with orange. Orange is also associated with the color that makes something stand out or requires attention. The *lemon* can be associated with a sour attitude or missing out on something and feeling jealous. Dreaming of *fruit* suggests that something exists within your reach and you need only "pluck it." *Meat* has an association with "hunting" or sexual nourishment, while *milk* suggests attainment and satisfaction in the sense of "the land of milk and honey" or "mother's milk" flowing from the breast.

**Foreign People and Places:** Going to a *foreign city* means that you are exploring social needs that are new or unfamiliar. Life is a constant learning process, and as you make changes, *all* aspects of who you are change too. Reflect on the nature of a particular city for clues about your current direction. Meeting foreign people, like **aborigines**, can suggest your more organic and natural elements coming forward. Cosmopolitan places and people will reflect the side of you that you associate with this group of people.

**Forest:** The tree often signifies the roots of who you are and the genetic heritage that grows within you. It is not uncommon to move through various levels of consciousness where you are lost, wandering or searching for something in a forest or cave. Sometimes you will meet the enchanting characters and animals that become archetypes during a period of transformation. Like the **Cave**, the forest is a powerful symbol of searching for your roots.

**Forget:** Since you are dreaming that you are forgetting something, you might explore its opposite meaning. Perhaps you are overly focused on something that some aspect of your higher mind finds trivial. On the other hand, you may be dreaming of what you are forgetting as a way of bringing it into a higher level of focus. Like dreams where you seem to be **Awake,** while actually asleep, dreams of forgetting show your **Anxiety** about having "so much on your plate" that you fail to "remember" the important things. The symbolism surrounding what you are forgetting will provide additional insight into what it is.

**Fork:** Kitchen utensils are associated with changes you are making. You use them to take what you need in order to find nourishment and self worth. Like food, the symbolism is exploring fulfillment. The difference between a fork and a spoon is their shape. A spoon suggests what you need to hold onto in order to feel satisfied, while the fork is more symbolic of taking a stab at something, or making a change in direction that will help you provide for yourself.

**Fountain:** As a majestic and endless flow of water, the fountain can represent your regenerative and free flowing feelings and your connection to your inner "wellspring." See **Water.**

**Four:** A dream that focuses on the number four is exploring a more earthy perspective. Four can represent the elements in terms of balance and the idea of getting grounded before moving forward. See **Numbers.**

**Fox:** The fox is associated with craftiness or sneaky behavior. Their refined instincts can symbolize intuition that is not being acted upon. See **Animals.**

**Friend:** All people in a dream represent various parts of your identity as you grow. Friends from childhood can portray characteristics that were adopted during those formative years, while current friends will portray that side of you that you associate with them. What is the one word you would use to describe this friend? Reflect on this characteristic within yourself.

**Frog:** See **Reptiles.**

**Front:** See **Placement and Perspective.**

**Frontier:** See **Border.**

**Frozen:** Anything that is cold or frozen in a dream represents the idea that you are cut off from your feelings, or you are keeping an idea 'on ice' rather than processing and releasing it. Seeing something frozen, or encased in ice and lifeless can signify your awareness that some aspect of you is inanimate, possibly because of fear: 'frozen with fear.' Explore the symbol that is associated with being frozen for additional insight into what you may need to thaw out and bring back to life.

**Fruit:** Since fruits are juicy and nourishing, they can be sexual symbols. As a food, they personify fulfillment and perhaps, 'taking a bigger bite' out of experience to know fulfillment. You may need to slow down and appreciate the journey. As the 'fruit of your labor' fruit can be associated with reward. See the individual fruits under **Food.**

**Funeral:** See **Burial.**

**Fur:** As a "protective covering that provides warmth," fur can be a symbol of seeking protection or security. It can also appear as a reference to sexual urges that are hidden.

**Furniture:** Often associated with a room, the symbolism of furniture can represent "where you rest" your ideas in relation to that area of the psyche described in **Houses and Buildings.** You may explore your idea of sexuality in a bedroom, although if the dream focuses particularly on the *bed*, it suggests that you are "trying out" a new way of understanding your sexual needs. Sometimes you will find yourself doing unusual things on the bed as your psyche exercises the opportunity to break you free from restraint, or to bring unacknowledged feelings to light.

A *chair* portrays the way in which you "rest" when you are not moving forward, and can symbolize the ideas from the past in which you take comfort. It's condition, colors and patterns can offer clues to the ideas you take for granted. The *couch* and *sofa* reveal a more relaxed attitude as you approach the idea of comfort and satisfaction. The *table* is a place where things are "out in the open" or displayed for public view, as in "out on the table." Items on a table can suggest the current way you are expressing yourself. A *lamp* provides additional light or insight, and can symbolize something from the unconscious that is attempting "to come to light." The *carpet* or *rug* is often a symbol of sweeping issues "under the rug" as you move forward. Patterns in a rug can portray how you are exploring the part you play in creating your circumstances. See **Houses and Buildings** for it's connection to furniture in dreams.

# G

The letter "G" can be associated with ideas that are stored, symbolizing concepts like garage and garbage. It can have a message about searching for the key to a breakthrough. "G" can stand for girl, sexual ideas like G-spot or G-string and can signify enjoyment or pleasure.

**Galaxy:** Dreaming of space can personify your need for space, but can also symbolize coolness or aloofness in your approach. Watching something unusual happening in space can portray your need for recognition. Stars falling to the earth can be symbolic of getting grounded or making your goals more attainable. A galaxy can symbolize aspirations and the patterns of tomorrow you are shaping through your beliefs. If you meet individuals from another galaxy, you are awakening to your unrecognized potential. The side of you that makes you different from others is being explored.

**Gallows:** Dreaming of gallows or witnessing a hanging can personify your feelings of guilt in some way. Why is the person being hung? Are they being punished unjustly? The person being hung can represent your own tendency to punish yourself with self criticism. Seeing a hanging can also portray feeling constricted or unable to freely expand your horizons. Dreams present a safe environment to explore conflict and crisis. When the setting of a dream involves gallows where someone is to be hung - the message can be that you are sabotaging some aspect of yourself. Examine the character that is being hung to see if it might represent a side of you that is feeling suffocated or unexpressed. Hanging is also associated with being in a state of suspension. You may also be harboring a sense of guilt that is undermining your ability to stand up for yourself.

**Gambling:** Going gambling can suggest a willingness to try something new. At the same time, dreaming of gambling can be an acknowledgement that you are taking unnecessary risks in some way. What was the outcome of your dream about gambling? This might provide a clue as to whether your current approach is too restrictive or needs a healthy sense of self discipline.

**Games:** Playing a game in a dream brings the idea of various aspects within you vying for competence. Just as you can dream of pursuing or being pursued by non-integrated or emerging aspects, the game shows a deeper movement toward integration. The type of game, players and your feelings surrounding the situation will provide additional clues as to how confident you are in bringing this new side forward. See **Attack or Being Chased.**

**Garage:** Combining the idea of a building (aspect of the self) and transportation (your drive to move forward) the condition and situation surrounding the garage will shed light on the side of you "that houses or protects your motivation." Garages can also be associated with what is stored or must be relinquished in order to move forward with a great sense of purpose or passion. See **Vehicles and Places of Transportation.**

**Garbage:** When you are dreaming of garbage, you are exploring what may have been "discarded," but is not really gone. The fact that you are dreaming of some type of symbolism associated with being garbage reveals how you are either still holding on to it or not appreciating its inherent value. Explore the symbol for further insight.

**Garden:** The garden can personify what you are planting and expect to harvest, as in how what you do today becomes the results you experience tomorrow. It can portray the idea of your potential and the ability to blossom. Caring for the garden in a dream can be symbolic of how you must care for your inner garden. See also Garden under **Houses and Buildings.**

**Gardener:** The gender of the character who comes to prune away old growth can symbolize the side of your nature (female/sensitive or male/assertive) and how you are currently caring for it. See Garden under **Houses and Buildings**.

**Gasoline:** Dreaming of gasoline can have two distinct meanings. On one hand, it is a combustible fluid, representing the danger of explosive emotions. At the same time gasoline is a fuel that propels the car forward, signifying the root of motivation.

**Gate:** The difference between a door and a gate is in how it protects you. Closing and locking a door presents the idea that you can open and shut some aspect of yourself at will. The gate often symbolizes more of a defensive structure. At the same time, the gate is a symbol of entering a new threshold or your movement into more profound and unknown level of awareness.

**Genitals:** Genitals have associations that transcend the simple ideas of sex. Breasts often relate to how you are exploring self-nurturing ideas and behavior. For a woman, breasts can symbolize what she gives of value to society, from the sense of how breasts nourish life. Female genitalia for a woman will signify her essence or deeper connection to life. To a man, female body parts reflect issues related to sensitivity while he explores the 'undeveloped' traits associated with femininity. Male genitals for a man can represent his power and life force, while a woman dreaming of male genitals can represent being more empowered or aggressive. See **Womb, Anima/Animus** and **Anatomy and Body Parts**

**Germs:** See **Bacteria.**

**Ghost:** When you dream of characters that are "not living," yet still have a presence, explore what they represent as a side of you that is unprocessed and may therefore, be "haunting" you. If the ghost frightens you or is hiding, that is all the more reason to self-integrate the power that this ghost holds "over you." If it is the ghost of someone who has passed, it can portray how you are processing the feelings associated with this passing or "adopting" their qualities. See also **Shadow** and **Nightmare.**

**Giant:** Since all characters in a dream represent you, dreaming of a giant or "larger than life" entity can personify the added emphasis you are putting on a certain aspect of your persona. The symbolism and behavior associated with the giant can provide clues as to whether this is healthy or destructive.

**Gift:** To receive something as a "gift" in a dream brings forward the idea that some side of you, particularly while dreaming, has the omniscient ability to provide insight, inspiration or intuition. Since the gift is often "packaged" for special delivery, the symbolism associated with being a gift will portray how the unconscious is delivering this aspect to you. You open a gift with careful consideration for the giver, therefore the character presenting the gift should also be considered as to how their characteristics pertain to you.

**Girl:** The girl can portray the innocent application of the feminine or sensitive nature. A man dreaming of a girl may be exploring sensitivity learned as a child, while a woman may be exploring aspects of actual `childhood. See **The Unknown Child** and **People.**

**Give:** When you give something, there is often the idea of sacrifice or an emphasis on balance. Who is doing the giving and what is being shared should be explored as the idea of integrating areas of life that are leading to imbalance. See **Gift.**

**Glass:** Like the **Cup,** a glass can be associated with the things you hold to be important. As a receptacle for liquid refreshments, it is associated with feelings or the intuitive flow of information. Dreaming of either can portray holding or trying to capture these things in an effort to gain insight about sustenance. A broken glass portrays a sense of pain or fear associated with feelings. Glass that acts as a barrier, such as a window, can symbolize the idea of blocking intimacy.

**Glasses:** A dream that focuses on eyeglasses can be offering a message about putting things in perspective or seeing more clearly. If there is something odd about the glasses, examine what makes them functional/dysfunctional as symbolism related to changing your perspective. Glasses in a cupboard can be associated with family dynamics, as in heirlooms and how our emotional responses are adopted from early upbringing. Sunglasses can symbolize diminishing the 'glare' when you are over reactive or unwilling to face something that makes you angry. See also **Binoculars, Glasses and Microscopes.**

**Gloves:** Since gloves protect the hands - you may be acting overly self-protective rather than reaching out to take what you feel you need. The idea of using 'kid gloves' in a situation can make this a symbol of using extra care in approaching an issue. Finding an unusual glove can represent new capabilities or learning a new skill in your work. Finally, the glove can symbolize an inability to receive from the sense of intimacy, as in being more able to feel. A sport type glove would have more of an association with integrating work with other responsibilities - or something related to balancing various aspects of your life. See also **Hand** and **Clothing.**

**Glue:** Glue in a dream can refer to the idea of attempting to make something stick that feels like it is broken or falling down. It can relate to insecurities in a variety of areas - so examine what you are gluing back together. A broken vase can represent relationships; a photograph can suggest a perspective you are trying to recapture. If the glue is on your fingers - you may feel you are attracting the very experiences you would rather avoid. Consider the ideas you entertain during the day - are they positive and optimistic? The glue is a symbol of why you attract or hold onto the same experiences.

**Goal:** The goal is an obvious symbol or where your actions are currently taking you. Since you are dreaming about it, chances are you are not aware of the root of your own motivation. See **Games.**

**Goat:** A goat symbolizes sexuality, impishness and playful curiosity. As a symbol associated with sacrifices, dreaming of a goat can be a message about sacrificing fun at the expense of duty. If the goat is associated with milk, it can be a symbol of maternal input as you explore a lighter to side to this influence. The Goat's association with the astrological sign Capricorn as an Archetype captures the idea of ambition, perseverance and/or you identity in the larger scope of society. See **Animals.**

**Gold:** Gold as a symbol has associations with extreme value. In life, there seems to be nothing that holds its value like gold. Searching for or discovering gold can be symbolic of tapping or recognizing your specialness and uniqueness. Although you may think that finding gold

143

means you will come into money, gold is something natural appearing in the earth and is associated with self-value. See **Colors.**

**Gorilla:** As a primate that resembles humans, this animal is very territorial and frightening. The gorilla can symbolize rage or anger or an aspect of power that is not being expressed. It is typical for a woman to dream of a gorilla or King Kong creature when she is approaching menstrual changes as a symbol of the immense power that her body holds over her. Kissing this creature can symbolize connecting with these life stages in a positive way. For a man, the gorilla can capture a sense of being overly-masculine at the expense of one's sensitivity. See **Animals**.

**Grandparent:** It is common to dream of grandparents during the later stages of a difficult transformation. Just as the Unknown **Child** in a dream can represent the birth of new sides of you, dreaming of the matriarch and patriarch of the family can portray the development of a more wise side of you that has been seasoned by the transformation. Often the grandparent can be viewed as the Wise One Archetype activated after a period of intense soul searching or difficulty, now awakened as an aspect of the Self. In some cases a grandparent can represent the objective exploration of dynamics associated with the parent that is related to them. In this case, you may not be acknowledging the positive characteristics inherited by this parent. See **Family** and **Archetypes and Universal Characters.**

**Grasp:** The idea that you are forced to "grasp" for something rather than just take it, brings a high level of focus to whatever the symbol represents. For example, drowning and grasping for something for survival brings forward the idea of being overwhelmed with fearful feelings. *That thing* you are trying to reach will provide clues to how you might integrate it to find wellness. The hand represents both taking and giving. Grasping something so that you do not lose it suggests desperation and perhaps, an unhealthy relationship to whatever you are holding.

**Grass:** The smell of cut grass and hearing the sound of lawnmowers usually coincides with the onset of summer. This can be a symbol of relaxation and a sense satisfaction. All things that are growing share the common symbolism of nurturing, however grass grows abundantly and multiplies quickly. It has the added feature of being somewhat "man-made" and unnatural.

**Gray:** See **Grey** and **Colors.**

**Grave:** See **Burial.**

**Green:** Green is a color of healing and renewal. It can represent being more natural or getting your feet firmly planted on the ground. A piece of clothing that is green is often a clue that your identity needs to become more closely aligned with who you really are. See **Colors.**

**Greenhouse:** Like dreams of the **Earth,** the idea of protecting the things that you are growing can be portrayed by the greenhouse. See Garden under **Houses and Buildings** and **Gardener.**

**Grey:** You can dream of the color grey as a representation of your mood. It can also symbolize the obscure or undefined that might require definition. Something that is grey is usually in a state of decay or undernourished and can symbolize the need to nurture and revive an area of your life. See **Colors**.

**Ground:** The ground is symbolic of the foundation of your beliefs. What is happening to the ground can personify changes that are taking place to your 'internal foundation.' Not being on the ground can be a message to become more grounded. Walking over an unusual type of ground can symbolize a type of inconsistency in your ideas. Ground that is giving way can symbolize a shift in perspective, while soggy or water seeping into the ground shows the incorporation of feelings into your perspective. See **Natural Disasters,** **Earth** and **Landscape and Scenery.**

**Group:** See **People** and **Crowd.**

**Gun:** The gun often appears in dreams when sexual feelings are leading to difficulty and pain. To dream of someone threatening you with a gun can embody the threat posed by these feelings. If you see guns buried under a house, you may not be giving free reign to your sexuality. Guns can also personify defense mechanisms at play. If you are looking for a gun, you may be exploring the root of feeling like you are sabotaging your relationships. See also **Defense Mechanisms** and **Weapons and Utensils.**

**Guru:** Interacting with a spiritual leader can have both positive and negative meanings. On one hand, this can represent a sense of enlightenment related to the other details of the character (man/achievement or woman/sensitivity). When the "spirit" awakens within, you have moved beyond family dynamics to explore your unique qualities. At the same time, this type of dream may be exploring the idea of following a spiritual pathway in a cult like fashion, perhaps denying more basic needs that have not been met. Remembering that all characters represent an aspect of you, explore the symbolism, behavior, and how this character left you *feeling* to understand its message. See **Wise Man** under **Archetypes and Characters.**

# H

Seeing an "H" in a dream can symbolize critical focus, since H can be a sign for Hospital or Help. It can also portray the way to happiness, haven and harvest and can symbolize the simpler things in life that bring nourishment.

**Hair:** Dreams related to hair symbolize attitudes and ideas that grow, must be groomed and how ideas fall out of fashion. The condition of the hair can symbolize how you currently relate to your ideas. If you are sporting a strange hairdo, you may feel that your ideas are crazy or not acceptable. If you have hair of an unusual color, explore the <u>color</u> for information about ideas that are being adopted or need to be considered. For example, if your hair is straight but you dream that it is curly, the dream can be guiding you to lighten up. If your hair is curly and you dream that it is straight, the dream might be suggesting that you 'straighten out' your thinking or tone it down. Changing hair color shows the shifting of focus in whatever you associate with the color. Body hair can portray a need to be more natural in your expression. See **Anatomy and Body Parts.**

**Hairdresser:** See **Barber or Beautician.**

**Hallway:** Buildings and Houses represent our inner architecture as it relates to work or simply being and expression. The various rooms will represent different aspects and the hall is the transitional space that joins them. When we dream of being in a hallway, we are opening to opportunities, exploring potential and the idea of making a change. See Hall under **Houses and Buildings** and **Corridor.**

**Hammer:** To dream of a hammer can portray how you are taking the initiative in some way to straighten out a situation or resolve it. The hammer shows a focus on power and cohesiveness - with the idea of 'hitting the nail on the head' or 'pounding out a solution.' If you are searching for a hammer or have misplaced it - you may feel powerless in a situation. If the hammer is deformed - you may not be seeing the situation in its proper perspective. See also **Weapons and Utensils.**

**Hand:** As an extension of the **Arm,** the hands represent the idea of taking and giving. Focus on a hand can symbolize the need to release something or that the power to change and know success is within your reach. See **Anatomy and Body Parts.**

**Handbag:** The handbag or purse combines the idea of identity with what you hold to be valuable, and therefore protect. It is common to lose or misplace your purse when your identity or self awareness is going through a transition. Consider where you lost your handbag for information about where you are placing your priorities. This is a very personal symbol that reveals who you really are and what you 'carry with you' daily. Losing the purse can also coincide with financial insecurity when you are exploring change in career pursuits. See **Purses, Wallets, Luggage, Jewels and Keys.**

**Hanging:** Dreams present a safe environment to explore conflict and crisis. When the setting of a dream involves gallows where someone is to be hung - the message can be that you are sabotaging some aspect of yourself. Examine the character that is being hung to see if it might represent a side of you that is feeling suffocated or unexpressed. Hanging is also associated with being in a state of suspension, while something suspended in the air can represent an opportunity that you are not seeing. Being hung can suggest how you may be harboring a sense of guilt that is undermining your ability to stand up for yourself.

**Hat:** Of all clothing symbols, the hat relates more to what you do to be acknowledged. Since it covers the head and therefore, the thoughts, the hat can signify how you express yourself or what you are known for. The type of hat can describe an area of thought: Baker's Hat: nourishment and fulfillment; Police Hat: discipline and abiding by the rules or conscience, Fire Hat: how your thinking can get you into trouble or how you hide your feelings by 'dowsing' them, or Helmet: protective or aggressive tendencies. Wearing a strange hat can portray how you are moving out of your comfort zone to express yourself differently. See also **Clothing and Makeup.**

148

**Head:** The head 'houses' your ideas. It is the seat of your personality and way of thinking. If the dream focuses on a head that is not yours, the message is that you have adopted ideas that are not yours. This type of dream can show the disconnect between what you are doing and saying and how your really feel. See **Anatomy and Body Parts.**

**Healing:** Symbols that are **Green** or associated with **Digging** or the **Earth** often portray how healing is taking place within you. Dysfunctional issues related to a house or vehicle will also point at the well-being of certain aspects of the physical body. Many times vehicle doors or lower and upper rooms of a house will depict aspects of the body, offering a message about your health and well-being.

      The *front door* can suggest arms and the *back doors* can represent legs. *Lighting* can be electrical circuitry or neurological, while *water* problems can be vascular or reflect "plumbing." Water appearing as a threat is usually associated with emotional issues. The *top floor* of a building can represent the head, while the *rooms below* can suggest various parts of the lower body. Protecting a *"treasure"* can signify repression at the root of illness, while searching for a *key* is often the clue to achieving wellness.

      If you are experiencing "dis-ease", *where* it is taking place in the body is as important as why. If the left leg is suffering, look for its representation in dreams of the back or lower left portion of a structure or vehicle. Sometimes before a physical manifestation will appear, you are warned of over indulgence or things that can impact our wellness. This is most obvious in the borderline alcoholic who is always dreaming of searching for something with images related to alcohol. Many therapists recognize repression at the root of illness. Since dreams portray what you are repressing, they are a profound tool in achieving wellness and balance.

**Hearing:** Dreaming of issues related to your ability to hear will often point directly to the idea that you are *not* listening. This could emerge from a situation of verbal abuse that is being ignored. Sensory tools allow you to take in new experiences. Communicating your ideas is important, but not at the expense of discovering new ways of understanding the world, you are growing into. When you are trying to communicate to others who are not listening, it portrays some part of you attempting to communicate with another side. What is being said and the other symbolism will shed light on the issue at hand.

**Hiding:** The idea of hiding something in a dream suggests the need to cherish or protect what may be given too freely. Finding something hidden is usually a reference to feelings or experiences that were long ago repressed, but are currently being explored. If you are hiding, see **Attack and Being Chased.**

**High:** When something in a dream appears higher than where you stand - the dream can be exploring ambitions or opportunities. The positioning of the symbol can place it in way that shows its influence, and in a sense 'hangs over you.' Like intoxication, these types of dreams can also be exploring the idea of releasing inhibitions. The idea of High in a dream is how you attempt to move beyond a sense of restriction. Your focus moves 'upward' as opposed to feeling grounded or rooted. See also **Placement and Perspective.**

**Hippopotamus:** The Hippopotamus presents a sort of hybrid, in that it is an animal associated with diving beneath the water, where its large size is indicative of the enormous emotions that can be submerged. See **Animals** and also **Reptiles**.

**Hold:** This is another dream of trying to "grasp" the importance of something you are holding on to. It may be important and require protection or may need to be discarded. What you are holding and the situation surrounding it can offer insight into whether this is a dream suggesting you resurrect or abandon something. See **Defend, Grasp** and Hand under **Anatomy and Body Parts.**

**Hole:** The hole is an obvious symbol that "something is missing" or "incomplete." As a hole in the ground, it can represent the idea that the foundation that you are standing upon may be unstable. At the same time, the hole is associated with the **Cave** or womb, so can appear as a way of combining the idea of incompleteness with motherly influences or nurturing.

**Home:** Dreaming of a home from childhood can represent ideas that were adopted at that point in your life. Dreaming of your home with rooms that do not exist in real life can be a way of exploring unknown potential described by the other symbolism in the rooms. Going home in a dream is a way of exploring your inner foundation and seeking to be centered. See also **Houses and Buildings.**

**Homeless:** Seeing a homeless person in a dream is an objective first step in exploring your own lack of fulfillment. A beggar or vagabond is a character that can portray a lack of self esteem or the ways that you kid yourself into believing you are happy. You may be going through some type of routine and not acknowledging your lack of fulfillment. The appearance of this character and how you relate to them allows you to explore your own sense of homelessness or the idea that you are not grounded. Sometimes this type of character will appear like the Fool or **Trickster** that trips you up in your inconsistencies. Often they will pester you as a way of making you look back at yourself honestly.

**Homonyms:** Since dreams have an uncanny way of breaking through your defensive barriers, often a homonym or word image will be used. A homonym is a word that sounds "like the same old thing" but offers a different meaning as a way of "tripping you up." For example: saying something *aloud* is the same as saying what may not be *allowed,* in the case of discussing difficult ideas you'd rather not face. Approaching the *altar* often coincides with attempting to *alter* or change your behavior; Inside of a *cell* can be a way of understanding the ideas that you *sell* to others, while authenticity remains a prisoner to convention. Someone may give you ten *cents* as a part of you explores the idea of *sense* or the increased ability to feel and acknowledge your worth. The idea of time and how you may be missing the importance of the present, can be symbolized by a *watch* and the idea of *watching*.

The dream can focus on a *duel* as a way of understanding *dual,* or the two conflicting ideas that have brought you into crisis. An *urn* can be a way of understanding what you *earn* as you explore self-worth. When a *maid* appears to make the bed, you are given the opportunity to understand what you have *made* of circumstances, in the sense of "making your bed and lying in it too." Hearing the word *morning* or a dream that is focused on the morning can also have an association with

151

*mourning* and feelings of sadness that remain unprocessed. You may dream of a *mummy* in the first stages of recognizing things that were adopted from *mommy* that may need to be relinquished. To *knead* bread is the same as the idea that you may *need* money or are overly focused on material security. The number *six* often appears as a cryptic way of exploring the idea of *sex*. Seeing a *knot* can suggest *not*, while undoing a knot is that same as undoing "not" and opening up. An *oar* can be *or*, offering the idea that the resolution is something you perhaps, are not considering. *Tents* can suggest nervousness or being *tense*, and focusing on a *vein* can signify being *vain*. If the symbol offers no obvious clues, explore whether it may also be a homonym.

**Homosexuality:** One of the most common and misunderstood aspects of dreams, performing homosexual acts while dreaming simply brings the idea of the "taboo" or disowned side of yourself forward for exploration. Mounting or being intimate with the same sex is a way of "incorporating" the deeper aspects of your feminine or masculine nature. At the same time, you may be exploring your hunger or lack of affection from either your mother or father, depending on the scenario. See **Affair** and Anima/Animus under **Archetypes and Universal Characters.**

**Honey:** Associated with the "birds and bees," honey can symbolize the sticky, but sweet nature of sexuality. See also **Cream.**

**Horse:** The horse is a 'spirited' animal and can appear in dreams when you are exploring issues of spirituality. Also associated with racing, the horse can be a symbol of enthusiasm and a desire to win. As an image of 'horsing around' the horse can also be a clue that you need to take life more seriously. See **Animals.**

**Hospital:** Dreams that take place in a hospital setting seem to suggest that a crisis may be taking place, although you may or may not be aware of it. As the last resort when we finally reach out for help, dreaming of being in a hospital can show very acute changes we are making within. The operation that can take place in a hospital is symbolic of making changes to the 'inner self' at a profound level.

**Hot:** The atmosphere of a dream portrays the condition of your inner landscape. To dream of being hot can suggest being angry or being filled with uncontrollable passion. At the same time, you can enter into a situation in a dream that feels unbearably hot as a representation of perhaps feeling like you are in 'hot water' or doing something out of the norm. Where dreaming of the cold or snow can symbolize being isolated or reserved - a hot landscape shows free movement in the area of passion. See also **Fire.**

**Houses and Buildings:** These are structures that represent aspects of you as you are changing. Commonly, you will dream of a house from childhood "with some new additions," representing the way that the self is constructed in childhood, although it continues to evolve and explore potential. Specific *rooms* are associated with aspects of the self and its decorations and architecture can portray your emerging "style." The *attic* signifies higher thought or spiritual ideas, but can also suggest the ideas you store and collect or how you must "climb upward" or raise consciousness to sort through what you no longer protect. The *basement* is usually the subconscious or area of the self that you keep "below the surface." New or *undiscovered rooms* will suggest aspects of the self you are unaware of, but currently exploring. The *"living room"* is a social place, while the *"bed"* and *"bath"* rooms are representative of "coming clean" or exploring your sexuality. The *"family"* room houses family dynamics at play in relationships and social situations, while the *office* portrays work and issues relating to how you are currently providing for yourself. The *hearth* or *fireplace* often symbolizes your sense of heritage and what you hold to be sacred.

Hallways are places of transition, where you meet others in "neutral space" and often appear when you are exploring choices or going through a transition. The *"front"* yard or *garden* is what you are making of yourself for "public view." The *"back"* yard is suggestive of more organic aspects, which are not made obvious to others. You often discover or search for something or explore the correctness of your behavior "in the *bushes*" or "in the *shadows*."

Buildings sometimes appear as *rickety structures*, representing how you grow to meet a future that has not yet been erected or "solidified." Buildings can be places in which you are *lost*, or *searching*, as in the case of searching for a new identity, by traveling to a specific

153

*floor* or level of consciousness. The *floor* of a structure can be indicative of levels of awareness or may be associated with the meaning of the number involved: See **Numbers.** You stand on the ground floor of awareness and travel upward to achieve your ideals, or downward to find those things that you keep hidden below.

The *roof* of a structure shows limitations. As a setting of activity, something taking place on a roof can portray your desire to break through barriers in achieving your ambitions. When the "sky is the limit" the *ceiling* can block your ambitions, suggesting how self-defeating ideas may be blocking your ability to discover success.

Opening a *door* suggests objectivity or discovery associated with the symbolism of where the door may lead. The door can lead to certain rooms as a way of *opening* to the area associated with that room. *Doors* can mean many things: boundaries and unblocking potential, while knocking is often a sexual symbol. The *"front"* door leads you "out" into the world, suggesting the barrier between the self and the social realm. The *"back"* and *"side"* doors allow for an "escape" or for the "intrusion" of characters who appear as aspects of your unacknowledged potential. See Intruder under **Archetypes and Universal Characters**.

A *church* is obviously spiritual, but can often suggest how religious ideas are holding you back in some way. Sometimes you may find yourself looking for a "key" in a church as a way of suggesting how a self-criticism and conscience are trapping your organic nature through illness or *dis-ease*. See Key under **Purses, Wallets, Luggage, Jewels and Keys.**

A *school* suggests learning experiences or being measured against others in your abilities. The *library* can represent your communication that is "out there" for public view. In the same way, a *gymnasium* is a place of competition in a more physical way. A *factory* is a place of "mass production" or the attitudes that you have "assembled" to fit in. It can also suggest what you are currently "making" out of your experiences. A *hospital* is a place of personal crisis; or where you might find "critical" care, as in understanding and re-writing your critical tapes. Hospitals can also represent "new life" or the place where you are "born" into a new way of interacting. When doctors and nurses offer you advice, you should give the message careful consideration as an aspect that may enhance your "well-being."

A *shopping center* reflects "shopping" for new ways of being and exploring the things you "need" against your values. It is a place of exchange, where you "buy" something by giving back another thing of equal value. *Restaurants* are associated with Food and nourishment. As a setting, the restaurant reveals how you are searching for sustenance or self-esteem. *Hotels, airports* and *places you visit while traveling* suggest experimenting with temporary ways of understanding experience or transient attitudes. See **Vehicles and Places of Transportation.**

**Hungry:** Dreaming of being hungry can symbolize a lack of fulfillment. It is common to be doing something work related in a dream - only to be focused on the food or eating when it doesn't seem appropriate. That is because your dream is connecting the idea of fulfillment to your need for recognition at work, or the need to find the more fulfilling work. Food related to riding in a car would be tying the idea of fulfillment to your drive. The ancient Chinese have a great saying: "nourish what is for the belly and not the eye." See **Food.**

# I

Seeing the letter "I" can be a symbol for the Self if you are currently not acknowledging or owning an issue. You may feel victimized and the dream is asking you to take responsibility for the situation. See also **Eye.** It can relate to a message to turn inward, with ideas like inspiration, insight, intuition. Its message can be how success is a path of self completion - and the seed is always within you.

**Ice:** Since water is often associated with feelings, ice can represent feelings in a frozen or inanimate condition. You may be cut off from your feelings, or you are keeping an idea 'on ice' rather than processing and releasing it. Seeing something frozen, or encased in ice and lifeless, can signify your awareness that some aspect of you is inanimate, possibly because of fear: 'frozen with fear' or because it is painful. Dreaming of walking on ice can show the precarious result of trying to skim over emotions. You can 'fall in' and be consumed by them - as in the case of holding in feelings only to explode at the least little incident. See **Frozen** and Ice-skating under **Roller-skating.**

**Ice Cream:** Desserts in dreams hold the same idea as **Food,** or how you are exploring nourishment and fulfillment from a more broad perspective. Associated with the idea of getting your 'just desserts,' these types of foods are connected to your idea of success and rewards in life. Since it is made of cream, it can have sexual meanings of release, however its coldness can embody how you are exploring sexual feelings that are 'on ice.' The cream aspect can also tie it to issues of maternal influences.

**Identity:** The most confusing aspect of dream interpretation is the idea that every character, symbol and even the landscape portray aspects of **you**. In waking life, you have the sense of being isolated or separate from everything around you, but at the molecular level, all of life can be observed to be interdependent and behaving as one giant organism.

When Einstein penetrated the secrets of the molecular world, he remarked: *"Nature does not distinguish between mass and energy but observes them to be one and the same."* He also revealed how our idea of space and time being distinct was incorrect: they are interwoven. His work transformed our understanding of the natural world, revealing our tendency to compartmentalize every aspect, as if each might exist independently. We now realize that there are no isolated building blocks, only the intricate relationship of how each part is an *observable* variation of a larger whole. It is we, who *"must become open"* if we are to understand nature's more holistic interconnectivity. Dreams operate from a more organic awareness and present the first clues that our normal perceptive orientation may not be accurate.

We are brought together propitiously to learn from each other. In dreams, we see how characters portray the emerging and changing sides of ourselves. Perhaps dreams can teach us how we can become more observant and learn from our interactions with others. See **Dreams as a model for approaching relationships** under **Dream Processing.**

**Illness:** When you dream of characters that are ill or handicapped, you may be exploring an undernourished part of yourself that requires healing. The thing about dreams is that since everyone is portraying you in some way - the message from this type of dream is how you are incapacitated or not up to par in some respect. See also **Healing.**

**Imitate:** If you dream of a character imitating you, it can be the Trickster archetype active, or that part of the self that challenges how absolutes limit us in our growth. In all of our serious attempts to be certain, we can get lost in our inconsistencies and there is a part of us that would help us break through to truth. This comical message is portraying how illogical ideas cannot be supported. If you are imitating someone else in a dream, you can be adopting or exploring traits you associate with them. The whole idea of imitation presents the consideration that something is not what it appears to be. See **Trickster**.

**Incense:** Burning incense in a dream can symbolize spiritual longing. If you are covering up a bad smell with incense, you may feel that something is wrong in your environment and rather than solve it, you

157

would rather cover it up. Incense can also be a cryptic way of exploring feeling 'incensed' or angry when you are not allowing anger to be expressed.

**Infection:**  The idea of infection can be both good and bad. We can be infected by laughter or become infected with something that makes us sick. The idea is that something that is in your environment is having an influence on you through osmosis. What type of friends are you surrounding yourself with and is it a healthy type of interaction? The infection had a cause and you are getting a message to explore where it came from. Only then can you solve the lack of wellness portrayed by this dream. See **Bacteria** and also, **Healing.**

**Inflammation:**  If you notice some part of your body becoming red or inflamed in a dream, you may have a 'sore spot' in relation to what the body part represents. In real life, inflammation is how the immune system rejects and processes toxins and dreaming of inflammation can have a similar meaning in helping you to achieve wellness. On the foot, you may be irritated with the false starts in your sense of direction. On the legs, you may be insecure about 'carrying your own weight.' If your arms are showing swelling in a dream, you may be feeling irritation about carrying the burdens of others. On your hands, you may be making choices that aren't appropriate for you. If your face becomes disfigured because of swelling - you may be exploring the idea that you are becoming someone you are not. The face is unrecognizable because it isn't healthy for you and isn't your 'real face.' Explore **Anatomy and Body Parts** for the part of the body involved for more information about what is 'festering' or in need of attention.

**Injection:**  Dreaming of getting an injection can show the difficulty you are having in allowing something into consciousness. This type of dream seems to suggest that healing and/or wellness cannot occur unless you become more open to: love, sex, feelings, enthusiasm, or optimism. See **Syringe, Vaccine** and also, **Healing.**

**Insects:** The vast majority of life forms are insects. Their longevity on this planet suggests that they will outlive us. They do not, however, demonstrate *our idea of intelligence* as something that would account for their longevity as a species.

They are operating in social structures that are similar to ours and can suggest getting caught up in what we believe is required of us.

As a symbol of unconscious processes, they appear "driven" like soldiers, without any sense of consciousness about what they are doing. When *ants* appear, they are pests and therefore, these dreams often suggest the nature of something "bugging" you. *Spiders* hide in webs and can bite, representing insecurity or feeling pursued or trapped in your growth by being afraid. *Larvae* and *flying insects* can portray metamorphosis and the ability to transform. *Moths* appear to be compulsively drawn to any type of light and can represent obsessively being drawn toward what you feel you need. Just as insects build their hives, webs and underground tunnels, insects appearing in a dream will often suggest how whatever is bugging you is self-created.

**Inside:** See **Placement and Perspective.**

**Insulation:** Dreaming of insulation signifies protective tendencies. It is something used in erecting walls that controls temperature. Therefore insulation can symbolize how one 'insulates' themselves from feelings.

**Insurance:** Negotiating an insurance policy in a dream brings forward issues related to security. If you have an accident and find out your insurance doesn't cover it, you may feel that you are setting goals that are unrealistic. The insurance policy can be understood in terms of what you are investing symbolically to ensure your success. Generally this type of dream is teaching you to be honest in understanding your capabilities. If the dream is resolved by getting insurance money, the message can suggest that you have more reserves (in terms of capabilities/self-esteem) than you thought possible. Insurance related to the home can embody the idea that life is a learning experience that requires continual transformation. Insurance related to the car revolves around the issue of drive and motivation. Insurance related to health can have a more literal message about the need to care for your body.

**Interpretation of Dreams:** See **Analyzing Dream** in beginning of book.

**Intersection:** Approaching an intersection in the road can symbolize changing paths or making choices about your life direction. Two roads are crossing and you may have to decide between two possible paths. If a car unexpectedly pulls out in an intersection, you may have conflicting desires and feel like you need to stop while you decide what to do.

**Intruder:** Having a dream of an intruder portrays an non-integrated part of you that is unacknowledged, yet seeks access into your 'house.' Since the house represents your inner architecture, dreaming of an intruder can symbolize the need to accept and find compassion for a part of you that may be in hiding. These types of dreams are common when early family dynamics may have labeled you a black sheep in some way. While you grow to become an empowered and caring human being, some part of you may still need to be resurrected and 'allowed in.' This is described under **Shadow**. See also Intruder under **Archetypes and Universal Characters.**

**Inventor:** To dream of someone inventing something reveals your ability to create something new of your life, even if you feel stuck. Whatever symbolism is being invented can shed light on what this area will be. Often dreaming of an invention is representative of the first level of incorporating change. Inventing shows the inspiration that is coming forward to guide you. Look at what is being invented objectively, and break it down to discover the sense of direction that is coming to you.

**Island:** The island is the foundation you stand upon that remains subject to the unpredictable behavior of the seas, (or emotions). It can also symbolize how your need to protect your feelings has left you feeling isolated and alone.

# J

The letter "J" can be associated with puns, jokes, the joker and jesters of the psyche that trip us up to dislodge us from stasis. This letter also inspires images of jails, jaywalking and juggling and can suggest the rules of society and whether or not we feel restricted by them.

**Jab:** To describe a movement like a jab in a dream can represent focusing on, and identifying what you want. Similar to a fork that allows you to take a stab at the idea of nourishment, a jab can be a wake up call to explore what you are not confronting. The character that 'takes a jab at you' might be considered in light of a tendency to be self defeating in some way. An unacknowledged part of you may be stirring and attempting to get your attention.

**Jack Hammer:** The jack hammer is a symbol of hardness in thinking. It often manifests during times when your 'inner architecture' is undergoing a type of renovation. If the jack hammer is not able to break apart the concrete - you may need to loosen your thinking in a way that allows you to see how difficulty is actually an opportunity.

**Jack in the Box:** As a toy and capturing the idea of a Trickster character, dreaming of a jack in the box can symbolize something from the unconscious poking fun at your need to establish absolutes in your thinking. This can be tied to thinking you have adopted from your parents, or a part of your nature that you are repressing that makes you different from others. The message is that this quality makes you unique and should be cultivated in acknowledging your gifts. See also **Trickster** and **Box.**

**Jacket:** The Jacket is associated with self-protection and can symbolize how you are 'covering' your sensitivity to what is happening around you. If you are finding an old coat in a closet, you may be exploring the defense mechanisms you established in childhood. See **Defense Mechanisms** and Outerwear under **Clothing and Makeup.**

**Jackpot:** Dreaming of winning the jackpot can symbolize financial insecurities. At the same time it is your intuition reassuring you that everything will work out. You may wake up disappointed that the dream was not true, but why not enjoy its subtle message of abundance? Perhaps you are missing all the little miracles of life by being overly focused on material rewards. The fact that everything always works out should be the real jackpot you discover in the message of this dream.

**Jaw:** The jaw is the part of the mouth that enables you to chew. As a dream symbol, the jaw can symbolize chewing on something. Often associated with unprocessed or unexpressed anger, the jaw can be a symbol that appears when you need to stand up for yourself. See **Anatomy and Body Parts.**

**Jaywalk:** When you jaywalk instead of using a crosswalk in a dream, the message can be about how doing the same thing often leads to the same result. The street symbolizes your sense of direction and where you are going. Crossing the street represents making changes in life direction. Not taking the crosswalk can signify breaking out of the pack - or overcoming old limitations. Even if you are approached by police (critical conscience) for doing something 'illegal' - this dream is actually a powerful sign that you are following your own sense of direction.

**Jellyfish:** Jellyfish are not easy to see and live just below the surface of the water. They can symbolize feelings and stinging activity just below the surface of awareness. You may have vague sensation of fear that is causing you to be over reactive - or you may not be aware of your fear and are taking pre-emptive actions to thwart any opportunity for success because of it. Explore your behavior and whether you are stinging others or yourself, because of insecurities. See **Water** and **Sealife.**

**Jesus:** Jesus is a common Archetype that allows you to explore the traits you have associated with him. He can be an image of patience and forgiveness at the same time that he can personify the idea of personal sacrifice. How you feel by observing this Archetype can allow you to understand why he is appearing in your dream. This side of you can be

162

awakening as you actualize your spiritual ideals. See Wise Man under **Archetypes and Universal Characters.**

**Jet:** The Jet can symbolize aspirations as you move into a new area of work. If it is a fighter jet, you may be exploring the idea of competition and how you might learn from it in order to perfect your skills. See also **Airplane.**

**Jewels and Jewelry:** Jewels, gold or precious stones show how you are exploring what is important/valuable to you. Sometimes this type of dream reveals issues that you are protecting. For example, you may be protecting a precious jewel or hiding it from discovery. In this case, the dream shows defense mechanisms or unresolved issues that you have hidden away. The dream allows you to see how you have given something value and protection - when the issue really needs to be processed. Explore the surrounding symbolism to understand what it relates to: house/idea, car/motivation, garden/expression, road/goals. In some cases, the jewel represents self worth and should be protected.

When you find a jewel - the dream is exploring how you might discover your own value - how you explore unknown potential or how you can recognize self worth by doing a little digging. When the jewel is associated with something you wear - such as jewelry - the idea of value and protection relate to the part of the body that is adorned. For example - a dream that focuses on earrings (ear) can be coaching you to listen more - a bracelet can have a message about giving and taking (hand/wrist) or providing for yourself. The bracelet can also have associations with being held back (restrained) because of values or priorities that are not healthy. A necklace can represent your core identity although it also covers the heart, which can be good or bad. The necklace can also have associations with responsibilities because it is 'worn around the neck.' While the jewel represents what you hold to be valuable - how it appears in a dream will describe its positive and/or negative meaning. See **Stones, Colors** and **Purses, Wallets, Luggage, Jewels and Keys.**

**Jigsaw Puzzle:** Assembling a puzzle can be a way of exploring how the different 'pieces' of experience fit together. The pieces can be square and linear as a representation of limitations, or round in certain places to symbolize wholeness. You may be feeling challenged beyond your capabilities but the puzzle is an uplifting message that everything does have meaning - and it does fit together in the end. Some side of you knows this, and is why you are being given this clue.

**Job:**  Since we spend so much time at work, it is common to have dreams that help us process what is going on in the work setting. Clues to how you can solve a crisis however, will come through in the interesting ways the work environment appears different. For example a dream of being at work that focuses on the ceiling - can be exploring your feelings about the 'ceiling' placed on your upward mobility. The telephone can symbolize communication issues. Weird things on the walls or strange walls can symbolize your self-imposed limitations or the 'ideal' you work to achieve and whether or not it is a good fit for you (pictures). The carpet can symbolize issues you are not facing. Unusual wall colors can be explored in terms of what the colors represent. Even your fellow employees can represent aspects that you attribute to them, as you explore adopting or discarding these traits.

**Jockey:**  This character is responsible for controlling how a horse behaves and the horse often personifies the spirit. Therefore, dreaming of a jockey can show the idea of restraining the spirit.

**Jogging:**  When you are jogging in a dream, you are exploring how you may be travelling to quickly - or too much in routine thinking or habitual patterns- as you move along your path. As a symbol, jogging can also have associations with the need to 'jog' your memory to reconnect with a past way of interacting that made your life experience more magical. Jogging can suggest that you need to slow down and smell the roses. Explore if you are too much in routines at this point in your life.

**Joints:**  Joints in the body can relate to flexibility and a new way of reaching for or attaining your desires. While the elbows can symbolize exerting your power as in 'elbowing your way in,' the knees have an association with groveling or not standing up for yourself. If you dream that your joints are moving in an unusual way, you are exploring changes in how you get your needs met (arms/wrists) or how you stand up for yourself to become more responsible (legs.) See also **Anatomy and Body Parts**.

**Joker:** See **Trickster.**

**Journey:**   Much of your life is spent focused on the future and organizing the days ahead. When you sleep, you are closer to the sense that life is an *unpredictable* journey and that *how it affects you* is more important than *where you are going.* You may dream of taking a journey where you are a passenger on a ship, train or on a bus to an unknown destination. This type of dream can be both prophetic in terms of offering glimpses into the future you are currently building, and revelatory in relation to understanding the mechanisms of how you are creating it. See **Vehicles and Places of Transportation.**

**Judge:** Like the committee of characters that can approve or disapprove of changes in your persona, the judge often represents the inner critic. If you are repressing a sense of guilt, it can be portrayed by the judge. Explore the other symbolism surrounding the dream for more insight into how you may be over-critical of yourself and others.

**Juggler:**   This character can be representing how you are trying to balance or juggle aspects of your life.

**Jungle:**   Since the setting of a dream embodies your 'inner landscape' - dreams that take place in a jungle setting can relate to how you explore your more wild or exotic self that seeks expression beyond the restrictions of conformity. It is common for dream themes to move into this more organic or earthy setting when you are going through a type of rebirth or actualizing (authentic) self expression. Trees can also relate to family dynamics. If the landscape is threatening - you may feel unsure about expressing your more 'animal' or authentic drives and passions. Exotic birds can tie the idea of exotic (authentic) expression with the idea of how it can help you 'fly.' See **Trees** and **Landscapes and Scenery.**

**Jupiter:**   Because the ancients tied benevolent events with the appearance of this planet - Jupiter has associations with grace, charity and positive or productive expansion. This planet also has a special significance to spiritual seekers - who will have this type of dream as the activation of the Buddha/Christ/Wise One Archetype within them. Associated with Jove, Jehovah and Zues, Jupiter can also relate to issues with the father and whether or not one feels protected and cared for by the father. Whether or not you understand astrology, the planet seems to emanate abundance because perhaps, of its size. Dreaming of traveling to Jupiter can be a message about expansion and can portray steps you are taking in becoming more giving of yourself.

**Jury:** Dreaming of being on a jury can be an objective portrayal of learning to operate in a group setting. You may feel that others are judging you but the jury setting is portraying your own tendency to judge. If you are being judged by a jury - the dream has more to do with gaining consensus from the different sides of you as you move through changes. See also **People**.

**Justice:** Sometimes you will awake from a dream with the sense that something bad was happening that had gone unpunished. In the dream, it appeared perfectly natural for the characters to ignore this situation. The natural world is blind to the idea of justice. There is only a movement toward balance and regeneration. Justice is a man-made illusion and since the dreamscape seems to have a more organic basis, it seeks only to "work through" the things that block you in your growth. This type of dream suggests that you might need to be more receptive to the way in which something may appear bad, when it is necessary for renewal.

# K

The letter "K" can be associated with leadership and the idea of being king. It can relate to keys, kites or be an affirmation in the sense of "okay." Its message can be that difficulty hones our greater capabilities.

**Kaleidoscope:**   The kaleidoscope is a type of seeing device with changing patterns. Looking through this instrument can suggest how you are beginning to detect patterns in your experiences. Since the 'real world' is not really visible when you look through it, the message can be about how you limit your view of life from a purely ego-centric perspective. This can also be a play on the word 'collide' and might suggest an awareness that is purely focused on conflict. Or, two conflicting ideas may be on the path of collision. Another message might be to open to the possibilities for new discovery.

**Kangaroo:**   The kangaroo can represent an unusual way of going forward that you haven't considered. Its large feet offer a message about the importance of walking your own path. Since it carries its young in a pouch, it can symbolize holding back expression or creativity in some way. Its large and powerful tail can tie it to the idea of having something to fall back on as you embark on a new direction.

**Karate:**   Karate is a martial art that relies on precision and one's own power to achieve unusual feats of strength, i.e: karate chopping a piece of wood. The message can be asking you to focus only on your power to achieve, and not on the obstacles, or the idea of failing. Failure is an illusion when you are focused on learning and succeeding. One does not learn karate overnight however, much practice and patience is needed.

Another aspect of karate is how one learns to use the momentum of another's attack to leverage and turn the force back on the opponent. If nothing anyone says or does can make or break your day - that is real power. Dreaming of karate can be a message about the Eastern philosophy of 'not doing' or not being so reactive.

**Key:** The key is often a powerful clue to what can unlock the doors of opportunity and happiness. Holding someone else's keys can represent giving them the power to orchestrate how the relationship unfolds. Finding a key in a church can tie wellness to overcoming a sense of guilt. Finding a key in a schoolyard can take you back to ideas of childhood and how you might need to release them. The key is also a sexual symbol and appears when you are denying your feelings - because it seems to say 'here is what is needed to open.' See **Purses, Wallets, Luggage, Jewels and Keys.**

**Keyhole:** Dreaming of a keyhole can represent small things that will lead to new opportunity. The door of opportunity may appear locked and requires a key, but if you are looking through the keyhole - you already know what you want. The key is merely your commitment to 'do it' rather than just entertain the idea.

**Kidnap:** Being kidnapped shows how you may be allowing your real nature to be 'kidnapped' by fear or the pressure of others. The threat of being abducted by **Aliens** and **UFOs** is a common dream theme arising from peer pressure or doing things that go against your sense of Self. Being threatened by a sinister character can portray the Shadow.

The Shadow represents the unacknowledged but powerful part of your nature that you are not allowing to have expression. Some part of you follows or stalks you and attempts to 'break in' to consciousness. In a sense, you are 'kidnapping' yourself or repressing some aspect of your real self. Being kidnapped by anything portrays the internal conflict created when one side of you is evolving, yet is blocked by your more ingrained or critical nature from the pressure of conformity. You may dream of being kidnapped any time you feel developmental pressure of this type. See **Shadow, UFO** and also **Abduction.**

**Kidneys:** Since the kidneys are associated with how the body removes toxins, dreaming of kidneys can be portraying the idea that you need to process something or how your own feelings can become toxic. A good

168

flush may be in order and you may need to release old feelings that no longer serve you.

**Killer:**  The idea that someone is a killer in a dream personifies how outworn aspects of behavior or thinking are being 'killed away' as you move toward a transition in thinking. Often blood is involved as the idea that authentic feelings must rise to the surface. See **Attack and Being Chased**.

**Killing:**  See **Attack and Being Chased, Murder** and **Corpse.**

**King:**  Dreaming of a King can be an Archetype that appears in the dreamscape when the Wise Man area of the psyche is becoming active. The King can personify maturity and wisdom. For a man, the King can symbolize issues related to the father, or how one is mastering the idea of success in a way that makes one a leader. For a woman, the King can appear when she is awakening to the type of potential that is associated with being 'masculine' but is applicable to either sex. She may be connecting with her ability to become empowered and to provide for herself. When the King appears in a dream, the message centers around empowerment. Depending upon the details of the dream, it can signify negative aspects of the ego, or positive qualities of maturity and wisdom.

**Kiss:**  This intimate gesture is deeply symbolic of integration. Who or what is being kissed, portrays a movement toward acceptance and union. Commonly a woman will kiss a beast during monumental stages in her development: puberty, empowerment and menopause. She is connecting with those aspects of her body that feel beyond her control. When she is integrating the Shadow or Animus in a movement toward empowerment, she may first encounter 'her power' as a monster that kisses her. A man may kiss a young girl as a way of embracing the birth of his sensitivity. See **Anima-Animus** and **Shadow**.

**Kitchen:**  Since rooms in a house represent our 'inner architecture' the kitchen has associations with nourishment from a more broad perspective. Whatever is happening in the kitchen has associations with our sense of well being or how we are feeling nourished in life. The kitchen sometimes appears in dreams when we are exploring family dynamics or changing patterns adopted in childhood. See rooms under **Houses and Buildings.**

**Kite:** Flying a kite symbolizes both the sense of exploring potential, but also, keeping your feet on the ground. Since you rely on the wind to keep a kite flying, the kite suggests how you are testing the waters of your ambition; going with the flow of events to see where they might lead. A kite can also symbolize reeling in your aspirations. You can be exploring whether or not you can get them 'to fly' by how well your kite is able to get lift. Just as the kite relies on the wind to keep it aloft - the message can be about moving with the changes while remaining open to opportunity.

**Kittens:** Seeing many kittens in a dream can symbolize innocence and the birth of your intuition.

**Kneeling:** To dream of kneeling shows a movement toward humility. The fact that you are dreaming about it, suggests that this quality may be underdeveloped in waking life.

**Knife:** Kitchen utensils are associated with changes you are making. You use them to take what you need in order to find nourishment and self worth. Like food, the symbolism is exploring fulfillment. The difference between a fork and a spoon is their shape. A spoon suggests what you need to hold onto in order to feel satisfied, while the fork is more symbolic of taking a stab at something, or making a change in direction that will help you provide for yourself. The fork can also symbolize choices or a crossroad, as in a 'fork in the road.' The knife can symbolize ideas that are painful or the cutting away of something. You may have to face the truth or eliminate outworn behavior. Since it is used as a weapon, it can symbolize allowing feelings to rise to the surface. A spatula is associated with turning something over or seeing another side of the situation. See **Weapons and Utensils.**

**Knob:** The knob can be a cryptic symbol that represents one's sexual feelings. The knob can also be a symbol that explores how the idea turning, or going after one's desires can open the doors of opportunity. It asks you to grasp something or identify what you desire so that you can achieve it.

**Knocking:** Knocking can be a message that something outside needs to be inside. This can portray how you project a sense of being a victim on events - when the issue might relate to your attitude. It is a classic symbol of sex as the idea of 'getting knocked up' or pregnant - but again, the knock portrays passion that feels beyond your control. The knock at the door can draw your attention to the need to 'open up' to discover something you are not facing. See **Door.**

**Knot:** You "tie the knot," as in commitment, the knot can portray things that are not easily undone. You can be "tied up in knots" and dream of the knot as an objective symbol of being overly caught up in a situation. The knot can be untied and suggests you may need to "detach." See Not under **Homonyms.**

# L

The letter "L" can relate to attraction and rejection with ideas like love and loss. It can symbolize the ideas of being lost, longing or feeling like you are late in terms of life stages. The shape of the letter can suggest a crossroad or doing something unusual or turning away from habitual behavior.

**Label:** The label brings greater emphasis to the idea of how symbols are used to get a message across during dreaming. Seeing a label brings its message to a higher level of focus. Whatever the label says and its association to the symbol portrayed will describe an aspect of you, of which you are unaware. Designer labels are a type of "stamp of approval." Wearing a label is your way of being recognized by your sense of style or how you express yourself.

**Ladder:** The ladder is used to access higher ground. To dream of a ladder represents your need to "get above something" or "climb out" of difficulty. See **Placement and Perspective.**

**Lake:** Unlike the ocean or traveling over the choppy waters of changing emotions, the lake is self-contained with definite boundaries. It portrays how you are composing your emotions; how you hold and protect them and how you must release or express them in order to be re-filled or renewed.

**Lamb:** A lamb or young sheep is associated with childhood comfort and the need for protection. It can symbolize being too passive or sacrificing happiness for security. See **Animals.**

**Land:** See **Earth.**

**Landscape** and **Scenery:** provide details about your relationship to your current environment. The setting can offer messages related to: how you are seeing clearly in the **Day** (consciously) or you may use a **Light** (exploring hidden aspects;) or whether you are not facing something in the **Night** or in the **Dark** (unconscious/unrecognized). In the *forest* (subconscious,) you often meet the **Characters** or Guide who can offer clues to your transformative processes. Approaching the forest, which grows from the roots of your beliefs, will always represent your attempt to overcome fear and unmask your greater power. *Trees* are stationary and rooted, suggesting the wealth of your genetic heritage. The *jungle* is that place within that remains uncivilized. Often you will dream of jungle patterns or decorations in a house as a way of exploring these natural and organic aspects of yourself. You climb *mountains* to gain a wider view, while the mountain can also represent how you can remain a prisoner of your beliefs. The *desert* returns you to an uncomplicated or barren landscape where you can discover the real roots of your sustenance.

Dreams about *water* occur commonly because water represents your emotions, and how you feel about *the changes* that you face as you move through life. To dream of *turbulent water* suggests a sense of emotional crisis associated with moving forward. Any time this type of dream occurs, later, you may dream about being on a similar ship and crossing the water that has become calm. This is representative of the emotional growth that you have achieved. In all of our ancient stories, water is the mysterious reservoir where the hero is to retrieve a treasure. Similarly, raging water often initiates you into a process of self-discovery. *Floods* and *tsunamis* demonstrate how emotions break free to undermine the foundation of your beliefs until you are forced to let go. What you thought was solid and what you thought you needed, is washed away as you pursue the basics of survival (well-being). Water can also represent health and wellness since it is a symbol of the elixir of life.

The *Great Sea* or ocean is a classic symbol of the home of the unconscious. You may approach its depth to discover its hidden treasures, such as: **Fish/Treasure/Sword/Jewels.** A symbol is brought forward as clues to your evolutionary journey. If you are in *quicksand* or "bogged down" in a *muddy swamp*, you may feel that your forward movement is impeded in some way. Because it is made of the earth, it represents your own ideas and how they may hold you back.

*Natural Disasters,* like *earthquakes* and *volcanoes* portray the transformative power or your emotions rising to the surface in the face of all that you believed to be static. The **Earth** can give way in *landslides,* which can destroy the structures you build. These structures represent the self and how it is evolving to meet the changes in your environment. Disasters associated with the *wind,* like *tornadoes* portray the movement of consciousness, and suggests how the hidden continues to stir within you. To dream of a *tornado,* signifies urges and emotions that have the potential to overwhelm you, and in a sense, you are picked up and placed into another context. You are released from your controlling and protective tendencies, which can only keep you re-creating the past.

All symbolism in a dream is important. As you explore the setting that reveals "your current mood," you will find a representation of where you currently stand in relationship to the changes you are facing.

**Large and Small:** When something appears in its unnatural size, it suggests how whatever the symbol represents is growing out of proportion or is moving toward being deficient. Life can teach you about maintaining balance and these type of dreams will reveal imbalances.

**Late:** It is common to dream of hurrying "somewhere," while knowing that you are late or about to miss something. This signifies your sense of passing time and not achieving those things that "you believe" are important to you. In some cases, you miss the event as a way of recognizing its importance or non-importance. See **Alarm, Arriving and Leaving, Placement and Perspective** and **Vehicles and Places of Transportation.**

**Laughing:** If you or someone else is laughing in the dream, there may be the need to take things more lightly. In daily life, you often laugh when you are uncomfortable and laughter in a dream can suggest looking objectively at your defense mechanisms.

**Laundry and Laundromat:** Because clothing represents the costume you wear or your attitude in the social setting, washing clothing can represent "coming clean" or revealing the essence of who you really are.

The Laundromat is a public place and therefore symbolizes what you are currently doing to gain acceptance. You may need to "air your dirty laundry" because you have no choice.

**Lavatory:** The lavatory brings forward ideas about revealing feelings or letting go. Searching for a bathroom to relieve yourself can symbolize holding onto feelings that need to be released. Often when you have revealed yourself to others in an intimate way, you will dream of 'losing your privacy' by urinating or defecating where others are able to see you. See also **Bath, Urinate** and **Defecate**.

**Lawn:** A dream that focuses on the lawn can symbolize how things grow or are interconnected, such as ideas. The front lawn will have associations with what you put out there for public view or what you are developing or growing in an effort to become more interactive with the world around you. The back lawn embodies ideas of a more private nature or what you hide from others. See Garden under **Houses and Buildings** and **Grass.**

**Leaf:** The leaf signifies the things that grow and fall to the ground from the tree of your beliefs. A dream that focuses on a leaf can suggest learning to let go. It may also have associations with care and pruning. See **Tree** and **Gardener.**

**Leak:** Like dreams about **Water** or faulty **Electricity**, observing a leak can suggest the first stages of emotions breaking through self-created barriers as you move toward transformation.
**Leaving:** See **Arriving and Leaving.**

**Left:** The idea of the left side of anything in a dream will have associations with something that has not been tried before or something different than what you normally do. Since the 'right' is the accepted path, going 'left' shows a new way or new approach 'the road not taken.' See **Placement and Perspective.**

**Left Behind:** When a dream leaves you feeling abandoned or left behind, it can be exploring how you have only identified with only one aspect of who you are. For example, you may be entering a new situation and dream that your family has gone on a trip without you - or you have gone somewhere without them as you explore insecurities about focusing on more personal matters. Sometimes you will be left behind because your path may need to be altered. The direction you assumed you should take may not be right and the dream is helping you to explore possibilities. See **Abandoned** and Forgotten under **Placement and Perspective.**

**Legs:** Just as the 'house' can symbolize your 'inner architecture' or the way you approach various aspects of your life, the body also portrays how you approach situations. Where the arms show how you give and take what you need, and the shoulders and neck relate to responsibilities, the legs root you to your foundation and carry you forward in life. Dreaming of something related to the leg can be a message about whether or not you feel autonomous or able to move forward freely. In a sense the legs reveal where you currently stand or what may need to be altered to allow for more freedom of movement. See **Anatomy and Body Parts.**

**Lemon:** Being a fruit, the lemon can relate to the fruit of one's labor, although its yellow color and sour taste might suggest not feeling satisfied with your accomplishments. At the same time, its color is vibrant and its taste jars the senses embodying an awakening or re-evaluation that allows you to find fulfillment. As a symbol, lemon is usually associated with feeling like you got an unlucky break or that something isn't working for you. See Fruit under **Food.**

**Lens:** See **Binoculars, Glasses and Microscopes.**

**Letter:** Writing and receiving letters can symbolize evolving communication skills and sharing information in a way that expresses new or unknown sides of you. If a character gives you a letter, there is a need to understand what part of you this person represents. Their communication or message can shed light on this
area of you that requires expression.

**Library:** Being in a library and looking through books is a common dream setting when you are changing your thinking or re-evaluating the past. In a sense you are looking through the ideas you have placed on the shelf, revisiting them to see what is necessary for the future and what should be discarded. If you are looking through books with the parent or in relation to the parent, you are examining their influences on your thinking. Seeing something in writing is often the first step in integrating a new idea into consciousness. The type of book will give you an idea of what part of your thinking is changing. See also **Houses and Buildings.**

**Light:** Dreams that focus on a light can be a way of bringing something to your attention for examination. A light shows the movement of ideas into conscious awareness. The light makes the less visible more visible, suggesting your attempt to become more aware. Symbols related to the light portray your attitude about seeing what they represent more clearly. Light surrounding another object can tie it to your spiritual path. For example, a glowing triangle can be a way of acknowledging spiritual insight with body, mind and spirit. A Ram illuminated in a glowing fire can symbolize spiritual perseverance. See Day and Night under **Placement and Perspective** and also, **Landscape and Scenery**.

**Lighthouse:** As a building that provides a sense of direction to boats moving across the water at night, the lighthouse suggests how you are finding direction within you. This is a symbol of your rising awareness as you search for a safe harbor during times of difficulty. You may have the sense of danger or that something beneath the water (unconscious) might harm you. The other symbolism in the dream can provide additional insight into what this danger may be. Since all aspects represent you, the lighthouse is how you are bringing light to your sense of direction.

**Lightning:** This 'bolt out of the blue' is a symbol of a 'charged' environment and its apparent dangers. The 'climate' can be 'heavy' and a downpour may be what is required to 'clear the air.' Seeing lightning hitting something can represent forces beyond your control that you believe are undermining your ability to build a solid foundation in your life.

**Lion:** This king of the jungle can represent harnessing your passions as a type of strength. As a feline, it can suggest a tendency to avoid domestication or conformity to express the power that comes from fearless expression. As a protector, it can be tied to the idea of parenting and your idea of love and passion learned from being a parent or through parenting. Its association with the astrological sign Leo as an Archetype shows it to be a highly creative symbol, where the lion often appears to explore issues related to self-expression and artistic expression. As a **Homonym**, it can suggest lies. See also **Animals.**

**Liquid:** Liquids are usually associated with feelings, sexuality and emotions. The container and the issues surrounding the liquid will shed light on how you are currently expressing these feelings. See **Cup** and **Glass.**

**Little:** When you are seeing something that is not its appropriate size, it can symbolize how you are viewing this aspect of yourself as being insignificant. See **Large and Small.**

**Lizard:** Reptiles and snakes in a dream relate to instincts and sensations that are somewhat unconscious and self regulating. As one of the oldest and most durable creatures, dreaming of lizards, salamanders or iguanas can portray the power of your survival instincts, both good and bad. In some cases, the message can be coaching you toward self preservation but more often than not, dreams of these creatures can embody the need to examine self destructive tendencies. Dreams of reptiles related to water can symbolize movement within the unconscious as something comes to the surface to reveal the power of your biological drives like anxiety and sexual impulses. As a symbol of transformation or how you can learn to shed 'your old skin' reptiles often have a message related to letting go of a dysfunctional approach to anxiety. On a grand scale, the Dragon is a symbol of metamorphosis and empowerment. The lizard, like all reptiles, can represent defense mechanisms or the flight or fight response as it is currently active. See also **Reptiles**, **Dragon** and **Unconscious.**

**Long and Short:** See **Large** and **Giant.**

178

**Looking for Something:**   Very commonly, you will find yourself "looking for something" in a dream. The fact that you have misplaced it reveals your current insecurities surrounding this symbol. If it is a purse or wallet, it can suggest financial insecurities. Looking for an heirloom or family treasure can signify your insecurities about your genetic heritage or chance to pro-create. Explore the meaning of the symbol for further clarification of what you are afraid you currently "do not have." See **Clothing and Makeup** and also, **Purses, Wallets, Luggage, Jewels and Keys.**

**Losing Something:** The anxiety of losing something precious can be so disturbing that even when you wake up, you cannot shake the sense of loss. The symbol may appear insignificant in waking life so you need to explore its deeper associations to see what you have currently "misplaced" or ignored. Often it is a clothing item or key. See **Clothing and Makeup** and also, **Purses, Wallets, Luggage, Jewels and Keys.**

**Lottery:**  We receive a prize usually because of our effort and tenacity. To dream of winning the lottery however, places the result of what you experience on others, fate or the outside and unpredictable forces around you. On one hand, dreaming of winning the lottery shows that you want to win or succeed - or get a lucky break. You can think of winning as giving you the opportunity to experience a sense of 'arrival.' It lifts you above all of your hard effort when you are too focused on the work - and not enough on the reward, or where the work may be leading you. It allows you to re-examine what you value in a way that might change your direction or focus.

Since dreams offer clues about how we can be more fulfilled, and we dream about what we are not facing - the lottery can suggest the need to take action or responsibility to claim your prize (fulfillment). For example, rather than succeed by 'the luck of the draw' explore whether you have a clear vision of what you want - the lottery can indicate how something fulfilling is within your reach - but you may be working so hard you are missing it.

As a symbol of balancing desires against experience - you may be taking responsibility for your success and blaming outside influences when you fail. An inconsistency in your thinking can undermine fulfillment. The idea of a lottery is showing how you are not owning

179

your accomplishments or seeing how failure is not punishment - but often a way of honing your continual success. The message coaches you to connect the outcome - to what you want, or what you are doing. If a specific number(s) was tied to winning - it should be explored as an aspect that is missing in your equation of fulfillment.

**Love:** Love is a complex idea in the dreamscape because dreams are portraying inner dynamics. You may be in a fulfilling relationship and dream of intimacy with past partners. At some point in your life - you projected the power for self love upon your mate. It is as if they hold/held the power to make you feel good about yourself. Consciously you may feel that you are functioning independently in a current relationship, but since you dream of what you are not facing, the appearance of an 'old flame' can be activated when you feel uncertain about your value in a current relationship. These past partners embody the idea of self love - they appear as we explore and merge (sexual intimacy) with this potential to love ourselves. This must occur independently from the feedback we are currently receiving.

All types of characters can appear in dreams in which you have a strong sense of attraction. Consider the adjective you would use to describe this person - or what they portray as a representation of you. A woman in a man's dream can portray the budding of his sensitivity - while the man in a woman's dream can portray her ability to be powerful and provide for herself. The attraction becomes symbolic of bringing some part of your own potential forward for exploration and integration. Intercourse symbolizes the merging.
The desire to be loved and accepted is a strong motivating force in life. When you dream that your love is rejected -you may be rejecting the idea of self love. Dreams are always a wake up call to be authentic, fulfilled and independent. Through the development of self love - you grow strong enough so that nothing anyone says or does can make or break your day. See also **Rejection**, **Sex**, **Anima/Animus** and **People**.

**Luggage:** Dreaming of luggage is a very common scenario because dreams often explore what we hold onto and what needs to be released as we grow. The situation surrounding the luggage will reveal what you are 'carrying with you.' In many cases, the luggage is lost as you become more open to the idea that you are carrying unnecessary baggage. If someone else is bringing your luggage in a dream, they may have a strong influence on your sense of identity.

If the luggage is associated with wrinkled or dirty clothes, you may have feelings of unworthiness that while carried with you, are being examined in preparation for release. If the luggage is associated with regal or formal clothing, your sense of self esteem is being examined. If the luggage reveals an unusual or inappropriate type of clothing, you may be opening to unexplored potential as your identity is undergoing transformation. Whatever is revealed when you open the luggage provides clues to the ideas that you are exploring. See **Clothing and Makeup** and also, **Purses, Wallets, Luggage, Jewels and Keys.**

# M

The letter "M" brings forward ideas like mom, matriarch, marriage and mate. Its message can be about recognizing how we give and receive in issues related to intimacy. "M" is also a symbol for male or masculinity and can be a way of exploring the idea of power or how one can provide for themselves.

**Machine:** When you dream of a machine, you may have the sense that your body is currently on autopilot. Chances are your imagination has come up with a comical or elaborate way of portraying how your inner processes are currently behaving.

**Magician:** The Magician as an Archetype that symbolizes being resourceful. The dream is portraying you as the Magician, so if you have been feeling stuck, the message is to trust in your abilities and be open to new ways of seeing old situations. At the same time, the Magician is a Trickster, so you may be exploring illogical thought patterns or inconsistencies in thinking through the character that asks you to 'defy logic.' If you dream of seeing a juggler or magician, you may be exploring the idea that the world you hold to be so solid and unchanging is about to reveal new possibilities. See **Trickster**.

**Magnifying Glass:** Dreaming of a magnifying glass can portray the need to focus more clearly on an issue. At the same time, it can have a message about seeing only the trees and not the forest. A magnifying glass is associated with scrutiny and close inspection. See **Binoculars, Glasses and Microscopes.**

**Mail:** All types of correspondence in a dream relate to communication. This can hold the idea of communication with others and also, communication from within - as in intuition or inner guidance. If you receive bizarre mail from someone you do not know, the message can be about inner guidance as you open to unexplored ideas. Receiving or sending something in the mail (as opposed to a phone call) can portray issues related to agreements and the idea that what you are saying or hearing might be inspected more carefully because you may be jumping to conclusions. The slowness and dependence on others to deliver what we send through the mail can portray how 'lines get crossed' or how some part of us (defense mechanisms) can undermine clear communication with others. See **Letter.**

**Mailbox:** Since correspondence in a dream represents communication - the mailbox can portray messages in the unconscious that are waiting to be retrieved. If the mailbox is defective, the dream can suggest that you need to pay more attention to inner guidance. If the mailbox is unusual in some way, you may be drawing conclusions when the dream seems to be prodding you to be more open or to take a different view or approach. If the mailbox is full - there may be issues that are blocking you from opening to opportunity.

**Mailman:** The mailman personifies how you express and take in information and new ideas. As an Archetype, he can symbolize the channel of communication between the unconscious and consciousness. Often the dream is helping you to open to a new way of thinking or communicating. If he has mail for you - unexplored potential is being activated through the dream. If there is a problem with the delivery - the message can be that you have shut down in some way and are not open to receive important guidance.

**Makeup:** Makeup is used to cover up the 'natural appearance.' Many times a dream that focuses on makeup has a message that relates to not expressing yourself authentically. You may be in a job that is not appropriate or that does not allow you to express your talents and real capabilities. If you are wearing heavier than normal makeup on the eyes - you may be exploring your ability to see yourself more clearly - or to give definition to your soul expression. If the dream focuses on lipstick, the message can relate to covering up expression in terms of what you say. Red lipstick that accentuates the mouth can be a message about 'speaking' what you are passionate about. If your cheeks are accentuated, you may need to open to intimacy or feelings that allow you to feel 'in the pink.' If you are going somewhere and realize that you have forgotten your makeup, the dream can be coaching you to move forward in a different way that better expresses who you really are. See also **Clothing and Makeup.**

**Male Genitals:** Whether you are male or female, dreaming of male genitalia relates to power, assertiveness and the penetrating force of feelings. For a man, these symbols can signify his vital essence or life force. He may dream of his penis as a way of exploring sexual drives or the need to activate his passion. For a woman, she may be activating power or need to assert herself with a more masculine approach. If the genitals are deformed or unusual, the dream can be coaching you to connect with your power in a more functional and less subterranean way. For a woman, if this type of dream appears threatening - she may not be comfortable expressing assertiveness and independence. Since ancient times, phallic symbols have portrayed dominating power and the life force that asserts, protects and defends. Since we generally dream about what we are not expressing or facing, this type of dream can be coaching your ability to become more empowered and passionate. See also **Genitals**, **Womb**, **Anima/Animus** and **Anatomy.**

**Man:** See **Anima/Animus** and **People.**

**Manure:** This is a more organic form of **Excrement.** Transcending the idea of simply letting go of what is no longer necessary, manure suggests fertilizing the future with aspects of what you are discarding.

**Marketplace:** This busy public place is a center where things are bartered or traded. One thing of value is traded for something equally valuable. Since it is a public scenario, usually the marketplace will signify the valuable part of your nature that you are trading for acceptance. You also explore your sense of value or self worth as it relates to work in a marketplace. Perhaps the routine of your current work environment is leaving you unfulfilled or feeling used. See Shopping Center under **Houses and Buildings.**

**Marriage:**  Often you will dream of attending a wedding that is not your own and have the sense of not remembering who the people were that were getting married. This portrays adopting behaviors that are not necessarily right for your. In this case, the other symbolism becomes important in recognizing how you may be going through the "ritual" or routine of public acceptance. If the wedding is your own, it becomes the classic representation of the merging or union of different sides of yourself, usually adopting the Anima or Animus. You may be making a commitment to adopt a certain behavior. See Anima/Animus under **Archetypes and Universal Characters.**

**Marsh:**  This is a common landscape in a dream when feelings are beginning to rise to the surface during therapy or when we are opening to intimacy. The marshy landscape blends the idea of green growth or natural expression and water (feelings.) See **Landscape and Scenery.**

**Martians:**  Dreaming of Martians portray how you are exploring aspects of yourself, which you find difficult to 'identify with.' Your sense of being different from the group (and how you feel about it) will be portrayed by how 'foreign' the characters appear in your dreams. As you move to fit in with the group, you may have a sense of how different others are from you, or how different you are from others. This is actually a good thing. All that makes you different can be harnessed as your gifts. Tap your unique qualities and express yourself fearlessly. There is nobody quite like you. Fitting in with the group often comes at the price of your real nature. An alien creature is a message that you should cherish what is unique and unchanging about you. See also **Flying Saucer**.

**Martyr:**  A dream that is focused on a sacrifice can portray an important side of you that you may be sacrificing because of the judgment of others. You can understand the Martyr or symbol sacrificed as representing some aspect of you. If you dream of persecution or being punished for your beliefs, you might explore the severity of your own inner critic.

To dream of someone being crucified can represent unprocessed guilt or anger and how self defeating thoughts stunt fulfillment. To dream of a hanging ties the message more to feeling trapped, an inability to communicate and the inability to breathe freely. In a sense, the weight of your own body is pulling you down. This type of dream often occurs when a child held the caregiver in contempt.

They may have felt crucified or unjustly punished. Some aspect of the parent can still influence their beliefs and at some level, we do identify with our parents. The conflict created by believing consciously that one is nothing like the parent, while unconsciously knowing they are the offspring can create unprocessed guilt and self-punishing behavior. One may say they have no guilt but if they explore whether they feel like an outsider or unworthy, they can begin to understand the nature of unprocessed guilt.

Being crucified or hung appears as the dream setting specifically because the ritualistic sacrifice of the authentic self is unacknowledged in daily life. The critical tapes of being unworthy heard as a child 'pull on us' and can 'tug us down.' The best medicine for a difficult childhood is forgiveness. See also **Shadow**.

**Maze:** When you are lost in a dream, you may not be recognizing how you are on the wrong path in daily life. To dream of a maze brings this idea into higher focus. Perhaps you have too many irons in the fire, or are embarking in too many directions to be effective. The maze suggests how you may feel overwhelmed by conflicting feelings. It is an objective representation of issues you are not recognizing.

**Medicine:** Taking medicine is usually unpleasant but necessary. If you dream of taking medicine, you may be exploring health and wellness from the standpoint of "ingesting" or "digesting" difficult choices in an effort to become "healthier."

**Meeting:** When you arrange to meet another, you are exploring the common ground that you associate with this person. This is a watered-down version of marriage and suggests the beginning stages of integration. Give careful consideration to all qualities of the person you are to meet. They represent an emerging side of you that you are exploring. See **Marriage** and Anima/Animus under **Archetypes and Universal Characters.**

**Melting:** When you move toward intimacy and become less "frigid," you may dream of something melting as a symbol of how your defensive tendencies are breaking down.

**Message:** Since dreams are always a vehicle of communication between the unconscious and consciousness, when you dream of a clear message, it should be considered in light of the other symbolism. The message may at first seem irrelevant, but if you explore the other symbolism, you will discover how the things that appear the most nonsensical are quite profound. When a character gives you a message, this portrays integration, and suggests issues associated with what this character represents. See **Answer, Letter** and Writing under **Colors.**

**Metal:** Metal is a substance that is tough and enduring. When it appears in a dream it can symbolize hardness or a lack of feeling that comes from being overly self-protective. Metal can still be weathered and worn by the elements to become rusty, where rust would signify how an old way of being may not be appropriate to the present. Metal is portraying something other than your organic nature because it is usually 'prepared' or shaped into something for use or display. Seeing a mesh-like object can symbolize mental dynamics or defense mechanisms at work. Metal objects in dreams are often a message that you are being too hard or not natural. See **Amulet and Necklace.**

**Milk:** See **Food.**

**Mirror:** The mirror is a symbol of self-reflection and can appear as a message about looking back at yourself. You may be blaming others in a situation when the reason you are feeling stuck may be your self limiting ideas. If the mirror is broken, the message can be about not being so self-focused. If you see something appearing in a mirror, explore the symbol as a message about your current sense of self-esteem.

**Money:** Dreaming of money shows how you are exploring what you value in life, and also, how you are seeking a stronger sense of self-worth. Since we dream of what we are not allowing into consciousness, dreaming of money can represent the part of you that is traded or bartered for acceptance, where the dream suggests a type of self worth that is undermined through conformity. While money has a high level of focus during daily life, in dreams, it often symbolizes 'false' values that gratify you in the short term, but leave you unfulfilled. Searching for money shows your desire to connect with a stronger sense of self-worth. At the same time, if you are dreaming of money, then you may be neglecting or not facing financial issues.

**Monkey:** A monkey is a playful primate that appears to have no sense of discipline. This animal can reflect a desire to approach life from a more playful perspective. It can also suggest 'aping' or mimicking others rather than expressing your authenticity. See **Animals.**

**Monster:** The good news about nightmares is that they are a sign that something powerful has begun to stir within you. A monster can appear in a dream as a representation of your power and how you may find this power frightening. Dream images can take on a Shadow form because we are unwilling to face something difficult or painful. For example, a person who was labeled a black sheep or 'a difficult child' can have two personas active: they can be a successful achiever by day but have unresolved tapes from childhood that undermine their sense of self acceptance or self worth. They may dream of a stalker trying to 'break into their house' (integration with Self) as a representation of this 'vagabond' identity and the need to understand, integrate it and 'let it in.'

A Dracula character can be a way of exploring how what your are doing might 'vampire' or deplete another area of your life because you are overly focusing on one thing. A Frankenstein character can represent moving through life without heart or sensation. The devil can personify being depressed or giving up on the goodness of life and feeling guilty about doing so or being unwilling to face depression. The monster is portraying you in some way.

Explore first the symbolism represented by the monster and observe how it might symbolize an aspect of you. The energy only appears as a monster because it has lived in the shadows for so long. In all cases, monster dreams should be viewed as a call to confront what you have hidden away. There is nothing negative taking place - it is an initiation that can lead to authentic power and increased self knowledge.

The monster can also represent what feels beyond your ability to manage such as: your temper or anger. The monster can be a way of releasing feelings that are considered 'unsavory' by day. A woman approaching menopause may feel her body doing things that seem beyond her power to control and she may dream of a monster kissing her as she attempts to integrate and understand the changes her body holds over her. At menopause stages particularly - the monster will have more of an association with being more male than female.

For a man who is not owning up to outbursts, he may dream of a monster or unsavory character stalking him. In all cases the 'bad and frightening thing' is merely representing aspects of you that are not integrated. This monster can also portray a type of power that once understood, can lead to greater empowerment and fulfillment. See **Shadow** and **Nightmares**.

**Moon:** The moon reflects the sides of you that you may not see because of its association with the Night. It is often a symbol of illusions, since it merely reflects the light of the sun. It also causes the tides to rise and fall and can represent responses and how you are pulled forward to behave emotionally, with feelings that feel beyond your control. Sometimes the moon can represent the critical nature or moodiness of the mother. If you see an eclipse, then expression and feelings are coming into alignment in a more natural way. Settings associated with the moon can represent the 'dim' exploration of information in the unconscious in the first stages of coming into awareness. See **Night** and **Unconscious.**

189

**Morning:** Dreams of morning often occur with the sense that you are awake and beginning your day, only to find that you overslept. This can symbolize how you are being swept up into routine, perhaps missing out on the more important things you are neglecting. If you dream of something and have a clear sense that it is morning, the dream may be portraying innocence or memories of your youth. See Day and Night under **Landscape and Scenery** and also, Mourning under **Homonyms.**

**Moth:** See **Insects.**

**Mother:** The mother appearing in a dream signifies how you were taught to express your feelings and sensitivity. While dreaming of the mother can portray how you are adopting or rejecting various aspects that are associated with her, she can also symbolize your ability to mother yourself. See **Family.**

**Motorcycle:** Since all transportation vehicles represent motivation and your ability to go forward in life, the motorcycle, being a 2 wheeled vehicle, requires balance. This type of dream can portray the need to balance two things in order to move forward productively. See **Vehicles and Places of Transportation.**

**Mountain:** Representative of pilgrimages to obtain a higher level of awareness both literally and symbolically, the mountain often signifies moving into higher levels of consciousness. Going inside of a mountain and into a cave, can represent climbing inward to retrieve subconscious information. The mountain remains stationary even while the landscape is changing around you and can portray a sense of what is solid in your life. At the same time, it can be indicative of a hardened perspective that may be blocking you in your transformation.

**Mouse:** See **Animals.**

**Mouth:** The mouth is associated with communication and the idea of nourishment. If a dream focuses on the mouth, you may be expressing yourself in a way that is not revealing what you really feel, causing a lack of real fulfillment. You may need to recognize the importance of truth in working through an issue. See **Anatomy and Body Parts.**

**Moving Van:** You may dream of a moving van when you are sorting through past ideas, or having difficulty letting go of past resentments. The moving van ties together the idea of moving forward with what you carry with you. Since furniture can symbolize the ideas that you rest upon, moving furniture is a message about sorting through past ideas and how you might release them. Explore the various symbols that are being moved for more insight into what part of your idea structure is being transformed. See also **Furniture** and **Luggage**.

**Mud:** This type of landscape appears when feelings (water) are coming to the surface (below the dirt) to allow you to express yourself or open to an intimate relationship. Often during therapy, one will dream of being in water up to the ankles or in a landscape of this type. See **Landscape and Scenery.**

**Mummy:** The mummy has been wrapped and preserved to experience an existence "other than real life" and signifies self-protective tendencies. See also Mommy under **Homonyms.**

**Murder:** When your life is threatened in a dream you are exploring change. Transformation means outworn aspects must 'pass on,' as part of your identity of the past may need to 'die away.' At the same time, being pursued by a murderer can portray one aspect attempting to kill off another, not always beneficial and so the symbolism surrounding the murder needs to be explored. If someone is 'assassinated' then you must consider whether you are doing something that is, perhaps, assassinating *your* character. See **Attack and Being Chased.**

**Music:** Playing a musical instrument or singing in a dream can represent your free flowing nature and how you are attempting to "harmonize" with the situations that you face. Playing a musical instrument is often a sexual symbol, again suggesting the free flowing aspect of your sexuality.

# N

The letter "N" can relate to ideas like nebulous, night, and negative, suggesting the subconscious themes of abreaction or defense mechanisms. Associated with nudity and natural - its message can highlight authenticity or how you explore inconsistencies presented in the theme of the Trickster. To achieve something in the 'nth' degree portrays achieving your highest potential. Its shape can symbolize the vicissitudes of life that lead you up and then down as you sometimes go backward in order to go forward. See **Defense Mechanisms** and **Trickster**.

**Nail:** If you are pounding a nail, it can represent "hitting the nail on the head" or the need to focus. See Hammer under **Weapons and Utensils.** If it is a fingernail, it can signify attitudes that grow and require grooming over time. See **Anatomy and Body Parts.**

**Naked**: Being naked or exposed suggests how you may be exposing the deeper or hidden sides of yourself. As you move toward intimacy, you may have dreams of being *undressed in public* or *relieving yourself* in *bathrooms without walls* as the result of having your nakedness exposed. As a child, you may have dreamt of *going to school in your underwear* when what you most wanted was to abide by the golden rule. In proportion to the rules you impose on yourself, you will find that dreams lead you toward the freedom to be yourself. To *"get naked"* or relieve yourself of your outer covering, you are allowing for the movement of other aspects of the psyche that had not previously found expression. This sense of being *vulnerable,* suggests how intimacy and exposing yourself is the only way of empowering authenticity.

Being exposed can also take place in dreams in which you feel *trapped* or *frightened.* Since the dream is bringing all that you *fear* to the surface, the symbolism should be given careful consideration so that you can transform the energy of fear into authentic empowerment. If the dream focuses on a *snake,* you might shed your skin and learn to express your natural drives; if it is an *intruder,* then you might try facing intimacy without feeling like others are intruding. When some part of you is being *revealed, stalked* and *discarded* or *killed,* you "get naked," confront the truth of what you fail to understand about yourself and learn to "let what is unnecessary go."

Dreams usually reveal the exact opposite of what you believe to be true about yourself. When you are frightened, it is a call to overcome your fear of being natural. If you feel ashamed, you may need to overcome shame to exist as a natural creature in a natural world.

**Name:** The focus on your name in a dream is a message to re-explore your roots. Your name is the "identity" that you have had your entire life. If you are trying to be someone that you are not, the name can bring that message home. Hearing a bizarre name in a dream happens when you are adopting new ways of interacting and experiencing life. This name is a "label" for the emerging side of you that has yet to be processed and integrated.

**Narrow:** If you are entering a space that you would describe as being narrow, it can represent how you have paved a way unwittingly that is *not* allowing you to express your full capabilities. Seeing a symbol that is narrow can reflect being "narrow minded" in your outlook or feeling hemmed in by circumstances.

**Natives:** See **Aborigines.**

**Natural Disasters:** Natural disasters, like earthquakes and volcanoes portray the transformative power or your emotions rising to the surface in the face of all that you believed to be static. The **Earth** can give way in landslides, which can destroy the structures you build. These structures represent the self and how it is evolving to meet the changes in your environment. Disasters associated with the wind, like tornadoes and hurricanes portray the movement of consciousness, and suggests how the hidden continues to stir within you. To dream of a tornado, signifies urges and emotions that have the potential to overwhelm you, and in a sense you are picked up and placed into another context. You are released from your controlling and protective tendencies, which can only keep you re-creating the past.

**Near:** See **Placement and Perspective.**

**Neck:** Focusing on the neck in a dream can represent feeling over burdened. Something can be serving as a 'pain in the neck' or you might be 'sticking your neck out' in terms of taking chances. The idea of 'being yoked' along with its other associations can make the neck a symbol of enabling behavior. Putting something around your neck can be a symbol of restriction or a lack of freedom in movement. If it is a pendant or necklace, you can be attempting to make your individuality more clear to others. See **Anatomy and Body Parts.**

**Necklace:** To dream of being given or wearing a special necklace with stones can symbolize how you are trusting in the direction of your Higher Self where the necklace becomes a symbol of your commitment to this connection. Since it covers the heart, it is a symbol of self acceptance and the discovery/commitment to inner beauty. In some cases, since it is worn around the neck, the necklace can have associations with being yoked by responsibilities. If the necklace is broken or lost, you may be coming to terms with letting go of something you have been committed to. See **Amulet and Necklace.**

**Needle:** The needle can symbolize ideas like 'the needle in the haystack' or a sense that something valuable is in front of you but you are not seeing it because you are focused only on loss. The message can be about overcoming confusion and the need to focus in order to 'sew' the seeds of success. If the needle pierces the skin, it indicates the need to allow your feelings and emotions to come to 'skin awareness.' It draws blood at the same time that it causes pain. Both ideas are associated with the activation of feelings. You may feel that opening to intimacy is painful, but being injected with a needle suggests the necessary healing that will allow you to move on. Threading a sewing needle is a symbol of creating a new identity. See **Drugs, Blood** and also, **Seamstress and Tailor.**

194

**Nest:** The bird's nest is often hidden in the branches of a tree, bringing forward both, the idea of your roots and the protective place that shields your spiritual nature. An insect's nest or hive is suggestive of the things that bother you, even while you cannot let them go. See **Tree** and **Birds.**

**Newspaper:** The newspaper is a symbol of having something "put out there" for public display. Seeing something very personal in the news can symbolize how you feel uncomfortable sharing intimate details about yourself with others. Seeing it "advertised" for public view, is often the first step in owning up to what you would rather not face. Whatever "has been published" is being examined in terms of how it can be applied during waking consciousness. See **Advertisement.**

**Night:** The setting of a dream is as important as the symbols that appear. To dream of something taking place in darkness or at night shows that you are unaware of the issue being explored. If a series of dreams moves from darkness to daylight, you are allowing this information to make its way into conscious awareness. See **Placement and Perspective.**

**Nightclub:** Going into a "dark place" to socialize with others, the nightclub can sometimes symbolize a lack of awareness of your motivations in social situations. This is especially true if it is a setting where you are being chased or pursued. The activity of drinking - along with the idea that we dream about what we are not facing - can sometimes be a wake up call to examine substance abuse. See **Alcohol, Night** and **Attack or Being Chased.**

**Nightmares:** Dreaming is a safe environment that allows us to explore our potential for change. When we are not open to change, or unwilling to acknowledge being in a rut, dreams often get extremely *colorful*. In an effort to get our attention, they can appear quite frightening. Nightmares are actually a good sign that something powerful is stirring within. Since we dream of what we are not facing, nightmares are a wake up call to take stock of what is blocking your growth and authenticity. Sometimes you may refuse to acknowledge that 'you are on the wrong path,' and often nightmares will recur until changes are made and the situation is resolved. It can be as simple as 'leaving something behind' while you hurry to your destination or as frightening as actually experiencing **death** or dismemberment. More than any other dream, the nightmare will disturb you so profoundly, that rather than run, you are forced to confront the truth. This is its simple goal: overcome your fear by seeing how 'unreasonable' it is. Once this fearful aspect that you are not facing is integrated, the nightmare will not recur. See **Shadow** and **Attack and Being Chased**.

**Nine:** Since ancient times, Nine has been a number associated with magic and mystery because of its peculiarities in mathematics. Dreaming of the number 9 can symbolize the Archetype of the Magician - or the profound ability to use what is at your disposal to achieve what you think is not possible. The cat has 'nine lives' to suggest how 9 symbolizes potential in the face of what appears to be an impasse. As the highest single digit number - and ideas like 'to the ninth degree,' dreaming of 9 can show completion or situations reaching an apex. In numerology it is the representation of a highly evolved spiritual awareness that points toward humanitarianism or a focus that transcends the sense of Self. See also **Magician**, **911** and **Numbers.**

**Nine One One (911)**: Like Red writing under **Colors,** when you are calling 911, you may be experiencing a  sense of crisis and are "calling" on the higher aspects of yourself to solve the problem. See Hospital under **Houses and Buildings.**

**North:** A dream that is focused on the direction of north can symbolize finding your bearings as in "true north" on a compass. Since it is associated with a cooler climate, it can also symbolize "cooling off" or getting control of your anger or other emotions.

**Noise:** See **Sound.**

**Nose:** The nose can be associated with a need to get at the bottom of something you are not facing. As the sensory organ most prominent on the face, the nose can symbolize your character and your need for acknowledgment. If the nose is bleeding, you may not realize how important passion is to your sense of success. See **Anatomy and Body Parts.**

**Nothing:** Anytime the dream focuses on emptiness or how 'nothing' was there – you are exploring substance or the idea of fulfillment in what you are doing.

**Nude:** See **Naked.**

**Numbers:** Not always obvious in a dream, numbers can appear in subtle ways. They can have universal meanings from sayings: *threes a crowd*; *seventh heaven*; or the *ninth degree*. They can also have personal meaning based on your past or actual experience.

Zero and *eight* often suggest wholeness and infinity because both appear endless. Like the circle or mandala, *zero* can be a composition of the self. *One* suggests aloneness or self-sufficiency; *Two* depicts partnerships, choices and integration; *Three* can be difficulty that requires integration, in the sense of a triangle situation, which demands resolution. It can also suggest getting the "third degree" or "threes a crowd;" *Four* can symbolize luck as in four leaf clovers, a symbol of the earth and elements; stability, as in "four on the floor" or crouching prior to moving forward. *Five* can represent fertility, abundance and like the digits of the hands and feet, issues related to taking, giving, holding and balance.

*Six* can be a way of getting the idea of "sex" out in the open or it can have mysterious or spiritual/psychic associations as in the case of extra sensory perception. *Seven* is associated with religion and stages or cycles in life as in seventh heaven. As mentioned, *eight* can represent infinity, eternity or wholeness, but it is also a symbol of evolution. Words that are **Homonyms** (like eight/ate) are the psyche's clever tools for slipping ideas past consciousness. In light of this, *eight* must also be considered in relation to **Food**. *Nine* is usually associated with a turning point or apex; being at the end of our rope as in "nine lives" or 911. It can signify excess or perfection since it is associated with "being dressed to the nines."

Ten can signify ambition because of its association with completion and arrival. It is a sense of having it all and integrating family and work in productive ways. You can dream of something related to the *eleventh* hour or it can be the non-integrated idea of one and one; *Twelve,* as in months, becomes completion or the beginning of a new cycle; *Thirteen* is odd, unnatural or unlucky and must also be considered in terms of integrating one (self) and three (eliminating or choosing).

Numbers can be associated with personal experience, age or they can also be reduced to units. *Fourteen,* as one and four suggests how your idea of independence (one), is currently challenged by issues of balance (four). *Twenty-five* becomes two and five, and can signify how partnership (two) leads to fertility or issues about giving and taking (five). *Forty-six* would be a message about stability (four) as you approach sex or increased "senses," or sensuality (six).

**Nun:** For a woman, the nun can represent a sense of protecting or covering sexuality in light of spiritual beliefs. She can embody a sense of what you hold to be sacred. For a man, the nun can represent an underdeveloped sensitive nature.

**Nurse:** The nurse can symbolize a need to retreat or rejuvenate. As an Archetype, this character is the part of the Self that ensures balance so that we can achieve longevity. Being cared for by a nurse can suggest that you are not caring for some aspect of yourself - or are focused too much in one area that an equally important aspect is in need of nurturing. See **Hospital** and **Houses and Buildings.**

**Nut:** The nut is a type of food that is encased in a protective shell. Since food represents nourishment, dreaming of a nut can symbolize how you are unable to find nourishment because of your protective tendencies. The nut is also associated with feeling that some side of you is 'nutty.' If it relates to nuts and bolts – you may need to get back to basics. The idea of opening to sexuality should also be considered.

# O

Seeing the letter "O" can have a message about openness and wholeness. It can symbolize opening the orifices from the standpoint of really listening or hearing what someone has said to you recently. It can also be associated with sex or enthusiasm.

**Oak:** The oak tree is valued for the strength of its wood. Trees carry the idea of your roots and foundation and the oak shows the stability of this structure. See **Forest.**

**Oar:** Like the bicycle that carries the idea of how you must propel your way forward, the oar brings this idea to the realm of the emotions. You may be going through extreme difficulty and dream of being lost on the water, unable to retrieve an oar. This is the sense of your current state of helplessness. The oar can appear as a **Homonym** of "or," representing a choice you may not have considered. Instead of wallowing in your misery, look for the opportunity that can help you paddle your way back to the shore.

**Obstacle:** When an obstacle appears in a dream, it presents you with an objective view of how you use the word "but" as a roadblock. Whenever this word is used in a sentence, it negates the power of whatever preceded it. "I want to be healthy, but..." I know I should study tonight, but..." Obstacles present a *tangible vehicle* that allows you to understand how you get stuck. In the dream, you are attempting to do something, *but there is an obstacle.* Rather than see it as a roadblock, look at it for the opportunity to transform or integrate this symbol into what you are doing. If the obstacle is a tree, explore your roots; it is a police barricade, explore how you might be too strict with yourself.

**Ocean:** Because the ocean is vast and we have a sense of the enormous life that stirs beneath its surface, this body of water is a classic symbol of delving into what lies below the surface of the **unconscious**. Being on a ship crossing the ocean can represent changes related to emotions and feelings. The behavior of the sea can reflect our emotional well being. See Great Sea under **Landscape and Scenery.**

**Octopus:** See **Sealife.**

**Odor:** When evolution led mammals to adapt to a nocturnal existence, olfactory bulbs developed, and smell replaced sight as the dominant sense. These aroma circuits or odor pathways are believed to have become the neural outline of the *limbic system* within the *mammalian* area. This is the emotional center that generates the parental care of mammals: playfulness, vocal calling and emotion. Emotion and mood originally evolved from neural structures, once allocated only to the sense of smell that merely *attracted* or *repelled*. Over time, these two simple responses became the complicated emotions we experience today.

Dreams that focus on an odor may arouse either a positive or negative response. The situation is "visible" only to the nose. "Something doesn't smell right" when you know it is bad, or "the odor may be pleasing" and attract you when it is good. The other symbolism can shed light on what you are "sensing" with your nose that you are perhaps not able to see. Attempting to cover body odor can signify hiding natural urges or sexuality from others.

**Office:** Dreams that take place in the office are generally exploring work issues when you want more in your career. All the little nuances of the office can provide direction about what is holding you back or what you can do to achieve your aspirations. Items hung on the walls portray beliefs and allow you to see the ideas that you 'surround yourself with.' Computers can reveal thought patterns and phones can symbolize communication. Focusing on the ceiling can portray what you believe are limitations to your growth and upward mobility. Going to the roof can show how you are exploring a new direction outside of your current work scenario. The rug or carpet can symbolize issues 'swept under the carpet' or what is at the foundation of the situation. Windows and doors allow you to explore new opportunities and their condition can show whether you are doing so. The desk is a symbol of being driven by a need for security. If you open the desk to find something unusual, you are exploring other talents or inner resources at your disposal. See **Houses and Buildings.**

**Oil:** This is a symbol that can have various meanings. Oil is a substance that "doesn't mix well" and can portray your inability to "fit in." It is associated with lamps and can suggest something inspiring you to "find your way" through the darkness. Finally, oil that is used in refineries can be black, sticky and smelly. In this case, the oil may signify motivations that are making you feel "dirty." See Black and Gold under **Colors.**

**Old:** See **Ancient.**

**One:** A dream that focuses on the number one describes exploration in the area of self-sufficiency. One, in association with other numbers points at the Self, and what you do or need to do to bring the situation to a successful resolution. See **Numbers.**

**Onion:** See **Food.**

**Operation:** When you undergo "the cutting" of your body, there is a sense that you are digging within to bring some part of you forward. See Hospitals under **Houses and Buildings** and also **Anatomy and Body Parts.**

**Orange:** As a color, orange is one that stands out. Its message can be either to alert you to potential danger or ask you to identify what is unique about you. Prison inmates often wear orange because it is an impossible color to hide in. This can tie the color to the fearless expression in being who you are. As a fruit, the orange represents wholeness and vibrancy. It also ties the theme of its color to the idea of your unique qualities, and how expressing them is healthy. See **Colors** and **Food**.

**Orchard:**  See Fruit under **Food** and also **Forest.**

**Organ:**  The organ is a classic symbol of genitals.  At the same time, the organ is also a symbol of the free expression of passion and pleasure. Playing any musical instrument symbolizes how you are attempting to give free reign to what you are passionate about. If the organ is part of the body, see **Anatomy and Body Parts** and see also **Music.**

**Orgasm:** Since we dream of what we are not facing, dreaming of having an orgasm can be a message about the need to open to your sexual feelings. The orgasm is also a symbol of achieving a high point and can symbolize a sense of being accepted or acknowledged for who you are. Pent up energy is released through dreams in all types of landscapes and symbols. Since the dream is focusing on your natural urges, you may need to get out of your head and recognize the basic needs of your body.

**Ornate:**  Commonly, you will dream of a familiar or new house with ornate decorations. Sometimes they are exotic suggesting sexual urges, and sometimes they are regal, portraying your desire for financial satisfaction. Whatever the symbol that is described as "ornate," it is still a representation of *you*. Explore the symbol for further clues as to how you may be blossoming.

**Oven:**  "When something is cooking" you may dream of the oven as an objective symbol of waiting for the fruit of your labor to 'rise.' Its association with **Food** makes the symbolism reflective of fulfillment and satisfaction.

**Owl:** An owl symbolizes the idea of aspirations mixed with intelligence or wisdom. The dream can be exploring intuition or a type of wisdom that might be activated in your work. The brown owl can relate to work that is practical, earthy or grounded, while the white owl can suggest healing work or spiritual aspirations. This nocturnal bird can also relate to messages coming from the unconscious. See **Birds.**

# P

Seeing the letter "P" can bring up issues of financial insecurities. It can represent patience or perseverance. It may suggest paying off debts that have left you feeling immobilized. There is a sense of paralysis or finality associated with this letter.

**Package:** Where the **Box** symbolizes what you store and protect, a package suggests something that is "wrapped up" or unexplored. It often appears in connection with the idea of sending or receiving (communication) and carries the idea of protection a little deeper. There are many symbols that can appear when you "open" the package. Transcending the idea of what is unknown, once you open it, the symbol is now making its way into consciousness and should be explored for further details.

**Packing:** The idea of packing reveals what you currently consider to be so important that you need to carry it with you as you go. Often you will "forget" to pack something or experience drama surrounding the actual packing experience as a way of exploring transition. Representing "baggage," or what you may need to release as you move forward, this is a classic dream that occurs during transformative periods. Generally packing **Clothes**, you are trying on new ways of interacting with the world around you. See **Purses, Wallets, Luggage, Jewels and Keys.**

**Pain:** Pain is the first signal of danger when "something isn't right." Proceeding without caution may bring harm to your well-being. If you are dreaming of being in pain, perhaps you are not recognizing this (emotional) sensation in waking life. If you dream that someone else is in pain, explore the side of you that this person represents. There is pain involved, although you are not "owning up to it." To dream of being afraid of something that *may* be painful, and yet doesn't really occur, suggests that you are holding back your feelings. See **Blood.**

**Painting:** As a symbol of expression and free flowing creativity, painting can symbolize the need to express all sides of you. If you are painting a wall, explore the color for clues to what you may be blocking. If you are looking at a painting, you are observing aspects of yourself in an objective format. See **Colors,** and **Advertisement.**

**Pan:** Using a pan to 'cook something up' can symbolizes steps you are taking to be more fulfilled. Often the pan is associated with family members as you explore the dynamics of your upbringing that affect your self esteem. Since food is transformed in the pan, this symbol can be a message about recognizing how self limiting ideas might be transformed into optimism ie: food for thought. You can see this symbol as having heavy associations with the ideas you were taught in early life - and you will often dream of a pot or pan when you are attempting to move beyond this conditioning. See also **Food** and **Cooking.**

**Pants:** A dream that focuses on pants explores your ability to provide for yourself or others as in "wearing the pants" in the family. Being dressed without pants can symbolize a change in career. In a sense you are disrobing an old **Persona**, revealing yourself openly and searching for a way of providing for yourself that is more revealing of who you are. See **Clothing and Makeup.**

**Paper:** See **Newspaper** and **Letter.**

**Parachute:** The parachute is used as a symbol of safety when you may be questioning your ability to "fly" or "land safely." See Airplane under **Vehicles and Places of Transportation.**

**Paralysis:** The human body is designed with a paralytic feature to keep you from acting out on your dreams. At times, you may awaken 'in between' the stages of full consciousness and sleep. You sense that you are awake but you cannot move. Although it can feel extremely frightening, it is not uncommon, and you are merely not fully conscious or awake. If you actually dream of being paralyzed, the dream is leading you to explore the idea of being stuck. See **Crippled** and **Anatomy and Body Parts**.

**Parasite:** This is a common symbol appearing in forms other than an insect. It brings forward the idea of the life that "grows" or is nourished by your suffering. The parasite symbolizes how you may be unwittingly doing something self-destructive because it "serves you" in some way. As a symbol of what may be draining your life force, it can represent a lack of fulfillment because you would rather ignore the problem. See **Blood.**

**Park:** See **Forest** and **Amusement Park.**

**Parking Lot:** As a place where cars are parked, the parking lot can symbolize a transition in your career as you explore new ways of moving forward. Cars represent motivation and how you are moving forward. When the car is parked, it is either because you are taking time to re-evaluate where you are going or are unaware of issues that are undermining your ability to succeed. Explore the other symbols and colors associated with the parking lot to understand what the dream is suggesting. See **Garage** and **Vehicles and Places of Transportation.**

**Party:** When you dream of a party, it can represent trying on new attitudes and ways of interacting. People gathering in a social situation that is less formal than a wedding shows the casual exploration of new sides of yourself and not necessarily actual integration. The more irons that you have in the fire, the more you will have dreams of this type of social interaction. See **People** and **Nightclub.**

**Passenger:** Having a passenger in your vehicle can represent your sense of responsibility to this person. They can also have an influence on your current motivation. Being a passenger rather than driving can portray a sense that you are not in control of where you are going. See Passenger under **Vehicles and Places of Transportation.**

**Path:** Following a path through the woods can symbolize how you approach the subconscious in the first steps toward exploring the unconscious. The path can represent your journey as you move toward transformation. See **Forest, Placement and Perspective** and also, **Landscape and Scenery.**

**Pay:** The idea that you have to "pay for something" can signify guilt or retribution. Dreams that focus on paying can also be exploring self value. Often there will be some confusion about 'the change,' as a message that something may need to change. Also explore the numbers associated with the 'change' to see what area of your life is undergoing change. See **Money.**

**Peacock:** The Peacock was Hera's favorite bird in Greek mythology and can embody arrogance or spite. It is associated with vanity and the outer expression of inner beauty. You may dream of a peacock as a message that you are relying too much on outer appearance and may need to turn inward to cultivate your inner beauty. Since it has eyes in its feathers - it can symbolize being too concerned with what others think. You may dream of the peacock when you need to develop self pride - or when you are too focused on it. The behavior of the peacock can tell you which is at play. See **Birds.**

**Pen:** A pen and pencil carry the idea of communication, while the pen can signify words that are not easily 'erased.' The pencil may be portraying words that have no commitment behind them. See **Weapons and Utensils.**

**Penis:** See **Male Genitals** and **Anatomy and Body Parts.**

**People:** All of the characters appearing in your dream represent evolving or transforming aspects of **you.** *Foreigners* and *aborigines* will represent unknown, or organic aspects of you that appear foreign, while still finding expression. *Males* appearing in a female's dream will represent her "masculine" aggressive and assertive personality functioning through immediate experience. A *female* appearing in a male's dream will represent his intuitive and sensitive side. *Kissing* these characters will reflect how you are exploring and integrating what they represent. When there is *attraction and rejection* involved, it reveals your desire or inability to "adopt these traits."

Running away from *unknown attackers* suggests how you can feel "pursued" by non-integrated aspects as you grow and evolve. The times when you are growing the most will be associated with these types of dreams because you are experimenting with "new" ways of interacting with the people around you. See **Attack and Being Chased.**

When you look at the dream as a plot where all of the characters are representing you, look beyond the character and ask: what *word* would I use to describe this person? How might this person be representing *a side of myself* that I might be failing to understand? *People from the past* can represent you at that point in life, and *family members* usually appear in a dream that is helping your to understand how a current crisis was created through your personal dynamics, and how it might be resolved (see Dream Cycles under **Dream Processing** in Introduction.

A committee or group of people represents the various sides of you that become, in a sense, the board members of your psyche. They can sit in judgment, as conscience, or negotiate important aspects of your unique needs against the consensus or "older members" of the group in terms of your past **Persona**.

*Famous people* take these issues to another level. On the one hand, they represent icons or display clear characteristics that you are adopting or need to adopt. Comedians can offer a message about the need to "lighten up." In a situation, you may find that you will achieve more if you can be less serious. The issues surrounding dreams of this type suggest that you are "trying on this public identity" in an effort to gain esteem or approval. Just like any other character however, the word you would use to describe them will shed light on this part of you that you are exploring. Ask yourself: "what is this famous person known for" in order to understand the dream's message.

**Pepper:** To dream of pepper can symbolize the need to "spice things up." Its association with the **Color** black (as opposed to salt, which is white) can represent spicy behavior that is also deemed to be dirty.

**Perfume:** Like makeup, you can hide your naturalness by covering yourself with a mask. Putting on perfume may symbolize covering up feelings to appear more amicable even though something 'doesn't smell right' or is bugging you. When your perfume or smell is the focus of a dream, you are exploring your magnetism or what attracts others to you. Smelling perfume that is sweet symbolizes attraction and a desire to experience beauty. Smell is a powerful memory trigger and the perfume may have associations with past experiences. A perfume bottle is delicate and can represent delicate aspects of femininity. Also see **Makeup** and **Odor**.

**Persona:** The word Persona comes from a Latin word that describes a mask used by an actor. The Latin word per sonare means to "sound through." As an aspect of dreaming, the Persona becomes the mask you wear in presenting yourself to the world. It often takes on the symbolism of **Clothing** where dreams of various types of clothing can represent changes you are making in expressing who you are. Carl Jung believed that dreaming was a way of compensating for the "one-sided" attitude that is often held in waking consciousness. Dreaming of sorting through old clothing can signify sorting through old ways of expressing yourself as you change and grow. Dreaming of packing clothing can symbolize the way you hold to just one way of expressing yourself. Often you will not be able to find some type of clothing when you are overly-identifying with only one aspect of who you are.

The Persona is also explored through the other characters that appear in your dream. If you stop and consider the adjective that you would use to describe the person, consider whether or not this aspect is currently being expressed. While we are awake, we tend to hold firmly to one image of who we are, while dreaming is ever leading us forward to explore new ways of tapping our potential. The other people we meet suggest aspects that are currently undergoing exploration. See also **Dream Basics** in beginning, **Packing** and **Purses, Wallets, Luggage, Jewels and Keys.**

**Pet:**  A household pet is different from wild animals because it is domesticated. Our pets can symbolize our own habitual or routine behavior. As a symbol, the pet can portray what you are nurturing and protecting - both good and bad. Their well being and behavior can embody how you may be neglecting aspects of yourself. Dogs relate to unconditional love but if you are afraid of a dog in a dream, you may not be feeling trusting in your current relationship.

The cat remains aloof and can symbolize a desire to be more self sufficient. Animals usually portray more natural or organic drives and passions - and when it is domesticated it can embody trading natural expression for security needs. Explore what type of animal is being portrayed as a pet for more information of the side of you that may be in need of freedom or nurturing. See **Animals.**

**Phone:**  Phones are a symbol of how various aspects of the psyche seek to communicate with you. The person who calls you should be considered in terms of the adjective you would use to describe them - they can be representing a side of you seeking expression. The message that they share with you should also be considered as a message that may be coming from the Higher Self.

**Photograph:** When you see a photograph in a dream, you are viewing a part of yourself in a very objective way, perhaps seeing something that is associated with the past. You may dream of issues in 'photo' form as the first steps in integrating something painful or difficult, sometimes when a loved on has died. The photo can be a 'static' representation of you in 'freeze frame' for exploration, similar to dreams of **Glasses.**

**Physician:**  See Hospital under **Houses and Buildings.**

**Piano:**  The piano, as a musical instrument can appear in dreams when you are becoming more open in expressing your passion. It embodies the idea of harmony and how and where it appears can describe where balance needs to be achieved. It can also relate to your mood depending on what type of music is being played. If the music is harsh or out of key, you may need to 'tone' how you are approaching experience -

either up or down, as in lighten up or get more involved with what you are doing. See **Music.**

**Picture:** Pictures on walls in a dream can portray your beliefs or the ideas you live by. Examining pictures in a book can be a way of seeing the past differently. Of all symbols, pictures and photographs provide an objective way of viewing a situation prior to making a change...as in 'picture this.' If there is something unusual about the picture - the message can be that the way you are viewing something isn't accurate. Explore what the picture presents as a symbol to understand what that is. For example: self/identity, parents/influences, car/motivation or house/thoughts, etc. See **Photograph**.

**Pig:** The pig is associated with satisfaction and enjoyment, sometimes at the expense of all else. You can be 'pig-headed' or too busy gathering creature comforts (working) to see how you are missing out the real joys of life. The pig can also suggest a sort of naturalness in being 'dirty' or the free flow of sexual feelings. See **Animals.**

**Pill:** See **Drug.**

**Pimple:** Whenever a dream focuses on the face - it can be a message about 'keeping face' or credibility. Generally your appearance in a dream is a way of exploring self esteem or your self image. If something on your face (like a pimple or acne) diminishes your attractiveness, you may be exploring the idea that you are not expressing your true self or acknowledging your own beauty. If you are picking a pimple or trying to remove a blemish - the message can be about releasing ideas or feelings that are undermining your self image.

**Pin:** See **Needle** and **Amulet and Necklace**.

**Pipe:** A pipe is a channel for water or gases and can signify either emotion or energy flowing through you. To dream of being in a pipe or enclosure of this type can have associations with birth and the idea of re-birth.

**Pit:** The pit can represent being in a situation that is not easy to get out of. Since it is usually a natural formation, some part of your own thinking is trapping you from moving forward. See Quicksand under **Landscape and Scenery.**

**Placement and Perspective:** Where you stand and perceive the symbols in your dream suggests where you stand in relationship to what they represent. *Ascending* or going upward suggests gaining a wider view or taking the steps to expand your awareness, sometimes intuitively or spiritually. To move into a position that places you *above* or *higher* than something, portrays your attempt to "rise above" it. Whatever is *beside* another symbol in a dream suggests some sort of connection between them; while something at the *center* represents the cause or how it affects you to the core.

What is *behind* you represents the past and circumstances that have passed, while it can also mean turning your back on what is important in a way that it stalks or shadows you. What is in *front* of you often suggests the direction in which you are going, or what you need to face, while something described as being *before* you, suggests that it may be blocking your movement. Something *next* to you or *near* you makes the symbol important, although you have not "owned" or integrated it. A symbol that is associated with being to the *right* can represent behavior that is correct or acceptable, while the *left* shows deviation from the norm and a movement toward authenticity.

*Descending* or going down can represent getting more grounded or returning to your roots. If you see something *beneath* the water or *lower* on a hill, it is sometimes indicative of bringing the relevance of this symbol to the surface, like *"below* the belt" can mean sexual feelings. Seeing something *up close*, in *daylight* or *under a light* brings all that the symbol represents into a high level of focus and suggests that you are conscious of it. Issues that you are not facing will appear as symbolism viewed at *night*, in the *dark*, or appearing *far away*. The low level of light suggests not recognizing its importance and so, it remains "out of the reach" of consciousness. Imagery that is associated with being *deep* portrays your sense of exploring the deeper aspects of the symbolism, while appearing *shallow* has the opposite meaning, in the sense of its irrelevance or the need to release it.

**Plant:** The plant is similar to the symbolism of the **Garden** and **Tree.** All portray growth and the idea of pruning or the things that you groom, such as children. It has roots and suggests the parts of you that were inherited from family genetics. When difficult childhood issues are being explored, the plant can symbolize your roots and desire to find your own way, aside from the demands of family.

**Plate:** Just as you can "have a lot on your plate," the plate can symbolize where you are currently focusing your attention. Whatever is "being served" can portray how you are currently finding nourishment and the way in which it may serve you." See **Food.**

**Plateau:** Moving upward in a dream is a way of exploring upward mobility. If you reach a plateau the message can be about taking time out for introspection or feeling like you have reached a stable position so you can explore new opportunities for growth. The landscape in a dream is every bit as important as the other symbols that appear - and its symbolism portrays the 'condition' of your inner landscape. See **Mountain.**

**Plucking:** Plucking hairs represents the difficulty you may feel in releasing an old perspective. Finding a strange hair growing on the face can symbolize your unique attributes that you are not considering. Attempting to pluck it suggests your desire to fit in. Hair has associations with ideas that grow and need to be groomed or released, since hair also falls out. Plucking your eyebrows represents changes you are making in perception and expression.

**Plumbing:** When you dream of faulty plumbing, there is a sense that your emotions have become uncontrollable. If you are inspecting the plumbing, you are trying to understand the root of your feelings. See **Faucet.**

**Pocket:** You fill your pockets with the things you need and therefore, the pocket can have associations with your values. The pocket can also represent the things you are hiding. Explore the symbolism associated with the pocket for further clues. See **Purses, Wallets, Luggage, Jewels and Keys.**

**Poison:** Feelings that are painful or difficult situations that are eating at you can be represented by poison. As something that is ingested against your will and potentially harmful, dreaming of poison can signify an unhealthy relationship or situation.

**Police:** Police dreams occur when one aspect of your evolving identity is challenged by the "critic" or the "patrolling" aspect of the psyche. Sometimes the message is important: slow down. At other times, the police will come to "inspect" the changes you are making, playing those time worn disciplinary tapes. Associated with the "inner critic," encountering police is often occurring because you may either need to step out of the lines to transform or some aspect of your current behavior is undergoing scrutiny. See **Vehicles and Places of Transportation.**

**Pool:** Like all bodies of water, the pool has associations with emotions, although in this case it takes on the symbolism of "being contained." Because it is maintained and kept clean, it can portray a clinical approach to feelings. If the pool is dirty or contains what shouldn't be there, it can be a message about a situation that is making you feel "dirty," like the feelings of uncontrollable sexual urges.

**Pot:** Like the pan, dreaming of a pot can symbolize early conditioning and your attempt to overcome self limiting ideas as you move toward fulfillment. Generally a pot is used to cook liquids and so the association leans more toward feelings. The idea of simmering and boiling are also associated with emotions - you may or may not be aware of feeling angry or resentful and the dream can be bringing this to your attention. If you discover a pot of gold, you are examining latent talents or moving toward a greater level of Self sufficiency. Pottery can have associations with the past, as something buried but discovered for its importance in the present. In this type of dream, you are resurrecting old issues so that you can find the hidden value of what you learned. See **Pan** and **Cooking**.

**Precipice:** Unlike the plateau that can show a period of arrival and reflection, the precipice can be associated with making a choice. You may be feeling forced to make some kind of change and are uncertain about it. The precipice represents conscious awareness as you explore transitions or a new pathway forward. If it is associated with descending a canyon you might need to come more 'down to earth' or move toward your 'center' to be more grounded in the sense of who you really are. See also **Ascending, Descending, Placement and Perspective** and **Plateau.**

**Precognition:** See **Prophetic Dreams.**

**Pregnant:** You can be "fertile" for a new way of interacting and understanding yourself. When you become pregnant, your rebirth has begun its gestation. To actually give birth, you are bringing this "new side" forward. See Unknown Child under **Archetypes and Characters.**

**Present:** See **Gift** and **Package.**

**Priest:** For a man, the priest can embody his spiritual nature and the mystery of sexuality. For a woman, the priest can symbolize the authoritative influence of the father. Your interaction with the priest will offer clues to how you are currently approaching your spiritual side. There is usually a sense of reservation associated with the priest.

**Prison:** You may not be aware of the limitations that you are currently facing in daily life. To dream of a prison suggests that you have lost your sense of freedom, although since you are dreaming about it, this may not be obvious to you.

**Prize:** Embodying the many things that you strive for, to dream of receiving a prize can signify whether or not your aspirations are realistic, attainable and healthy. Explore the symbol that is portrayed as the prize for clues about how you are currently approaching ambition. A prize or treasure emphasizes a goal or something that is an important aspect of your fulfillment. Discovering treasure or something buried usually has associations with what is repressed (guns/sex - gold/self-value.) We receive a prize usually because of our effort and tenacity. To dream of winning the lottery however, places the result of what you experience on others, fate or the outside and unpredictable forces around you.

On one hand, dreaming of winning the lottery shows that you want to win or succeed - or get a lucky break. You can think of winning as giving you the opportunity to experience a sense of 'arrival.' It lifts you above all of your hard effort when you are too focused on the work - and not enough on the reward, or where the work may be leading you. It allows you to re-examine what you value in a way that might change your direction or focus.

Since dreams offer clues about how we can be more fulfilled, and we dream about what we are not facing - the lottery can suggest the need to take action or responsibility to claim your prize (fulfillment). For example, rather than succeed by 'the luck of the draw' explore whether you have a clear vision of what you want - the lottery can indicate how something fulfilling is within your reach - but you may be working so hard you are missing it.

As a symbol of balancing desires against experience - you may be taking responsibility for your success and blaming outside influences when you fail. An inconsistency in your thinking can undermine fulfillment. The idea of a lottery/prize is showing how you are not owning your accomplishments or seeing how failure is not punishment - but often a way of honing your continual success. The message coaches you to connect the outcome - to what you want, or what you are doing. If a specific number(s) was tied to winning - it should be explored as an aspect that is missing in your equation of fulfillment.

**Prophetic Dreams:** See **Types of Dreams** in **Introduction**.

**Prostitute:**　This character is trading the ability to experience *real intimacy* for money. Perhaps you have a sense that you are sacrificing something special for work or material gain. The idea of "paying for sex" can have two interpretations:

Either sex is associated with pain or intimacy is easily traded for insecurity. In either case, being intimate with a prostitute will show how you are currently exploring the *real value* of intimacy.

**Pull:**　Pulling something in a dream can signify unacknowledged burdens. The symbol you are pulling should be explored for further clues to what this is.

**Puncture:** Puncturing something shows an attempt to "break through." What is being punctured will reveal what this area is.

**Punish:** Being punished in a dream can be the personification and work through of guilt. If you are not aware of how guilt can undermine your sense of self esteem or success, you can dream about punishment as an objective portrayal of how you are punishing yourself by not letting go. See **Justice.**

**Puppet:** Usually a puppet symbolizes a way of being that is not natural. As an aspect of you, the puppet can be the first *objective representation* of difficult issues that you are not facing. Because it is animated by another, it can signify "cutting the strings" that tie you to them.

**Purses, Wallets, Luggage, Jewels and Keys** can represent the valuable part of your nature, or what you protect and carry with you. They become the subject of many dreams where you are "embarking" or traveling in a new direction, as things that are often lost or left behind. In this way, *luggage* can suggest baggage that needs to be released during a transformative process.

As the essence of the genetic traits that are bequeathed to your children, protected items, like *jewels* can represent responsibility or issues related to childbearing. In some cases, looking for or protecting jewels or *treasure* can symbolize the healing that can take place one after you discover what you are repressing; usually childhood pain. The *purse* and *wallet* portray your sense of self-worth and how protective you are of them will show how you protect *who you are* against *who you might become.* Changing careers often coincides with these types of symbols, where losing or searching for them is similar to searching for your new identity. These symbols also appear in dreams during times when you are feeling financially insecure.

Searching for a *key* often suggests that you are exploring your relationship to your sexuality. The key can also symbolize your desire to "unlock" the doors that hold you back as you explore direction to find increased meaning in life.

**Push:** Like **Pull,** pushing can represent an unacknowledged burden. The extra energy required to push shows that something is not flowing easily.

**Pussycat:** A cat that would be referred to as a pussycat is a cryptic way of exploring sexuality. See **Cat** and **Animals.**

**Pyramid:** Associated with mystery and exotic or bygone cultures, the pyramid can symbolize the search for deeper meaning in life. Its triangular shape can also represent the idea of *three* or conflicting ideas that require integration. A triangle is also highly spiritual, so dreaming of a pyramid can portray the condition of your spiritual ideas and how you are blending material experiences with spiritual pursuits. Since it has four sides, it can also symbolize balance or issues that need to be brought together to achieve harmony. Associated with mystery and exotic or bygone cultures, the pyramid can symbolize spirituality or the search for deeper meaning in life. See **Egypt, Mummy** and **Numbers.**

# Q

The letter "Q" conjures ideas of the strange, bizarre and dramatic as in 'curly Q.' You may feel that there are strings attached to being open, or embarking on a new sense of adventure may require that you stay grounded and practical. It can also suggest elegance and grace. This is a regal letter that can also pose a question in a type of initiation where solving a puzzle leads to Self actualization. In this case the letter Q can relate to the idea of being given a cue or clues.

**Qtip:** Using a Q-tip in a dream can symbolize changes to how you take in information by listening. In a sense, you need to 'clean' your ears so you don't become dismissive or quick to jump to conclusions. The message is to take an active part in the listening process. Perhaps you missed a valuable cue or clue because you dismissed the opportunity to explore it as something new.

**Quadruplets:** Any time a symbol associated with four appears in a dream, the message is about balance and earthiness. Just as there are four basic elements and directions, dreaming of quadruplets shows the activation of all sides (mental, spiritual, emotional, physical) and how balance is being achieved within. See also **Four** and **Numbers**.

**Quail:** The quail is often thought of as a type of bird that doesn't fly, but hides in the brush. It can symbolize aspirations that are grounded - in both a positive and negative sense. The quail does fly for short distances, and may appear in a dream as a message about taking a more grounded approach. Their unusual top feather can symbolize a desire to 'have a feather in one's cap.' Like the chicken, it is more wild and exotic, and the quail can symbolize unusual **defense mechanisms**. See also **Birds**.

**Quaker:** Dreaming of a Quaker character can symbolize your own ideas of purity or chastity. There may be something unusually 'puritanical' in your current approach. The religious association can tie the Quaker to the exploration of your spiritual ideas. The image of the Quaker related to the oat cereal brand can be a way of exploring why 'sowing your wild oats' may be under a type of 'house arrest' related to critical conscience. Another theme that the Quaker can personify is the 'quaking' or movement of urges that have been 'under wraps.' Associated with 'oats' – it might suggest the idea of sowing your 'wild oats.'

**Quarantine:** The idea of quarantine represents taking special care when approaching something that might be 'infectious' like runaway feelings or affections. While the dream has little to do with the actual idea that your health is threatened, the action of placing something in quarantine allows you to examine how you enact 'compulsory isolation' when you might find more happiness by opening up. You may not be giving free reign to your feelings. Dis-ease can objectify how you are feeling uneasy - or how you might release the tendency to hold back. When your feelings seem beyond your control - the idea of avoiding infection can symbolize your fear of 'affection' or intimacy. If you are being quarantined because you may be a threat to others - the dream can be suggesting that your behavior or thoughts are blocking your development. This type of dream can be a 'time out' while you re-examine unproductive thought patterns. You may also need to examine your self esteem to ensure that you are not harboring feelings of inadequacy.

**Quarrel:** During the day we can meet people that challenge us through a type of conflict. It is usually not the easy relationships in our lives that keep us growing, but the challenging ones. In the same way, characters that challenge you in a dream are attempting to bring something new into awareness. The particular character challenging you can represent a side of you that is undergoing exploration. Explore an adjective you would use to describe the person you are quarreling with in a dream. How does the character portray an aspect that you may be discarding, adopting or perhaps ignoring? The quarrel brings this issue forward for your consideration. See **Attack and Being Chased, People** and **Shadow**.

**Quarter:** To dream of a quarter symbolizes a sense of inadequacy. As the idea of 1/4th, you may be giving too much consideration to only one aspect of a well rounded life. Also explore whether the quarter might be representing your current living arrangement or 'quarters.' An idea you might not want to face by day, can be captured in the symbol of a quarter.

**Queen:** The Queen in a dream can symbolize the Wise Woman Archetype. For a woman, she can embody power and wisdom becoming active. For the man, she can embody one of the last stages in his initiation into the feeling realm. The Queen can portray the negative aspects of what is associated with the feminine as well- such as manipulation, gossip and being overly dramatic. Explore what qualities are undergoing scrutiny by the Queen - and how this scrutiny is self inflicted. Her message is a powerful one and her appearance usually ushers in heightened creativity, intuition and sensitivity. See **Wise Woman**.

**Question:** Words that stand out in a dream are usually a clear message describing something that needs to be heeded. In fact, often you will wake up with words on your mind as the dream state changes into waking state. These words are capturing the dream imagery so stop and observe if you can see this happening upon waking. These words will sometimes become prophetic (capturing events that will unfold during the week) and is an interesting exercise that allows you to see how dreams have a different time sense.

When a question is asked of you in a dream - explore this question as if it is something your higher self is asking of you.

A good trick to enhance dream recall: use the state prior to waking to transfer the imagery in your dream into words. You dream in right brain holistic imagery yet usually awaken into left brain logic. The transition back to the left brain logical side can make the imagery evaporate. By transferring the images into words, you can then explore the symbols. You don't need to remember everything. You will generally dream of the same themes in different settings during the night. See also **Answer.**

**Quicksand:** Dreaming of being trapped in quick sand can be a message that the foundation of your established beliefs is undergoing a type of implosion. While self limiting ideas may be trapping you, the solvency of the foundation is actually a good sign that the foundation is being reworked. See **Landscape and Scenery.**

**Quilt:** A quilt can represent the need for security in both positive and negative ways. If you cover yourself with a quilt to be warm, you might examine if you are feeling a sense of coldness around you because you are remaining distant from others. If you are making a quilt, you are taking steps to incorporate security in your life. A blanket can also show how you may be covering or protecting something that needs to be explored. If it is the blanket or quilt of your childhood, you may need to examine whether your fear of intimacy stems from the type of love you received as a child. The dream is showing your desire to bring warmth into your life.

**Quiver:** A dream that focuses on the Quiver that carries bows and arrows offers a message about focusing on what is important. You may need to establish goals or examine what you are working to achieve - and whether or not it is right for you. Carrying bows and arrows on your back can also be a message about being too defensive. See also **Arrow** and **Bow**.

**Quiz:** See **Test**.

# R

The letter "R" can be associated with seeing how 'what is - is' from the standpoint of acceptance. It can ask a question of you related to whether or not you are really happy in a situation as in 'are?' It can suggest release or the removal of what stands in the way of your happiness. It can ask you to retrace your steps or 'return' in some way to see the truth of what is unfolding.

**Rabbit:** A rabbit is a rich dream symbol and can combine the idea of sex, magic and its appearance or disappearance in your life. As a symbol of the mystery of life, the rabbit is a symbol of pro-creation, both in terms of children and the re-birth associated with transformation. See **Animals.**

**Race:** There are several interpretations for the idea of racing or being in a race. First of all, you can be "pressed for time" and racing to get somewhere as a sense of feeling that you are not reaching the plateaus in your life fast enough. See **Late.** If you are racing in some type of vehicle, it has more to do with motivation and your drive to move forward. See **Vehicles and Places of Transportation.** Finally, you can be racing another character as a way of feeling "overwhelmed" by a side of you that is moving forward without integration.

**Radar:** This is a tool that allows you to observe what cannot be seen with the eye. Offering a message about intuition or guidance, you may dream of radar as a sense of acknowledging what may be coming at you "from left field." Usually offering details related to things that fly, the symbolism can suggest ambitions.

**Radio:** Sometimes hearing a radio is a representation of "ambient noise" or the idea that something is simply playing in the background. If there is a message that becomes loud and clear on the radio, it can offer symbolism as to what you are missing because of your daily routine.

**Railroad**: Railroad tracks portray a sense of direction as if it has been laid down for you and is not easily changed. It can show the expectations placed upon you by others. See Train under **Vehicles and Places of Transportation.**

**Rain:** After the sky has filled with clouds or condensation, rain is released. To dream of rain can symbolize the need to let go of painful emotions that can lead to depression. There is a sense of renewal associated with rain. It offers a message about the need to see the silver lining in every cloud.

**Rainbow:** Representing wishes and the promise of well-being, you may dream of a rainbow as a symbol of hope. The more "tangible" the rainbow appears in the dream, the more it reflects how you are currently achieving your ambitions.

**Raincoat:** See Outerwear under **Clothing and Makeup.**

**Ram:** A ram is a powerful symbol of the drive to achieve. Associated with perseverance, the ram symbolizes the need to push beyond obstacles. If the ram is associated with fire, it can represent a necessary transformation that is taking place. A masculine symbol, it embodies traits adopted by the father, where the goat and its connection to milk, personifies characteristics associated with the mother. The goat is also mischievous and overtly sexual and can represent this quality and whether or not you are open to playfulness and sex. The Ram's astrological relationship to the sign Aries as an Archetype captures the idea of the Self, or the mask you wear as your **Persona.**

**Rape:** When you are not giving free reign to your emotions or urges you can dream of being "dominated" by a character in a sexual way. Sleep becomes the only "natural" way that your consciousness can process this energy and there is really nothing sinister involved. If you are dreaming of being raped because of actual trauma, consciousness may still be attempting to process these difficult memories. See Shadow under **Archetypes and Universal Characters.**

**Rat:** Rats and mice are often 'pests' or associated with what is 'unclean' or forbidden. Rats can be 'stowaways,' hiding in ships, or in the shadows, representing abandoning something, sneaking around or escaping like a 'dirty rat.' Used in scientific laboratories, both can symbolize 'experimenting' in the expression of feelings. See **Animals.**

**Raven:** See **Birds.**

**Read:** Dreams of reading show how you are exploring ideas in an objective format. Seeing something printed is the first step toward integrating this new idea. Reading also portrays your feelings and insecurities about 'revealing' yourself to others. See **Advertisement, Books** and **Newspaper.**

**Receive:** To dream of receiving something shows how you are not open to receiving whatever this symbol represents in daily life. Explore the symbol for clues about what this is.

**Recurring Dreams:** You will experience recurring dreams as story lines or themes that repeat themselves over weeks, months or even years. Sometimes they leave you feeling puzzled because they seem meaningless and at other times, they will be extremely frightening. Since dreams are suggesting what you fail to acknowledge in daily life, whatever you are avoiding or not integrating will continue to be the subject matter of your dream until it is resolved and integrated. Like nightmares, (See **Nightmares** under types of Dreams in Introduction.) once the resolution or transformation takes place, the dream will not recur.

**Red:** This is a color that symbolizes passion and enthusiasm. It can also appear as a warning and direct you to play closer inspection to what is going on in the dream. If you are currently cut off from your feelings, red can symbolize the need to re-connect with purpose and passion. See **Colors.**

**Reflection:** Two of the most important symbols that appear as you move toward self-actualization, is to hear your name and to see your reflection. In both cases, the dream is offering a message about cultivating who you really are. Seeing the reflection of something else can show a 'disconnect' related to the symbol. A time for reflection may be necessary to see clearly. See also **Mirror.**

**Refrigerator:** This appliance combines the idea of food with something that is cold or frozen. Representing how you receive nourishment, at some level, you are aware of what you have "put on ice" or in a state of suspended animation. In other words, you are not finding nourishment because of your need for preservation or protection. Whatever symbol is associated with the refrigerator can portray what may need to be "thawed" in an effort to achieve fulfillment. See **Food, Cold** and **Frozen.**

**Rejection:** Dreams explore inner dynamics through the costume of other people as they appear in the dreamscape. Feelings of love for someone in a dream when this love is not reciprocated can be symbolic of how we undermine our power for self love. Characters can make advances or seek intimacy with us as the representation of the **Anima/Animus** awakening within. We may reject these advances when we are not quite ready to make the transformation. See **Love** and **People.**

**Relatives:** When you describe characters in a dream as relatives, often they are appearing as family members in a dream, although in real life you don't know who they are. This type of setting usually reflects an experience that has left you wondering about your behavior and dynamics. Relatives not included in the immediate family can represent that side of you that you believe might "rescue" you from the family dynamics that you inherited. Aunts, Uncles and Grandparents usually provide care in a more unconditional way. See **Family Members.**

**Renovate:** Buildings symbolize aspects of our inner architecture. When we are undergoing change and transformation we may dream of making renovations to specific areas associated with the rooms or type of building. We may remodel the kitchen when we are making changes to how we move toward greater fulfillment. We can renovate a bathroom as a way of 'coming clean' of self-defeating behavior or fears of intimacy. If we renovate the bedroom, we can be making changes to how we approach sex or changes to our beliefs as in 'we made the bed we lie in.' Renovation to commercial buildings can represent changes in how we approach work. Renovation usually leads to a more comfortable expression of who we are. See various structures and rooms under **Houses and Buildings**. See also **Demolish** and **Furniture**.

**Rent:** Looking for a place to "rent" can symbolize not wanting to establish roots. In daily life, you may be putting a lot of energy into forming intimate relationships only to find yourself alone. This type of dream seems to suggest that your fear of intimacy is at the root of the rejection you may experience. Renting a room can also represent trying out new or temporary attitudes as you move through changes.

**Reptiles:** Reptiles and snakes in a dream relate to instincts and sensations that are somewhat unconscious and self regulating. The reptilian portion of the brain is the oldest and is associated with autonomic reactions, sex and survival mechanisms. Often dreams of reptiles will portray organic and autonomous functioning that remains unconscious to you. Our most ancient evolutionary processes are captured by the image of reptiles. They shed their skin and move around on all fours in a fight or flight posture, symbolizing insecurities or a sense of panic that may need to be controlled. This primitive side of your autonomic functioning and your relationship to it, will be portrayed in the type of reptile and your interaction with it.

*Frogs* emerge from tadpoles that resemble sperm and often signify reproductive elements or sex. *Lizards* keep close to the earth and require sun or shade to regulate temperature, often symbolizing biological or evolutionary processes connecting with consciousness. As one of the oldest and most durable creatures, dreaming of *lizards*, *salamanders* or *iguanas* can portray the power of your survival instincts, both good and bad. In some cases, the message can be coaching you toward self preservation but more often than not, dreams of these creatures can embody the need to examine self destructive tendencies.

Dreams of reptiles related to water can symbolize movement within the unconscious as something comes to the surface to reveal the power of your biological drives like anxiety and sexual impulses. As a symbol of transformation or how you can learn to shed 'your old skin' reptiles often have a message related to letting go of a dysfunctional approach to anxiety.

On a grand scale, the *Dragon* is a symbol of metamorphosis and empowerment. *Snakes* can have sexual meanings, although their ability to renew their 'protective covering' suggests transformative aspects currently taking place. They can also represent the biting or poisonous side of your instinctual nature, which you try to repress, and thus, it recoils to 'hurt you.'

Unlike warm blooded and emotionally reactive mammals, reptiles are associated with being cold blooded and seeking protection. The *turtle* can portray covering your feelings or insecurities when you are hurt or feeling shy. How big (*dinosaur/dragon*) or self-destructive they appear will suggest the level of repression as your unconscious processes seek wellness and expression. Their vigilant behavior and ancient associations with transformation will portray your physical well being and bio-physical processes. When a reptile is injured in a dream, it can portray how your defensive mechanisms are actually hurting you.

*Alligators* and *Crocodiles* move below the surface, but are carnivorous, and suggest something painful stirring beneath the waters of the unconscious that can bite you to draw blood or *allow you to feel*. Experiencing fear associated with of any reptile will portray just how 'tightly' you are blocking your natural and instinctive processes. See also **Dragon** and **Snake.**

**Rescue:** If you need to be rescued in a dream, chances are you are unaware of a similar need in daily life. When one character is rescuing another, it portrays the side of you that is weak, being compensated for by the side of you that is strong. Explore the imagery associated with the characters or symbols for more clues. See **People** and **Animals.**

**Restaurant:** The restaurant is a common dream setting because our lives are so focused on actualizing fulfillment. The events that happen in a restaurant should be explored in terms of steps you are taking to be more fulfilled. See **Food** and **Houses and Buildings.**

**Ride:** Being a passenger in a vehicle shows how you are not currently acting autonomously in your decisions to move forward. The type of vehicle and characters involved should be explored as a way of moving toward empowerment. See **Vehicles and Places of Transportation.**

**Rifle:** See **Weapons and Utensils.**

**Right:** Anything described as being to the right in a dream represents conformity and the search for acceptance. When it is on the left, it shows the road less traveled. See **Placement and Perspective.**

**Ring:** The ring combines the ideas of something of value that is bequeathed, and the idea of eternity and the circle. It can symbolize commitment, or how it is lacking in a situation. As an heirloom, it can represent family dynamics or what is passed on to your children. See **Purses, Wallets, Luggage, Jewels and Keys**.

**Ritual:** See **Ceremony.**

**River:** The river carries water from one place to another. It can reveal the flow of emotions or a sense of what sustains your passions. Since it has a tendency to pick up the earth, stones and debris that it place upriver, it brings forward the idea of the things that you are doing in the present that create your future. The river can also be a symbol of learning to "let go" and move with "current" trends or changes.

**Road:** You may have forgotten that you are a "traveler" on a journey through life that is ever changing and not static. Dreaming of roads can show you how you are "paving" your future with your thoughts of today. It can offer a message about how you are making your way forward. See **Crossroad.**

**Robot:** When you dream of a robot or "mechanical way of being," you may have the sense that you are doing things by routine without fully participating in life. Observe your patterns of behavior and routine to see if the robot can shed light on this aspect of your nature. See **Machine.**

**Rock:** The rock holds the element of the earth in its most "concrete" form and can be associated with what was once earthy and malleable, which has hardened and become inanimate. When you are "stuck between a rock and a hard place," you experience the sense that either choice has difficult consequences, therefore the rock is often a symbol of difficult transitions. You may dream of carving something from a rock as a way of giving new definition to a way of being that has become hardened. If the rock appears valuable or sacred, then the message suggests the need to "hold to" the things of value that you may be ignoring or discarding.

**Rocket:** Unlike the UFO, which appears to "**Abduct** you" when you behave in an **Alien** or unusual way, the rocket is a supercharged "**Airplane.**" It is associated with extreme drive in achieving your ambitions. In some cases, the rocket can be a symbol of male genitalia as you explore your assertiveness from a male perspective. See **Vehicles and Places of Transportation.**

**Roller-skating**: Dreaming of roller-skating or ice-skating ties together (1) the idea of moving forward, (2) the feet or the path, and (3) a sense of skating or skimming the surface. You may be exploring moving forward more easily or with a more carefree attitude at the same time that it can be a message about going too fast. Ice skating adds the added dimension of coldness and can be a message about skimming the surface because of feelings you would rather not address. The items that allow us to propel ourselves forward have significance related to ambition, motivation and self direction. See also **Feet, Shoes, Ice** and **Vehicles and Places of Transportation.**

**Roof:** When the dream setting focuses on a roof, there is a sense that you are moving beyond the 'ceiling' or the limitations that previously held you back. Just prior to make a career change, you may dream of being on the roof of your work building as a symbol of gaining a broader perspective and going 'outside' of the work environment. The roof of a house can portray ideas or the philosophy that helps you weather the vicissitudes of life. Since the roof protects us from bad weather and allows the elements to 'roll off,' dreaming of a roof can be a message about going with the flow as much as it can symbolize the limitations you put on yourself. See **Houses and Buildings.**

**Room:** Rooms can portray how we compartmentalize different areas of our mind. The *bedroom* has associations with sexual feelings, but can also include issues related to identity exploration since the bedroom is where we store our clothes. The *kitchen* symbolizes how we can be more fulfilled and 'nourished' in life. Often we are in the kitchen in a dream when we are learning to overcome negative conditioning or past self defeating beliefs. The utensils can symbolize our ability to take what we need to be fulfilled. We can take unusual things out of the refrigerator as a way of no longer keeping old issues 'on ice.'

The *living room* is where we explore how we bring others into our sense of intimacy. The office is usually work related. We might explore the *ceiling* or climb to the roof when we are ready to expand our capabilities.

*Hallways* represent transitions and appear when we are making changes. The *windows* and *doors* can symbolize how we meet opportunity or move to expand our perspective. If we are unable to 'see out' or 'open' the door - the message can show us what we fear. The *stairs* can represent going up in terms of aspirations, or going down to explore what we store in the subconscious area of the mind. The *attic* can symbolize spirituality or conscience, and the *basement* usually becomes thematic when we are digging below our habitual behavior during periods of intense transformation.

The *bathroom* appears when we are becoming more truthful with ourselves - we 'come clean.' The *family room* and *hearth* are classic symbols of family patterning. If a person other than a family member appears near the hearth, we may have adopted them in some way as a parent. The *garage* stores the car, so can appear when we are exploring our motivation or how we are moving forward in life. See various Rooms under **Houses and Buildings.**

**Root:** The root is a figurative symbol representing the cause of something. It nourishes something that is growing and dreaming of a root can portray how you are exploring the basis of your feelings or the cause of your behavior. See **Garden, Tree** and **Seed.**

**Rope:** A rope is usually associated with safety, as in "throw me a rope." You can unwittingly hang yourself "given enough rope." It can be a symbol of a barrier if it is blocking your way. See **Knot.**

**Rowing:** There are not many ways of propelling yourself forward with your arms. The psyche is very 'economical' in how it can suggest two principles with one symbol: moving forward and the idea of personal effort. Because of its association with the arms, it can represent the idea of give and take as you move forward. At the same time, you must rely on the 'current' or be present enough to maximize your efforts. You may be questioning your ability to pull your own weight. Rowing can symbolize moving forward from a better sense of who you are and what you need in life. See **Water.**

**Round:** See **Circle.**

**Rubbish:** See **Garbage.**

**Rug:** See **Carpet.**

**Ruins:** Visiting ruins suggests both, outworn structures that may no longer serve you and the idea of **Ancient** or the those things that endure through time. If you are uncertain about the direction to take, seeing ruins suggests that the "old way" is no longer working.

**Running:** When you dream of running, you may be looking objectively at your motivation and desire to move forward too quickly, or you may be running away from something that you would rather not face. Running utilizes the legs and so, has associations with exploring your ability to move forward. See **Attack and Being Chased.**

**Rust:** Seeing something that has become rusted, shows how the "elements" or experience have worn you down. It can sometimes portray feelings that have become "mechanical," or routine and is not unlike a complex or abstract view of blood, as in your life force that has run dry. See **Metal.**

# S

The letter "S" can be associated with flexibility that will make you stronger. It can have a message about standing up for yourself or the idea of stopping from the sense of overlaying the present with ideas of the past. There is a sense of lightness associated with this letter in ideas like satisfaction and silly. It can also capture the idea of the higher Self or Spirit that guides you in your dreams.

**Sacred:** You can dream of a symbol as being sacred, even while in real life, it may appear unimportant. Explore the symbol for insight into the part of you that may need to be resurrected or cherished.

**Sacrifice:** As a type of **Ceremony,** the sacrifice is a ritual where something is eliminated for the well-being of something else. This can portray the integration and elimination taking place within you. Explore the symbol that is being sacrificed for clues to the part of your nature that is no longer necessary.

**Saddle:** Dreaming of a saddle can show how you are seeking a good fit with your spirituality. You can also be 'saddled' with responsibility and the dream can portray why and whether or not that is good. One uses a saddle as a way to drive the spirit (horse) forward. As a seat - it can show ideas that you rest upon. See **Horse** and **Animals.**

**Safari:** Dreaming of being on a safari shows the current setting of you 'inner terrain.' You may be allowing your more organic or wild urges to have expression. Explore the animals that you see for more information. You may be feeling a bit 'uncivilized' as you move away from conformity. A journey through this type of wild and exotic terrain can reveal your budding sense of emotional or sexual authenticity. See **Animals**.

**Sailing:** Crossing the water in a vessel that relies on the wind to move forward can portray your sense of moving with events to harness difficulty and transform it into opportunity. If the water is calm, you may have moved out of a difficult period and are feeling more in control of your emotions. If the water is choppy or frightening, it can portray your current sense of fear that you are not feeling self directed. The message of this type of dream can be about trusting that the path is leading you where you need to be, where the wind can symbolize fate. It can also be coaching you to let go and allow events to lead you forward. "If you cannot change the direction of the wind, adjust your sails and let it guide you." See also **Vehicles** and **Water.**

**Saliva:** As a "wet" substance that comes from the mouth, seeing saliva can symbolize superficial communication when a deeper exchange of feelings might be necessary. To see someone "spit" can represent unacknowledged anger or the idea that something said has left you with "a bad taste in your mouth."

**Salt:** Rubbing "salt on wounds" compounds pain. Dreaming of salt can symbolize making a difficult situation worse. Its association with the **Color** white (unlike pepper, which is black) can represent purity or "renewing" your outer covering. Being "salty" or "overly seasoned" can also portray being jaded.

**Sand:** Associated with passing time and sleep, sand is a classic symbol of "having sand in your eyes" or not seeing clearly. Sand at the seashore can represent steps taken to move closer to the **Unconscious**. Walking on sand, and making footprints along the water's edge can symbolize your journey through life..

**Satan:** In the book of Job, the hero laments his 'satan' which means 'any adversary.' The word Lucifer meant Bearer of Light and in ancient times, was the name of Venus, the star that rose as the Morning or Evening Star. Lucifer is used only once in the book of Isaiah when he describes "Lucifer who has fallen." Isaiah was writing about an historical and prideful Babylonian king, Tiglath Pilesar III. He used the word Lucifer to compare this arrogant king to the planet Venus, when it boldly rose before the sun in the morning.

As the Morning Star, Lucifer or Venus was always viewed as an imposter of the sun. Because of mistranslations, we have a mythical symbol that gives us permission to remain victims. Yet, our dreams reveal how light always overcomes darkness and in the end, the hero is redeemed when the monsters (transformation barriers) are vanquished.

Meeting a devil or satan character is a common Archetype explored in dreaming. One can have unconscious associations with the devil because it can represent a type of power within that is unexpressed and appears frightening or disturbing. This power is usually associated with all the wonderful things that were viewed as making us different from others, and were therefore repressed. Resurrecting this part of our natural vitality and power is important in helping us to actualize our destiny. See **Devil, Evil** and **Shadow.**

**Satellite:**   A satellite is a symbol of communication, although its position high up in the sky can portray the sense of wanting to rise above a situation to see and understand it objectively. Since it revolves around the earth - it can embody how patterns unfold or how a situation is circular and always brings us back to ourselves. The satellite enables communication over unseen distances and can be symbolic of the Higher Self and its guidance. See also **UFO**.

**Savings:** Since dreams often embody insecurities, dreams portraying "savings" usually unfold with the theme of loss, representing current financial insecurities. If you are aware of "socking something away" for a rainy day, you may be exploring how you protect the things you value at the expense of living fully in the moment. See **Credit Card.**

**Scales:** Scales on creatures portray defensive tendencies or being overly self-protective. As a type of armor, the scales can be hiding your ability to feel or interact more deeply. Scales used to measure weight can symbolize how you are exploring the idea of balance in your life. Associated with the astrological sign of Libra as an Archetype, dreaming of scales can represent weighing two ideas or the idea of relationships where you must balance your needs with those of your partner. See **Reptiles** and **Justice.**

**Scar:** A scar is a clear representation of prior trauma that does not go away. Seeing a scar or wound can portray past hurts that have not been acknowledged or processed. If the scar is associated with a sinister character, see **Shadow.**

**School:** Dreaming of being at a school is a common dream because life appears to be a perpetual learning experience. Sitting in a class setting can symbolize the exploration and merging of various sides of you. The teacher is often a symbol of expanded awareness or the activation of the **Wise Guide** within you. As one of the first places where you developed your social skills, being at a school can be a way of observing the early dynamics behind your interactions with others. The anxiety associated with 'fitting in' and 'being measured' against others, can make the school the representation of what you feel to be your shortcomings. See School under **Houses and Buildings** and Going to School in Your Underwear under **Naked.**

**Scissors:** Utensils represent what you hold in your hand to express, feed, defend or build something. The scissors association with the hand can suggests letting go or cutting away the unnecessary so that you can take what you need from life. Cutting tools are used to cut through restraints or to shape something new from the old. Scissors combine the motion of grasping and letting go with the idea of cutting to symbolize 'cutting away' the things that bind you. Whatever you are cutting with the scissors is undergoing some type of change just as we prune away branches so new growth can occur. See **Weapons and Utensils.**

**Screw:** An obvious way of getting the idea of sex out in the open, you can dream of a screw and have no idea that your thoughts have turned sexual. If you are attempting to screw something to make it secure, you may be using sex as a way of exploring the idea of security. See Spiral under **Shapes.**

237

**Scorpion:** Whenever you dream of small creatures that have a tendency to hide and suddenly strike, you are exploring your own tendencies to keep your instinctual nature under wraps and the ways in which it can bite back. Since the scorpion is associated with the desert, it can symbolize the 'inner wasteland' that is created by not engaging fully with life. The scorpion resembles a reptile in that it can have associations with the more autonomous functions of the brain, like fear responses, sex and/or heartbeat regulation, but it is actually a spider, bringing forward more of a web weaving tendency or the way you trap yourself in your growth. Its astrological association with the sign Scorpio as an Archetype brings forward ideas related to the deeper elements of sex and the transformative power of experience. More often than not, scorpions are on paths and bite at the lower extremities bringing forward the idea of a sense of fear in moving forward. See **Reptiles** and **Insects**.

**Sea:** The sea is a classic symbol of the depths of the **Unconscious** and the unknown, untapped or fearful aspect of the psyche. Water dreams are very common because water represents your emotions, and how you feel about *the changes* that you face as you move through life. To dream of *turbulent seas* suggests a sense of emotional crisis associated with moving forward. Any time this type of dreams occurs, later, you may dream about being on a similar ship and crossing the water that has become calm.

　　　　The sea is representative of your emotional condition and feelings about what is going on around you.  In all of our ancient stories, water is the mysterious reservoir where the hero is to retrieve a treasure. Similarly, raging water often initiates you into a process of self-discovery. *Floods* can undermine the foundation of your beliefs until you are forced to let go. What you thought was solid and what you thought you needed is washed away in the pursuit of basic survival. Water can also represent health and wellness since it is a symbol of the elixir of life.

**Sealife:** The creatures that live beneath the water combine the idea of unconscious stirrings "below the surface" with the idea of emotion. All creatures associated with the sea generally portray the life that stirs beneath the unknown waters of the unconscious. Since ancient times, the *fish* has been associated with the idea of "trapping fate" or luck. It symbolizes a sense of knowing that a situation is becoming favorable. The swimming fish can represent your evolutionary journey, while the *dead fish* symbolizes your inability to grow. The different types of fish and their **Colors** or behavior can shed light on how you are currently "connecting" with this information about you from the unconscious.

To dream of a *crab* can suggest moving back and forth indecisively or defensively as you bring emotions forward. This is a highly self-protective creature that can be "weighed down" by its own armor. Dreaming of a crab can be a message about moving beyond insecurity and fear. The dolphin is playful, and could be classified as "the dog of the sea." Like dogs, who are "faithful" and represent the easy expression of feelings and love in your relationship *to others*, dreaming of a dolphin suggests this loving connection taking place *within you* as you move to access your deeper layers.

*Jellyfish* are not easily seen, and have long tentacles that can sting you. They can portray fear of delving beneath the surface to trace the roots of your feelings that are painful. Their transparent skin associates them with the idea that you may be "thin skinned" in your emotional interactions or unaware of the part you play in meeting difficulty. The *octopus* has "clinging" and "sucking" arms that come from every direction and can drown you. It can symbolize clinginess or jealousy and guilt associated with the mother. The *seal* spends large amounts of time on land and can symbolize making practical use of unconscious information that is rising to the surface. Like the dolphin, they appear to be content with the simple things in life. Because they come out of the water they can symbolize a rebirth.

*Sharks* instill fear because of their razor sharp teeth. They can represent aggressive behavior that operates unconsciously below the surface, threatening "to tear you apart." The *whale* is an enormous fish that is associated with overwhelming urges and grand scale movement within the psyche.

*Plant life*, which thrive beneath the surface of water and wash ashore when dead, can symbolize what is growing and being nurtured or neglected within you. *Corals* are stony structures, which can threaten ships approaching a harbor and can represent the defensive structures you build to keep others from getting emotionally close to you. If the coral are colorful and appreciated in the depths of the water, the message is more about the beauty and complexity of your own inner depths.

**Seamstress and Tailor:** These characters mend clothing and work to make your outer covering more specific to your unique body. Since **Clothing** represents your persona or costume you wear in public, dreaming of the seamstress or tailor can show how you are working to bring forward a more authentic way of interacting with others. They can also portray how you are giving shape to a new idea or way of providing for yourself. The issues surrounding these characters will reveal where you stand in relation to donning a new persona, which is more reflective of the person you
really are.

**Searching:** See **Looking for Something.**

**Seaweed:** See **Sealife.**

**Seed:** A seed is the power of potential in its most compacted form. You can be planting seeds as a way of "sowing" your potential to reap the reward of authentic expression. You can discover a seed as a way of seeing your potential objectively or you can witness the seed sprouting because you are exploring yourself in an environment that allows you to thrive and blossom. Negative associations with the seed are similar to dreams of roots. See **Roots** and **Garden.**

**Sell:** See **Buying** and **Marketplace.**

**Seven:** Seven is often associated with cycles in life as in seven year itch, seventh heaven. It is also symbolic of luck or that part of life that we would call fate. See **Numbers.**

**Sewer:** The sewer combines the idea of **Plumbing** or emotions and **Excrement** or eliminating the unnecessary. Seeing the sewer reflects how you are not *really* letting go of something unpleasant. Perhaps you need to find the learning experience behind a difficult situation so that you can process and release it.

**Sewing:** See **Seamstress and Tailor.**

**Sex:** Since dreams allow for the free exploration of feelings, it is common to dream of sharing affection, sex or intimacy with people other than your mate. As you 'role play' by experiencing the different aspects of yourself, it can be portrayed by various characters, where you sometimes behave in a masculine way or mounting dominating another masculine character (your aggressive and assertive nature.) You are merely exploring your desire to be more aggressive. You may dream of being unusually sensitive or affectionate with another woman, or in a feminine way, as a way of 'embracing' or exploring the idea of increased sensitivity within you. The side of you this person represents and how you approach them in the dream, will feel 'clandestine,' only in proportion to how you are currently not 'embracing' or integrating this side of yourself in waking life. See **Affair, Love** and **Anima/Animus.**

**Shadow:** Shadow dreams include a stalker, intruder or other frightening monsters hiding in the shadows, stalking you or attempting to break into your home. Since all characters in a dream represent sides of you and the house represents your psyche, this type of dream can represent difficult ideas that you are not assimilating or integrating into consciousness. Some side of you simply wants to be acknowledged in consciousness. It only stalks you because you do not allow it.

The Shadow embodies the rejected or repressed aspects of your more natural expression that was sent underground. At some point, you may have decided (or were told) that some part of you was unacceptable because it suggested weakness, fear of fitting in with the group, and can create unresolved anger. In actuality, these aspects become the power of your untapped potential. It appears frightening because you do not understand it.

As a child, you may have been labeled the 'black sheep' or were a caregiver to the caregiver. A difficult relationship with a parent can be at the root of Shadow dreams. One part of you is a pronounced nurturer but you are unable to nurture yourself because of old tapes play and suggest you are not worthy. You grow to become empowered and successful, but the part of you that is disowned (unprocessed) can continue to stalk you. Look at this type of dream as your misunderstood value, which is trying to be understood. Since we role identify with the parent, if we hold them in contempt, there may be an alter identity that is unacknowledged, and yet, stalks us.

Repetitive dreams of this type can be solved by understanding the nature of forgiveness. You may not approve of how you were raised but compassion for another's shortcomings goes along way in helping you to release these non-integrated feelings. Simply denying and repressing it is what causes this 'neglected' Self to stalk you. Any time powerful aspects are not allowed expression, they come forward as something powerful that pursues you. This can happen when you are in a disempowering relationship as an adult. You believe another holds power over you, when you have simply given them this power.

As a type of defense mechanism, Freud believed repression worked to keep the truth inaccessible. He also explored fixation and fetishes as being organized by ideas that evoked a sense of attraction and repulsion at the same time. An urge that initially sought pleasure brought instead, displeasure as the pathway from urge to satisfaction was distorted. Fixation is the way in which we are drawn to the type of situations we would rather avoid. Energy repressed within is always seeking to be understood and integrated.

This convergence of feeling is at the root of the intense emotional response or charge that is created when you encounter your Shadow in another. Understanding the Shadow is central to your empowerment and wellness. When you can understand and transcend the initial displeasure arising in this type of encounter, you are able to access the truth of what you fail to acknowledge about yourself. See Shadow under **Archetypes and Universal Characters.**

**Shampoo:** Washing hair with soap can be a way of "cleaning up" your attitude. Grooming hair suggests the need to "prune" outworn perspectives. See Hair under **Anatomy and Body Parts.**

**Shapes:** A *circle* represents wholeness and closure, and like the *crescent*, is associated with femininity or sensitivity. The *square* can symbolize being grounded and more literal in your approach, while the *star* is a symbol of ideals and aspirations or being recognized for your accomplishments. When you are dreaming of this type of symbol, there may be insecurities surrounding your sense of self-esteem. The *spiral* can show how you are moving in circles and not necessarily getting anywhere. Something that is *flat* can portray a one-dimensional outlook that lacks vitality and leaves you unfulfilled, while being *full* can symbolize a "puffed up" version of reality or fulfillment. *Phallic* shapes are masculine and therefore show penetration or your need to break through restrictions by being more aggressive. If the phallic shape is threatening, then you may need to curb your aggressive tendencies.

**Shark:** When you are making strides to understand your capabilities and feelings, the dream setting will involve water, which can represent feelings and what lies hidden 'below the surface.' Fish are a representation of your potential for new life and can also represent opportunities. When the fish appears threatening, you may be uncomfortable with your own anger or the power of expressing your full capabilities. If you are being attacked by a shark, the dream can be blending a message about the need to feel (blood) your feelings (water) in order to achieve your potential (fish.) See **Sealife.**

**Shave:** To dream of shaving can symbolize your daily routine or the sense of "grooming outworn attitudes." Removing unattractive whiskers is a classic symbol of the way you groom your organic nature to "fit in." See Hair under **Anatomy and Body Parts.**

**Sheep:** The sheep is a classic symbol of passivity. Examine whether you are being too passive in a situation or whether you are following the crowd to the extent that you are not expressing your individuality. See **Animals.**

**Shell:** A shell can sometimes portray listening skills in discovering unknown potential. It can also symbolize protective tendencies that keep your real feelings hidden. See **Sand, Sea** and **Sealife.**

**Shine:** Seeing something shine is an objective way of exploring your desire to be appreciated. To shine an object is a way of removing what is hiding your potential.

**Ship:** The ship combines the idea of moving forward with a sense that you must follow unfolding events to find your way. Travel by water is a way of exploring the unknown and how you navigate the depths of your emotions. See **Vehicles and Places of Transportation** and **Sea.**

**Shirt:** The shirt is an aspect of the **Persona** and symbolizes the role we have adopted in expressing who we are. It has associations with responsibilities and can sometimes appear in a dream when we are learning to let go of obligations or issues that are no longer serving us. It appears frequently when we are changing careers or 'trying on' new attitudes and potentials. The **Color** of the shirt can be important in understanding how you are changing or what you are carrying with you as a sense of obligation. See **Clothing and Makeup.**

**Shoes:** Shoes cover the **Feet** as a symbol of your path and ability to move forward. Searching for shoes can symbolize looking for meaningful work or the means to achieve your ambitions. Strange shoes describe the unusual opportunities you are missing by seeing only the paths of the past. The type of shoes can shed light on what is needed to 'walk' forward in a more fulfilling way. See **Clothing and Makeup.**

**Shooting:** Guns are associated with sex. Shooting is the classic representation of the painful emotions that can arise from sexual feelings. You can 'shoot yourself in the foot' when you cannot let something go. Knowing you are about to be shot and allowing it to happen is a way of allowing painful feelings to have expression so that you can move beyond them. It is almost as if going through difficulty reaches such as stage that you can no longer ward off the transformation and the ability to accept and become mature is symbolized by accepting the situation or 'biting the bullet.' Seeing another person being shot portrays your denial of the situation or how you place the responsibility of your pain 'outside,' when this other character is actually you. See **Weapons and Utensils, Attack and Being Chased** and **Corpse.**

**Shop:** Shopping in a dream can be a way of exploring a new identity. The type of shop will correspond to what area of your life you are exploring. For example a shop that sells food can relate to fulfillment; a shoe shop symbolizes seeking a new path; a bike shop can show how you want to move forward by balancing differing aspects; a clothing shop will show how you are making changes to your **Persona.** See **Marketplace** or Shopping Center under **Houses and Buildings.**

**Shoulder:** Like the back, we can shoulder responsibility so this symbol suggests burdens. To dream of aching shoulders is a way of exploring releasing responsibilities that have been imposed on you. See **Anatomy and Body Parts.**

**Shovel:** This is something used to "dig beneath the surface" of the earth, representing the need to resurrect your more organic nature. See **Weapons and Utensils.**

**Shrink:** See **Large and Small**

**Shutters:** Shutters cover windows and in a dream, the shutters represent something that may be blocking your perspective of ability to see something clearly. Dreaming of shutters can relate to the eyes and your ability to meet experience without expectations or fear.

**Sick:** When you dream of being sick, you may be "sick and tired" of something you are unable to process. A lack of wellness associated with a symbol can portray your desire to work through it. See **Healing.**

**Signature:** The signature captures the image of "signing on the dotted line" or making a commitment to something putting your reputation up as collateral. Seeing another's signature can be the first steps of integrating issues that you are not owning. See **Label** and **Name.**

**Silver:** See **Colors.**

**Sing:** The joyful expression of your sense of harmony with the things around you. See **Music.**

**Sink:** The sink captures the idea of how feelings are retained, and turned on and off, since water generally symbolizes emotions. The sink itself, is usually where we wash or remove unnecessary residue as a symbol of washing away difficulty or outworn ideas. If it is a kitchen sink, the dream can be exploring fulfillment and how holding onto feelings is affecting your sense of happiness and fulfillment in the present. Often the kitchen ties dream imagery to what is adopted from family dynamics. If it is a bathroom sink, the idea is more personal in your desire to be more intimate or revealing of yourself. Turbid water in a sink symbolizes painful feelings that need to be released.

Sinking portrays the idea that your foundation is not solid. As a message about your 'internal architecture' sinking can symbolize feelings of insecurity or a sense that you are being undermined in your efforts. Associated with moisture, it can represent how emotions or feelings are undermining your ability to stand up for yourself, or on sure footing. See also **Faucet** and **Quicksand**, and Muddy under **Landscape and Scenery.**

**Sister:** See **Family Members.**

**Size:** See **Large and Small** and **Placement and Perspective.**

**Six:** Dreams are very clever in bringing 'taboo' subjects out for

246

inspection. Six can be a way of getting the psyche to explore the idea of 'sex.' It can also have associations with ideas that transcend sensory experience, as in sixth sense, spiritual or transcendental ideas. See **Numbers.**

**Skating:** If skating is associated with ice, you can have a sense of "skating over the issues" or finding a way to move easily away from emotional closeness. If you are roller-skating, you may be approaching difficulty in a childish or innocent way when a more mature approach might be required. Associated with shoes, skating often portrays *how* you are moving forward.

**Skeleton:** You may wonder where the saying about the "skeleton in the closet" came from. The skeleton can represent your fear of mortality, and since it is associated with intrigue, it is usually a representation of what you are "hiding." Bones portray the foundation of who you are and what you are built upon. To see a skeleton can symbolize getting back to your core essence. See **Anatomy and Body Parts.**

**Skin:** See **Anatomy and Body Parts.**

**Skirt:** See **Clothing and Makeup.**

**Sky:** Dreams that involve the sky have associations with ambitions. If you are watching something moving through the sky, you are exploring your aspirations objectively and whatever happens will reflect your hopes and fears.

**Sleep:** Dreaming of sleeping is a double dose of a message with a wake up call. The dream seems to suggest that you are unaware of something and "dozing" when you should be paying more attention.

**Sleep Paralysis:** The human body is designed with a paralytic feature to keep you from acting out on your dreams. At times, you may awaken "in between" the stages of full consciousness and sleep. Although it can feel extremely frightening, it is not uncommon, and you are merely not fully conscious or awake.

**Smell:** See **Odor.**

**Smoke:** Smoke can be a "smoke screen" that blocks your ability to see or a warning that something neglected is in peril. Unlike **Fog,** which is cold and damp, smoke is the result of fire and has an opposite meaning. Where water represents feelings, something may be smoldering that might be better extinguished. This is also a case of knowing that "where there is smoke, there is fire."

**Snake:** The snake is one of the most common symbols that people dream about. It can have associations with sex because of its shape, but also the biting and poisonous way instinctual behavior causes us to recoil and ultimately 'bites back' at us. In this way the snake is a classic symbol of defense mechanisms. Since ancient times, the snake has personified the need to 'shed the old skin' and transform. The feminine centered fertility and snake worshipping cults of antiquity were so powerful at one time that a mythology of evil was implemented to combat them during the rise of the Patriarchal religions. Just as the snake is associated with evil, it represents feelings or urges that you deem unacceptable for expression. When you dream of a snake, you are actually making strides to break free of self imposed restraints. See **Defense Mechanisms** and also **Reptiles**.

**Snow:** Snow is a frozen form of **water,** and can symbolize frozen feelings. Rather than the sense of renewal that comes after a storm, snow shows how the feeling of coldness can linger. As a landscape, it can portray entering an area of the psyche or facing emotions that are somewhat "frozen," cold or on ice. See **Frozen.**

**Soap:** Coming clean or attempting to remove the sensation of "feeling dirty." See **Shampoo,** Bathroom under **Houses and Buildings** and **Bath.**

**Sock:** See **Clothing and Makeup.**

**Soldier:** Dreaming of being a soldier can portray acting too defensively in a situation. Since soldiers wear the same uniforms and are stripped of their personal identity, this type of dream can represent how you are not living authentically. Like **Attack and Being Chased** where your identity is undergoing a type of change, this dream can also be accompanied by bombs or the symbols that represent the release of what you are protecting/repressing. Being a soldier can represent the first steps in allowing for the uprooting of fear in preparation for a more authentic way of expressing yourself. See **Bombs** and also **Army**.

**Sonar:** Like **Radar**, which suggests the appearance of something 'out of view' as it relates to ambitions, dreaming of sonar has more of an association with feelings that you are not acknowledging. You are being told that there is something there although you may not be aware of it. To dream of being in a submarine shows how you are exploring the unconscious or what lies below the surface of consciousness. Using sonar shows active steps you are taking in to follow intuition or inner guidance.

**Sound:** Dreaming is a highly visual and emotional sensory process. When sound becomes a focal point of the dream, it still has the effect of stirring your emotions, which leaves you *feeling* something. Over and above the dialogue and interaction with other characters, to actually focus on a sound requires a deeper exploration of its symbolic representation.

**Soup:** See **Food.**

**South:** Depending upon where you are from, the south can be associated with appreciating the simple things in life or giving of yourself. Like the back doors in cars and houses, the idea of "south" can also represent the lower portion of the body, particularly the sexual region.

**Space:** Any setting that presents the idea of vast space can suggest future potential as you explore the unknown aspects of yourself. It symbolizes openness. The universe and dark space can represent your fears about the future and a sense of not being anchored or grounded.

**Spaceship:** You may dream of being in a spaceship when you are exploring aspirations that you feel may not be grounded or practical. If the spaceship is descending to the earth, you may be finding ways to make your goals more attainable. Something about what you are doing may not be supported by those around you. Unlike the plane, which signifies moving to achieve your ambitions, the 'space' association of this type of vehicle can show the need to approach your goals in a more practical way. See also **Aliens** and **Rocket.**

**Sperm:** Seeing sperm can depict your life force or desire to create something lasting.

**Spice:** Your desire to experience more excitement or dimension in life can be represented by spice in the sense of "spicing things up a bit."

**Spider:** Spiders are similar to insects in that they can portray the unseen, yet destructive tendency to allow something to bug you without addressing it. Since spiders make webs, they are a clear portrayal of how you weave your own difficulty through insecurity or fear. Lots of tiny spiders can symbolize how whatever is festering below the surface seems out of your ability to control. To see one or a few large spiders can represent a larger issue created by getting caught up in a type of web or the dynamics of others. Spider dreams are a call to acknowledge a sense of hiding or entrapment that is stunting you or your ability to be truthfulness, since the spider is symbolizing your behavior too. Dreams often use symbols that are the most frightening to us simply to wake us to our own self destructive behavior. See **Insects.**

**Spoon:** Kitchen utensils are associated with changes you are making. You use them to take what you need in order to find nourishment and self worth. Like food, the symbolism is exploring fulfillment. The difference between a fork and a spoon is their shape. A spoon suggests what you need to hold onto in order to feel satisfied, while the fork is more symbolic of taking a stab at something, or making a change in direction that will help you provide for yourself. The spoon can also personify your desire to be cared for and nurtured. See **Eating Utensils**.

**Spots:** Spots are usually associated with *dis-ease* if on the skin, so can represent uneasiness. They can portray "breaking out" of your protective tendencies. Spots on a creature can represent a sense of wholeness associated with the symbolism that the creature represents.

**Spring:** Springtime is a time for renewal and the beginning of your blossoming. A spring where water comes forth portrays inspiration and inner guidance. See **Sea.**

**Squirrel:** As an animal that knows how to plan ahead for tough times, a squirrel in a dream can signify being too security driven or fearful. Their association with the tree and also burrowing, can portray the idea of family influences or the root of behavior operating below the surface and currently undergoing transformation. See also **Tree** and **Animals.**

**Stairs:** Dreaming of steps or stairways can represent your sense of how you are currently moving through life. Going up would symbolize aspirations, while going down can represent feeling the need to dig beneath your motivation to understand what is important to you. Steps in a shopping center can signify assessing your values or self worth, while steps in a public building can represent work issues. The condition of the stairs can shed light on how you feel about your current opportunities and challenges. Winding stairs can have associations with backtracking or recognizing the circular aspect of life where you look to the past to understand the future. See **Houses and Buildings.**

**Statue:** Observing a statue captures the objective exploration of what is unchanging about you or "set in stone." The statue can portray a sense of being inanimate or "stuck." It can also symbolize how the person you are becoming is shaped by experience. As something made of stone, it can also signify a hardened perspective.

**Steal:** If you dream of stealing, you might consider the symbolism of what is being stolen as a way of recognizing its importance in your life. If someone else steals from you, there may be conflicting needs and a lack of balance and integration within you. Explore the symbolism stolen for additional insight.

**Steam:** The condensation that emerges from heat portrays how emotions that are not easily expressed are coming forward in the form of anger. As pressure rises, this energy finds expression in the only way it can.

**Sterilize:** The idea of clean and unclean usually have to do with "dirty thoughts" or sexuality. The symbol that is being sterilized needs to be explored to understand your current relationship to what it represents.

**Stick:** Sometimes a phallic or symbol of assertiveness, the stick can also be associated with a branch of a tree or the idea of breaking away from your roots. Dreaming of a stick can also be a message about sticking to something or exploring commitment. If the symbolism is more associated with something sticky or the idea of sticking, then you are attempting new ways of thought (head) or relating (hands) or moving forward (feet) etc. Explore the part of the body associated with sticking under **Anatomy and Body Parts**. Also See **Tree** and **Weapons and Utensils.**

**Sticky:** Dreaming of something that is sticky can embody the feeling that you are attracting undesirable situations. You are dreaming about it because you may need to explore how these situations are the result of your thinking. What you would call a 'sticky' situation is one that has allot of 'charge' to it. You carry an extra dose of 'something' and you need to explore what the 'something' is. Items that appear to stick to you in a dream should be explored as a type of baggage related to what the symbol represents. See also **Glue.**

**Sting:** A sting from an insect can portray how your personal dynamics are coming back "to bite you." The sting doesn't draw blood but only causes an irritation, suggesting your inability to see these dynamics at play. See **Insects.**

**Stomach:** Since emotion is associated with 'gut feelings,' dreams of the stomach can represent feelings that you are not acknowledging. The condition of the abdomen and whether or not it is yours, suggests how you are owning or acting on your gut feelings. As a symbol of digestion, it can represent unprocessed issues. See **Anatomy and Body Parts.**

**Stones:** A stone appears to be "lifeless" although depending on the type of stone, it can have tremendous value, portraying self-esteem. Dreaming of a stone can symbolize how you are approaching life to recognize the difference between what is transient and what is solid or unchanging. Like the other elements, this is a "solid" part of you that continues to be shaped by experience. See **Purses, Wallets, Luggage, Jewels and Keys.**

**Store:** Going into a store to buy something can symbolize how you are exploring the reserves within you. Often you are exploring ideas from childhood that are 'stored' in memory. Shopping seems to suggest that you are 'in the market' for a new way of doing things. See **Marketplace.**

**Stove:** You can use a stove to cook various types of nourishment so the stove can portray what you 'are cooking up' or making of experience to find fulfillment. Something can simmer on the stove as a way of capturing feelings that simmer beneath the surface, yet play a part in shaping your experiences. Cooking is also a symbol of alchemy where feelings have yet to gel or solidify. Dreams of something cooking on a stove often take place when you are exploring childhood feelings and family dynamics to find the recipe for your happiness and current fulfillment.

**Stranger:** Just as a movie would never introduce a character without them having some type of meaning or role to fulfill – just because you would call someone a stranger in a dream – doesn't mean they are irrelevant. They are representing an unknown aspect of you. See **People** and **Shadow.**

**Strangle:** There are many ways of experiencing how sides of you pass on. The idea of being strangled suggests that perhaps an important aspect within you is being "cut off" as another side achieves temporary prominence. See **Attack** and **Being Chased.**

**String:** The string carries the idea of how things are connected.

**Submarine:** This vehicle allows safe passage below the water. As a symbol of exploring unconscious motivation, its shape can suggest the idea of masculine traits, such as assertiveness and aggression. See **Vehicles and Places of Transportation, Sonar** and **Sea.**

**Subway:** This underground transportation system carries the idea of "tracks" or your sense of going with what is expected of you with the added image of delving below the surface. The idea of a subterranean way of moving forward is also captured in the idea of not recognizing what is driving you forward. Since it is a mass transportation vehicle, the issue of conformity that is undermining your true sense of self expression needs to be considered. See **Vehicles and Places of Transportation.**

**Suck:** Sucking is an infant's first instinct and can portray very basic needs that are not being met.

**Suffocate:** As the idea of not having enough air, being suffocated can suggest the anxiety associated with your inability to achieve your aspirations. See **Air** and **Attack and Being Chased.**

**Sugar:** This white powder combines the idea of sweets or finding pleasure and purity. See **Colors** and Desserts under **Food.**

**Suitcase:** A suitcase is a common dream symbol because at some level, we are aware of how our identity must undergo change as we grow. Since **Clothing** is associated with the **Persona,** we often dream of packing and unpacking when we are releasing an old identity or trying on a new one. The dream of rushing to the airport symbolizes changes in aspirations and ambitions and our feelings about achieving those aspirations in terms of life stages. The idea of baggage can portray old ways of being that we might need to discard and how we feel an urgency to carry 'our costume or mask' into every new situation. Not being able to find something related to packing can be a message that you are overly identifying with only one role, when your greater needs might be sacrificed because of it. See **Purses, Wallets, Luggage, Jewels and Keys.**

**Sun:** The sun can represent the ultimate symbol of the self. Dreaming of a sun can symbolize your sense of wholeness and how you shine. If the dream portrays the sun as destructive, you may be shining and seeking acceptance at the expense of allowing for balance in your life.

**Surgery:** Dreaming of surgery often coincides with periods of making tough changes to how you feel about yourself. You may know that you need to let go of something - although the process can be difficult for you. Having surgery on a particular area of the body will be how the psyche attempts to 'cut away' feelings or ideas that are not healthy. If you have an abnormal growth that is being cut away - the message is that a past issue has taken on a life of its own and needs to be released. Sometimes it relates to forgiveness. Explore the part of the body to see what it relates to. See **Hospital** under **Houses and Buildings, Anatomy and Body Parts** and **Weapons and Utensils.**

**Swallow:** When swallowing is the subject of a dream, you may be finding something "is hard to swallow" or emotions can be stuck in your "throat," meaning that you have difficulty in expressing them. An aspect of the situation remains "undigested" as you continue to process it.

**Swamp:** See Quicksand and Mud under **Landscape and Scenery**.

**Sweep:** Any type of cleaning in a dream can suggest "cleaning up" or removing outworn ideas and attitudes. You may be sweeping to clear the "house" or inner self of the buildup or "dust" or residue that accumulates from experience.

**Sweets:**  See Desserts under **Food.**

**Swimming:** Associated with Water, swimming and enjoying yourself in a dream can portray your easy movement through the changes you are going through. If swimming seems difficult or is required to find "safety" then the changes are bringing forward emotions that feel overwhelming.

**Swimming Pool:**  See **Pool.**

**Swing:**  Swinging brings together the idea of movement and furniture. The furniture aspect represents the "ideas you rest upon" and swinging can suggest finding movement or a shift in these ideas. The playful aspect of swinging like a child can suggest innocence. The idea of adult "swingers" can signify exploring sexuality.

**Sword:**  See **Weapons and Utensils.**

**Syringe:**  You may dream that someone is trying to inject you with a syringe if you have given this person an unusual amount of power over your feelings. If your blood is being drawn, you may feel that circumstances are no longer fulfilling. If you are injected with a healing substance, the message is offering you the promise that difficulty will soon be transformed. If you believe the substance will harm you - consider how the influences of others are changing you in ways that do not support who you are. See also **Injection** and **Drugs.**

# T

The letter "T" can be associated with crossroads or impending changes. It can symbolize difficult communication or the idea of speaking the truth. The crossing of the letter "T" is often used in handwriting analysis, and can have a message about what makes you unique or exploring talents and gifts. You may be facing a situation in which you must choose between the idea of going right (associated with conforming) or going left (taking the road less traveled.)

**Table:** Since we use expressions about putting something 'out on the table' as a way of being out in the open - the table can represent being forthright in communication. It can also show the part of you that you are displaying to others, where items on a table can represent aspects you consider important. See also **Furniture.**

**Tailor:** See **Seamstress and Tailor.**

**Talking:** Information is conveyed through dreams in many ways. Just as you are moved by the words of others, in dreams the person sharing information with you can be viewed as another aspect of yourself bringing light to something you may not recognize. See **Answer.**

**Tap:** See **Faucet.**

**Tapestry:** Observing the intricacy of a woven fabric can portray your sense of exploring how things are connected. This type of dream can be a message about slowing down to observe the little things that can give you a greater sense of value in life.

**Taste:** You can have a "nasty taste in your mouth" over a difficult encounter or you can long to "taste" something fulfilling. This can also be a way of exploring your "tastes" or values. See **Food.**

257

**Tattoo:** Like the label, having a tattoo is clear way of advertising your character. Even if you would not have a tattoo in real life, dreaming of having a tattoo shows how you are "wearing something on your shirtsleeve." The symbol or design and the part of the body that is tattooed can portray information about the side of you that requires expression and acknowledgement.

**Taxi:** See **Cab.**

**Teacher:** The teacher delivers educational information in an effort to enlighten you. When you dream of a teacher, you may be seeing the side of yourself that "thinks you have all the answers" and continues to operate on "rote" or routine. If the teacher offers you words of wisdom, then some aspect is coming forward as a guide. Even if you are not open to the teaching – you will find that this Archetype works patiently and persistently. See Wise Man and Wise Woman under **Archetypes and Universal Characters.**

**Teeth:** Losing Teeth is a common dream that occurs at monumental points in life. Just as you lose your baby teeth as a child, wisdom teeth as an adolescent and perhaps all of your teeth when you are old, teeth are associated with letting go of old ways of "chewing on things." The way that you approached situations in the past will no longer do. Teeth can also represent credibility. As you smile, you may suddenly look stupid because your teeth are missing. This demonstrates how losing teeth can be an aspect of the *Trickster,* or transformative power, humorously tricking you toward authentic behavior. About to say "the same old thing," you can only mumble because your mouth is suddenly full of your own teeth. Whatever you were about to say would not be considered the truth. See Trickster under **Archetypes and Universal Characters** and Mouth under **Anatomy and Body Parts.**

**Telephone:** The telephone is a more focused representation of the sharing of words and ideas. Like **Talking,** having this information conveyed over a telephone can portray either the need to recognize the importance of what is being said or your "distance" from acknowledging the information as being relevant to you. See also **Cell** and **911.**

**Telescope:** See **Binoculars, Glasses and Microscopes.**

**Television:** To see something happening on television or in a movie shows how you have not yet integrated or accepted it. What is it that is playing on t.v, and how is it portraying an aspect of you? Whatever is playing on the t.v might be new information that you are exploring objectively. The television acts as an 'alternate reality' where the idea is making its way into consciousness. Many people who lose a loved one will dream of seeing them on t.v. as the first steps in dealing with and accepting the loss. See also **Advertisement**.

**Temperature:** When the temperature becomes a subject of a dream, it can portray 'cooling off' in an emotional situation, or 'heating up' as your passions are ignited. Sometimes as the 'atmosphere' changes you may dream of changing body temperature. In either case, the message is the same. If the environment seems cold and wintery, the message can be about being aloof or detached, non committal and avoiding intimacy. If the atmosphere is hot, the message can be about getting in over your head or not acknowledging your passions. A fiery setting in a dream shows a type of passion, anger or feeling that is not being expressed by day. See also **Landscape and Scenery.**

**Ten:** Ten has associations with arrival and satisfaction in life. It can represent self fulfillment, combining the idea of one (self-sufficiency) and zero (infinity and wholeness.) Ten symbolizes our greatest goals and desire to achieve social acclaim. Ten can be a threshold or plateau before we embark in a new direction. See **Numbers.**

**Test:** Dreaming of taking a test or exam can have several messages. On one hand, you may dream of returning to school if your current situation poses a challenge that needs to be solved. The message would be to remember that life is a learning experience and that you are still growing. You may have shut down the idea of growth and learning in some way - holding to rigid thinking. Taking a test can symbolize a sense of feeling tested currently.

Taking a quiz or exam in a dream can be a type of initiation to examine whether your beliefs are serving you in a productive way. If you are late for the test and therefore fail, your own insecurities are undermining your ability for success. A person doesn't succeed in life if they believe they will fail. Failure is a prerequisite for success. All accomplishments are achieved after a series of trials that include missing the mark. If you have suddenly forgotten what the material is about, you are being given the opportunity to let your old way of thinking go.

Being quizzed by an unusual character can also be the activation of the **Trickster** archetype. You are tripped up in your inconsistencies of thought, so that you can start with a fresh perspective. The quiz measures what you know - and sometimes it is better not to know so that you can discover.

Dreams of tests and exams often remind you that life cannot be learned through answers but through experience. Your thought patterns may have become a card catalogue file over time - these types of anxiety dreams are helping you to loosen rigid thinking so that you can grow and continue to be fulfilled. If you are supposed to be in a class and cannot find it, or are late, you may feel insecure about where you are in terms of life stages. The idea that you should be in class underscores learning - perhaps you are dismissing a situation that is meant to teach you something.

**Text:** Messages that come over the phone are a symbol of how various aspects of the psyche seek to communicate with you. The person who is texting you should be considered in terms of the adjective you would use to describe them - they can be representing a side of you seeking expression. The message that they share with you should also be considered as a message that may be coming from the Higher Self. If you are reading the text of a book, you may be going through a type of change that is allowing you to explore the past objectively. See also **Abbreviations**.

**Thaw:** Something that is "**Frozen**" can also thaw as a way of portraying how life or energy is returning to what was once inanimate.

**Theater:** Being at the theater in a dream allows you to examine your behavior objectively. Whatever is transpiring on the stage or in the movie is allowing you to examine how you are currently 'acting.' Exploring thoughts and behavior in this manner can be the psyche's way of communicating to you beyond your usual defenses. See **Film and Television** and **Audience.**

**Thief:** If you are dreaming of another character stealing something, you might explore how some aspect of you is forced to operate 'in the dark' to get its needs met. Rather than take what you deserve from life, you may be forced to sneak around to get your needs met. Explore the character that is stealing and the symbol stolen for more information about what you are denying to yourself in terms of greater fulfillment. See Burglar under Archetypes and **Universal Characters.**

**Thirst:** Unlike **Food,** which symbolizes how you find nourishment in life, liquid refreshments generally portray emotional needs. Being thirsty can portray how you are recognizing the need to give your emotions free reign.

**Three:** A dream that focuses on the number three is exploring integration or a triangle situation where one aspect needs to be let go of to achieve balance. See **Numbers.**

**Throat:** A dream that focuses on the throat can be exploring difficult communication. Something may be 'hard to swallow' or words can be 'caught in your throat.' The throat is a part of the body that makes you vulnerable - so dreaming of a throat can represent 'sticking your neck out' in a way that puts your credibility on the line. To dream of a cut on the throat can symbolize tendencies that might be called 'cut throat' or underhanded. Finally, seeing the throat cut in a way that a head topples, shows the release of outworn ideas associated with the person who's head comes off. Losing one's head is also another way of exploring fanatical behavior. See **Swallow** and **Anatomy and Body Parts**.

**Thunder:** Hearing thunder in a dream can portray how you are recognizing an "imbalance in the atmosphere." The threat of rain can suggest how you are holding back emotions that will soon be released.

**Tiger:** A tiger is a symbol of non-conformity and the free expression of passion. It can symbolize unrestrained anger or an outburst that occurs during the day and then appears to 'come out the woods' to bite you when you dream. The message teaches you to process anger and not hold it in. See **Blood** and **Animals**.

**Time:** See Time of Day under **Landscape and Scenery** and **Morning, Day** and **Night.**

**Tipping:** To dream of something described as tipping shows an imbalance that is not natural. For example a house that is tipping can show how you are giving too much consideration to only one aspect of life, as in caring too much what others think of you. A building would have a similar meaning that is tied more to work. Anything that is tipping will eventually succumb to the force of gravity that reveals shoddy construction. You may have built the 'foundation of your beliefs' in a way that cannot support your success. See also **Abnormal.**

**Tire:** Like the **Shoe** that brings a high level of focus to the things you use to find your way forward, the tire can represent how your motivation and experiences are leading you forward. Inspecting tires on a car can symbolize making changes in a career, while a flat tire can suggest insecurities about your ability to succeed. You may not feel the inspiration or competence necessary to make the transition. The roundness of this symbol has associations with harmony and balance. Used as a symbol of motivation, it can also tie in the idea of being tired or unfulfilled. Tires separate us from feeling the effects of the road we travel, and can personify feeling disconnected from what you are doing or where you are going. If the tires are unusual in some way, explore whether there may be a message or clue about how you can feel successful and fulfilled by doing something different. See **Vehicles and Places of Transportation**.

**Toilet:** See **Bath** and Bathroom under **Houses and Buildings.**

**Tools:** See **Weapons and Utensils.**

**Tornado:** When you are moving through difficulty, there are many ways that you are carried forward, or in some cases, forced to let go. The tornado represents how events feel beyond your control and in a sense, you are being "swept up" to be placed in a "different perspective." The tornado can portray the intensity of your emotions and how they are constrained in a way that "will break free."

**Touch:** You touch things to make contact with something to allow for your "deeper interaction" with it. Explore the symbol that you are touching to understand how you are exploring and integrating what the symbol represents.

**Tower:** The tower is a structure that offers a point of view combined with the idea of protection. You may be dreaming of a tower as a way of exploring how your "current viewpoint" is limiting your freedom. See **Houses and Buildings**.

**Town:** See **City.**

**Toy:** The toy can represent how you are re-visiting aspects and character traits adopted in childhood. The condition and type of toy can shed further light on what this is. For example, a train is representing how you move forward on a proven track. The doll can symbolize your need to be nurtured and protected. Being a toy, it can suggest a childish approach that might require more maturity.

**Track:** See **Vehicles and Places of Transportation.**

**Train:** The train, as a transportation symbol, personifies motivation and direction. Because it is following a track, you may have the feeling that your path has been laid out before you and is not within your control to change. Missing a train can symbolize fear of failure in light of expectations that have been imposed upon you, perhaps by your employer or parents. Jumping in and out of trains can symbolize how you are trying to find your own way. The train station is a place of transition and has a specific schedule, portraying your feelings about your ability to meet your own expectations. Dreaming of trying to catch a train can personify how you are caught up by the current demands of your schedule.

Boats, buses and trains, in which you are a 'passenger,' suggest how you are following a course that is not self-directed and not easily changed. See **Vehicles and Places of Transportation.**

**Trapped:** Being trapped in a dream suggests how you feel trapped in daily life. The other symbols in the dream can shed light on why this is happening. See Quicksand and Mud under **Landscape and Scenery.**

**Trash:** See **Garbage.**

**Travel:** A dream about travelling is a message about expanding your horizons. Pay close attention to whether what you are doing while travelling is going 'right' or going 'left.' Often going right suggests habit - while going left can suggest a new way - or that you might explore the 'road less traveled.' You are exploring potential and opportunity by visiting places that might be classified as 'foreign.' If you are traveling by boat, you are taking stock of your feelings. If by train, you have a sense that a course can be set that is leading you forward. By plane can symbolize exploring or changing your ambitions in some way. By car - you are getting at the root of your motivation. See **Vehicles and Places of Transportation** and also going **Abroad**.

**Treasure:** See **Purses, Wallets, Luggage, Jewels and Keys** and **Prize.**

**Trees:** The tree is a classic symbol of your heritage and roots. Dreaming of trees can symbolize how you are exploring your legacy or the "stem" of everything you are.  See **Forest** and Garden under **Houses and Buildings**.

**Trespassing:** Whether you or someone else are entering "forbidden territory" the dream suggests those places within that are guarded and therefore, out of reach of consciousness. This is actually an empowering dream about breaking through defenses or barriers within.

**Triangle:**  Dreaming of a triangle can symbolize triangulation or the unknown potential that exists between two extremes. Just as progress springs from conflict, a triangle asks you to consider how a difficult choice is often the happy medium between opposing ideas. Two can represent choices and balance, although the idea of Three sides often signifies an imbalance that needs to be resolved. The triangle or the theme of three is also common in spiritual ideas as the direct awareness of the trinity, where body, mind and spirit thrive in harmony. See **Three** and **Pyramid.**

**Trickster:**  The Trickster is an Archetype that is the cosmic jester of the dreamscape, and portrays the unconscious active in consciousness. The psyche has an amazing and clever way of injecting humor into dream symbolism in an effort to jar the status quo. You will know the Trickster because this character is odd and pesters you in a way that demands your attention. Trickster is like a Freudian slip and traps us in our inconsistencies. The part the Trickster character plays in the psyche is to use humor to trick us into being honest with ourselves.

There are many roads and the right road is sometimes just the pathway exposing the contradiction inherent in your absolutes. In the middle road between good and evil is your willingness jump into the unknown. When someone is tricking, testing or pestering you in a dream, examine whether you need to let go of rigid thinking. See also Trickster under **Archetypes and Universal Characters** for more information.

**Truck:**   The truck symbolizes motivation and your desire to move forward. Unlike a car however, driving or seeing a truck can be exploring what you are carrying with you that may need to be released. See **Vehicles and Places of Transportation.**

**Trunk:**   See **Chest** and **Purses, Wallets, Luggage, Jewels and Keys.**

**Tsunami:   Water** represents your body of emotions. A deep shift below the surface, or an "enormous wave" can threaten to overwhelm you. At the same time, there will be an "enormous wave of relief" as you allow your emotions the freedom to be released.

**Tunnel:**   The ground usually symbolizes your foundation of beliefs. When you are tunneling "below the surface" there is the sense that you are finding ways of circumventing "daylight" or "getting around" something as the idea that you are not consciously facing difficult issues.

**Turtle:** See **Reptiles.**

**Twelve:** See **Numbers**

**Twins:**   Dreaming of two of anything often embodies choices. Associated with the astrological sign Gemini as an Archetype, dreaming of twins can show diverging sides of your nature that need to be synchronized. The Twins appear in many mythical stories around the world representing the childish inquisitiveness that is sometimes necessary for a more meaningful relationship with life. If the twins are a boy and girl, the dream can be exploring the merging of masculine and feminine traits so you may become more sensitive, yet empowered and assertive in achieving fulfillment. See also **Unknown Child** and **Two**.

**Two:**   Two often symbolizes making some type of choice or the idea of balancing extremes. If it is two people in a dream, consider the characters as how they might portray conflicting sides of you that need to be integrated. See **Numbers.**

# U

The letter "U" can signify making a 'u-turn' to go back to something you abandoned. It can embody the idea of 'you' in a cryptic form. Since U-boats travel underwater and UFO's are things that cannot be validated, there may be something unusual you are exploring as an idea that can lead you to unify or balance all the sides of you. This letter can suggest that you might celebrate the quirky things that make you who you are.

**UFO:** Dreaming of UFOs or being threatened by aliens portrays how you are exploring aspects of yourself, which you find difficult to 'identify with.' Your sense of being different from the group (and how you feel about it) will be portrayed by how 'foreign' the characters appear in your dreams.

    Unlike family (genetic or inherited self-dynamics,) friends, people (acquaintances that change you) and even aborigines (the more organic side of you,) aliens would be considered natural creatures, they are just 'not from around here.' Being abducted by aliens is actually suggesting how you are being 'kidnapped' by your fear of conformity and not being authentic. Fitting in with the group often comes at the price of your real nature. A robot would also be offering a message that you are not being authentic or are just going through the motions to fit in. See also **Aliens** and **Flying Saucer**.

**Umbilical Cord:** The umbilical cord is a classic symbol of the thread that binds and nurtures you within. Having a baby usually portrays how you are "giving birth" to a new side of yourself and the umbilical cord is both, what connects these sides of yourself and how they are nurtured. It can also represent the traits adopted from your mother and how they are currently influencing you.

**Umbrella:** Dreaming of an umbrella can symbolize how you are currently protecting yourself from difficulty rather than processing what can be learned from it. The issues surrounding the umbrella will portray how you are doing this.

**Uncle:** See **Family**.

**Unconscious:** One theory of the mind separates it into three aspects: consciousness, the subconscious and the unconscious. When you are a child, your mind has free reign to explore all sides of who you are, but as you grow older, a type of subconscious barrier develops. As you come to understand "the idea of who you are," those elements that are "unacceptable" or denied can remain within an area that is called the unconscious. As these feelings and ideas seek expression, the subconscious net blocks them in daily life. While you sleep, the barrier dissolves and this information rises freely into the mind for exploration.

**Under:** See **Placement and Perspective.**

**Undress:** You can remove you "protective covering" to reveal the more intimate sides of yourself. If the dream brings pleasure, then you are embracing intimacy openly. If you are uncomfortable, then you may feel that you have been "exposed" or revealed in way that did not feel comfortable. See **Naked** and **Clothing and Makeup**.

**Uniform:** See **Clothing and Makeup.**

**Universal Symbolism of Dreams:** See **Archetypes and Universal Characters** and also the book, *The Mythology of Sleep: The Waking Power of Dreams by Kari Hohne.*

**University:** You dream of visiting a university or school as a representation of how you are 'learning' or adopting new attitudes. Being in this classroom setting reveals how you are going through changes or learning something new about yourself. The university can be an objective portrayal of your beliefs and the other students can represent balancing conflicting needs and roles. See School under **Houses and Buildings.**

**Up:** See **Placement and Perspective.**

**Urinate:** Feelings that need to be released since liquids are generally associated with emotion. Not being able to find a place to urinate can symbolize how you do not feel the environment allows for the expression of feelings. See also **Defecate** and **Bath**.

# V

The letter "V" can relate to affection or suggest sexuality when it is not being expressed. Like "A" it is another symbol that can look like an arrow - only it is pointing downwards as a message about feelings stirring in the lower regions; ie: sex.

**Vacant:** If you are entering a vacant house or building in a dream, you may have a sense that an old way has come to an end. At the same time, the vacancy can also symbolize potential that is not immediately obvious. Exploring rooms that are empty of furnishings shows how you are opening to new possibilities that couldn't have been possible without learning to let go of the past. If it is an apartment that is vacant, it can symbolize a transitory perspective as you move through a type of transformation, as in changing jobs, relationships or moving toward a more spiritual awareness. Dreaming of something that is vacant can also personify the sense of emptiness that comes from pleasing others or doing things that are not fulfilling.

**Vacation:** These types of dreams are very common and portray a landscape where you can be free of the daily regimen. Going on "vacation" captures the dreamscape where you can escape from the "daily constraints" of consciousness. See **Traveling** and **Landscape and Scenery**.

**Vaccine:** Getting a vaccine in a dream can portray your defense mechanisms as you ward off facing something that threatens to 'invade' your privacy or emotional aloofness. In many cases you will be getting a vaccine for something that seems like nonsense, as your mind shows you there is no reason to be afraid of intimacy. Since a vaccine is meant to boost an area of 'weakness' within you, the dream can be helping you to understand an area where you might grow stronger. See also **Syringe** and **Drugs**.

**Valley:** This landscape between mountains can represent the female body and the budding fertility of your inner reserves and transformative potential.

**Vampire:** This is a character who is sustained by "**Blood**" or the need to get below the surface to find nourishment through feelings. While it may seem grotesque, there is a message here about your need to find sustenance through feelings. See **Shadow**.

**Van:** See **Moving Van.**

**Vase:** Like the **Womb**, the vase can symbolize your feminine heritage or the idea of holding feelings. The condition and appearance of the vase will reflect your current relationship to these characteristics within you.

**Vegetables:** Vegetables often have associations that relate to their shape and color. They can represent the idea of fulfillment from an organic level, as in health, sex and general well being. Unlike fruit, vegetables often grow beneath the soil and can represent digging within to uncover unrecognized talent and potential. Your fulfillment and potential is often personified by the type of vegetable that is being presented. See individual vegetables under **Food.**

**Vehicles and Places of Transportation** are common dream themes. These types of dreams suggest the condition in which you are currently moving forward. The type of vehicle, and whether or not you are driving, in control or being driven, will portray your present sense of direction and autonomy.

   ***Boats, buses*** and ***trains***, in which you are a 'passenger,' suggest how you are following a course that is not self-directed and not easily changed. ***Travel over water*** is indicative of emotions and how the 'flow of events' or 'current' is leading you forward into the future, and often represent the internal drama of uncertainty. The water can be ***dark, calm*** or ***choppy*** in relation to how you feel about where you are currently going in life. The ***train*** follows a proven track as a representation of how the course has been laid down for you. The train can symbolize other's expectations and not necessarily your own.

Missing a train can symbolize fears of failing in the eyes of what is expected of you. Jumping in and out of trains can symbolize how you are trying to find *your own* way. If you dream of a **box car on a train**, the dream is exploring the idea of other's expectations and the baggage you carry because of it.

The **bus** is a classic image of conformity where a **school bus** is what you adopted or learned. You will often dream of being on a school bus when you are learning how to assert your uniqueness in relation to conformity. You may move f**orward and backward on the bus** as a representation of your progress. A **public bus** shows how you mould your way of being into what you believe is expected of you. It reflects how you may have become a 'passenger' rather than blazing your own path. Since the **taxi** portrays a ride with usually one other character, the driver should be given consideration as the side of you that is currently *driving you forward*. **Paying a fare** for any type of travel shows issues related to self-worth and what you trade in order to move forward in life. **Being driven** by anyone in a dream portrays a need to become more autonomous.

A **bicycle**, because it is propelled forward by your actual effort, can suggest vitality and issues related to health. As a child, perhaps you learned to ride by balancing your weight against movement, so it can also suggest balancing well-being with motivation and drive. The bicycle often appears as a representation of following a path that better reflects your *natural* potential. In a sense, you are slowing down your pace to connect more with experience and get in touch with who you are.

**Go-carts** offer a similar message although they also reveal a sense of competition. **Bumper cars** and other **jalopies** suggest how you are moving forward, sometimes in comical or dangerous ways. A vehicle without protection or some of its parts missing can symbolize scarcity or dysfunction operating in your motivation. The **motorcycle** is also associated with balance and precision.

**Trucks** suggest how you are moving forward while carrying a 'load' or attempting to 'transport' what is important to you, rather than being free to move forward. **Moving vans** take carrying unnecessary baggage to a higher level of awareness. They usually appear when you are sorting through old ideas and making changes in preparation for moving forward. Where the bus shows conformity and social demands, the van full of people can represent the various sides of you collectively.

*Airports* and *train stations* are places of transition, and therefore are associated with hopes and ambitions. You can *'fly'* to your destination through expanded awareness and insight, or find your *compartment* or 'place' on a train that follows a 'proven track' as in expectations. You can be going *up, down* or in *circles*, as a way of following inspiration, overcoming repression, or revisiting the past. *Danger* and the idea of *crashing* suggest how you are not in control of where you are going and are therefore, feeling uncertain about your direction.

Being *stopped by police* or *traffic lights* show how you are obeying the disciplinarian controls of conscience.

A *delivery truck* can signify being given or receiving some type of insight that you may be missing. The package can provide clues to what is hidden. *Hitchhiking* can represent not taking responsibility for where you are going in life. *Giving a ride to an unknown passenger* can represent integrating or understanding an unknown part of you at work as the root of your motivation.

A *parking garage* or seeing a *parked car* reflects how your motivation is currently parked, sometimes because of changes your are making, and at other times, because you might not recognize how and why you undermine your ambition. *Fender benders in a parking* garage are usually the result of colliding sides of you coming out for consideration. A *race car* or *red sports* car can symbolize a competitive streak in your motivation. See **Color** for other associations of aspects related to motivation.

**Victim:** See **Attack and Being Chased** and **Shadow.**

**Vine:** The vine captures the idea of roots, growth and how things are intertwined. Dreaming of a vine is a symbol of your heritage and your interconnectivity with the world around you. See **Gardener**.

**Violin:** Because of its "strings," the violin combines the ideas of free flowing sexuality and a sense of "the strings that are attached." See **Music.**

**Volcano:** Capturing how emotions are repressed and will break through your calm exterior, dreaming of a volcano can suggest the need to express difficult feelings so that you don not "explode." See **Landscape and Scenery.**

**Vomit:** Anything associated with the mouth usually represents communication. If you are unable to "digest" process or express yourself, you may dream of vomiting *something*. The symbol that is vomited will shed light on what this may be.

**Voyage:** Combining the idea of Water with transportation, a voyage can represent the condition of your emotions as you move through life. See **Water** and **Vehicles and Places of Transportation**.

**Vulnerable:** Since dreams often are a way of processing **Anxiety,** feeling vulnerable or scared is a common theme of dreams. See **Attack and Being Chased.**

**Vulture:** A vulture combines the idea of "flight" or achieving ambitions, with being an "opportunistic scavenger." To dream of a vulture can symbolize a side of you that is "preying" on another weakness, as in the case of an inferiority complex that leads you to become an unfulfilled overachiever. Since this Bird appears after something "has died", it may be calling you to recognize how some aspect of you is thriving at the expense of another equally important aspect. See **Birds.**

# W

The letter "W" can be associated with ideas like words and writing as a symbol of communication. It is a letter that is associated with waiting, washing (releasing) or questioning, as in What, Where and Why? It can show how two symbols are related in the dream. The message is that there may not necessarily be a choice - you can do both. Finally, "W" is a symbol for women or the idea of femininity when one is exploring sensitivity, intuition or traits that would be considered feminine.

**Waiter:** This character is responsible for bringing you nourishment. Dreaming of a waiter can be an objective portrayal of how you allow yourself to be fulfilled or nourished. Explore the characteristics of the waiter for information that might lead to greater fulfillment. See **Food.**

**Waiting:** Since dreams usually represent the *opposite* of what you believe to be true about yourself, a dream where you are forced to wait can actually suggest a need to slow down in a situation where you are too *busy* to notice that you are unfulfilled. Waiting associated with transportation shows your dependency on circumstances that allow you to understand the roots of your motivation. See **Late** and **Vehicles and Places of Transportation**.

**Wake up:** See **Awake.**

**Walking:** There are many ways that you move forward in life. Transportation vehicles and shoes can reveal your motivation or sense of empowerment in moving forward. When you are walking, the dream seems to suggest that you are currently moving slowly and *perceptively* through the changes in your life in order to learn more about yourself.

**Wall:** Associated with **Houses and Buildings**, a wall suggests what you have "erected" to hide behind. Climbing a wall can portray your desire to transcend your these boundaries. Relieving yourself in a bathroom without walls can portray your movement toward intimacy. Any dream involving walls shows both the barriers you construct and how they block your natural expression. See **Bath.**

**Wallet:** The wallet is associated with your identity and ability to provide for oneself. Losing a wallet or searching for a wallet is common when we are changing jobs. We keep our valuables in a wallet and keep it protected, so it can be a message about protecting your sense of values or exploring self-worth. See **Pocket** and **Purses, Wallets, Luggage, Jewels and Keys.**

**Wallpaper:** You may build walls that protect your current ideas and then cover them with colorful paper as a way of entertaining yourself while the world outside passes you by. The wallpaper is a symbol of "covering up" the idea that you are hiding behind a superficial perspective. Seeing a tear in the wallpaper can symbolize the first stage of transformation as you transcend the walls that hold you back.

**War:** Being in a war in the dreamscape embodies the idea that various sides of you are in conflict. You may be embarking in a new career direction and worry about its influences on the family. You may be entering a relationship and worry about its affects on your emotions. You may be rising above a conflicted situation or emotional abuse and dream of war as a way of processing these feelings. Examine your current situation to see if open communication can alleviate your fears. See **Army** and **Atomic Bomb.**

**Wardrobe:** See **Clothing and Makeup.**

**Warehouse:** We dream of warehouses when we are sorting through the past or exploring our 'reserves.' See **Houses and Buildings.**

**Warning:** Being warned by **Police** is a common theme as some emerging side of you is transcending your critical tapes. See **Answer** and Red, Yellow under **Colors**; also **911.**

**Washing:** The idea of "coming clean" or removing "dirt" from an object can suggest either being intimate, truthful or avoiding "dirty" or sexual feelings. The symbol that is being cleaned can shed further light on what this is. If it is clothes, then you are "renewing" an outworn attitude. If it is dishes, then you are washing away an outworn way of being fulfilled to allow for growth. See **Clean.**

**Watch:** See **Clock** and **Homonyms**.

**Water:** Water dreams are very common because water represents your emotions, and how you feel about *the changes* that you face as you move through life. The sea is a classic symbol of the depths of the unconscious and the unknown, untapped or fearful aspects you hold within the psyche. To dream of *turbulent seas* suggests a sense of emotional crisis associated with moving forward. Any time this type of dreams occurs, later, you may dream about being on a similar ship and crossing the water that has become calm. This is representative of the emotional growth that you have achieved. In all of our ancient stories, water is the mysterious reservoir where the hero is to retrieve a treasure. Similarly, raging water often initiates you into a process of self-discovery. *Floods* can undermine the foundation of your beliefs until you are forced to let go. What you thought was solid and what you thought you needed, is washed away in the pursuit of basic survival. Water can also represent health and wellness since it is a symbol of the elixir of life.

**Weapons** and **Utensils** represent what you hold in your hand to express, feed, defend or build something. Guns can represent defensive tendencies and are sometimes sexual. *Cutting tools* are used to cut through restraints or to shape something new from the old. *Scissors* combine the motion of grasping and letting go with the idea of cutting to symbolize "cutting away" the things that bind you. The *hammer* allows you to "nail something" of get it right, while you may also be pounding out your frustration. A *sword* can be sexual, although a sword or *knife* can suggest defensive tendencies or cutting through something to see the truth. An *arrow* can represent your desire to "hit the mark" in your aspirations. A *fork* can represent the ability to gain fulfillment, but can also suggest a "fork in the road" or choice. *Artistic tools* are associated creativity and any item that is held in the hand will have an association with self-creation. A *pen* and *pencil* carry the idea of communication, while the pen can signify words that are not easily "erased." The pencil may be portraying words that have no commitment behind them. See **Attack and Being Chased**.

**Weather:** See **Temperature** and **Landscape and Scenery**.

**Web:** See Spider under **Insects**.

**Wedding:** Often you will dream of attending a wedding that is not your own and have the sense of not remembering the people that were getting married. This portrays the integration of qualities that were not integrated before and the idea of allowing more freedom of the unknown in your current relationship. If the wedding is your own, it becomes the classic representation of the merging or union of different sides of yourself, usually adopting the Anima or Animus. You may be making a commitment to adopt a certain behavior. See Anima/Animus under **Archetypes and Universal Characters, Bride** and **Ceremony.**

**Weeds:** Something is *growing* within that may not be fulfilling and may strangle your ability to find sustenance. See Garden under **Houses and Buildings**.

**Well:** As the wellspring of your inspiration and intuition, the well can symbolize how you are approaching unconscious attitudes in an effort to understand your feelings. See **Water**.

**Werewolf:** This character combines the idea of unrepressed urges and how they can come to overwhelm your need for control. See **Animals** and Shadow under **Archetypes and Universal Characters**.

**West:** Going west can symbolize how you are exploring the "frontier" of your potential. Associated with what is modern and driven to achieve success, the direction of west can point to these qualities within you.

**Whale:** Since fish are often symbolic of opportunity and how you resurrect your potential by exploring what lies hidden below the unconscious, the whale can symbolize this part of you stirring. If you are frightened of the whale - you may have reservations about enacting the power of the **Shadow**. Since water is associated with feelings - dreaming of a whale can show the enormity of emotions that are stirring 'below the surface.' See also **Sealife**.

**Wheel:** You may have a sense that you are "coming full circle" or that you may need to move forward. See **Circle**, **Tire** and **Vehicles and Places of Transportation.**

**Whirlwind:** See **Tornado.**

**Whistle:** When the whistle blows, something usually begins or ends. Like **Alarm**, you may need to pay attention to the idea of beginning or ending something.

**Wig:** Since hair represents how you groom your ideas over time, a wig carries the idea of "donning" a false persona, perhaps for acceptance.

**Wind:** The wind has a way of stirring things up and moving what remains stationary, like the branches of trees. It removes the seeds of the future and returns them to the ground. Like **Tornado**, the wind can portray a force beyond your control that is moving you forward.

**Window:** Windows are associated with the ability to see clearly. If you are cleaning the window, you are increasing your awareness or ability to see something. If you are in a room without windows, the area of the psyche that the room represents is being shut off from everyday experiences. To open a window, you are opening to new ideas and perspectives. See **Houses and Buildings**.

**Wine:** See **Alcohol.**

**Winter:**  Associated with **Cold** and **Ice,** a winter landscape can represent feelings that remain below the surface, as you move across what appears to be a barren landscape. If you are working through issues that are difficult for you to face, often you may find yourself in this "cold" environment initially. In reality, there is an enormous amount of creative energy "below" waiting for the spring of your "rebirth."

**Wise Man or Woman:**  Often associated with older characters and especially grandparents that have passed away, meeting these characters can portray how all that they represent  has become active within you as a type of internal guidance.  See **Archetypes and Universal Characters.**

**Witch:**  See Great Mother under **Archetypes and Universal Characters**.

**Wizard:**  See Wise Man under **Archetypes and Universal Characters.**

**Wolf:**  See **Animals.**

**Woman:**  See **People** and **Anima/Animus.**

**Womb:**  Dreaming of caves or openings in the earth can be representative of the womb and feelings associated with the mother. For a woman, traveling into a cave can represent her exploration of sexual urges. For a man, it can signify a movement toward sensitivity.

**Wood:**  Like **Metal** and **Stone**, wood is an element that signifies what is most natural within you. When an object is made of wood, it represents the suppleness of your authenticity, portraying an element that is most susceptible to the changes in your environment. Explore the other symbols for more clues.

**Work:**  There are often challenges in the work environment and dreaming of work allows you to work through these challenges. To dream of doing work that is not what you are currently doing, suggests the symbolism you are currently "working on." For example dreaming of serving food can represent self-nourishing thoughts, while driving a bus can suggest "hosting" the integration of all sides of you as you explore your motivation to move forward.

**Worm:** Generally unpleasant, the worm is a living thing beneath the soil and can represent feelings of being unworthy or ignored "crawling" beneath the surface. These feelings of insignificance can rise when you are moving toward self-acceptance. See **Insects.**

**Wound:** See **Scar.**

**Wrinkle:** Time marks itself upon the skin with wrinkles and seeing something wrinkled can represent your sense of passing time. A "wrinkle in the fabric" can suggest difficulty or that something is amiss that you are failing to recognize.

**Write:** See **Letter.**

# X

The letter "X" often marks the spot and can be directing you to look closely at the symbolism to find direction. It can also symbolize closing or blocking yourself from opportunity that is right in front of you. If you explore the symbolism surrounding this letter, you will discover something that you are not seeing during the day. In the same sense, it can be a covert way of getting the idea of sex (or its absence from your waking mind) out into the open.

**X-ray:** To see something revealed by an X-ray can portray your desire to look deeper at a situation. Seeing the outline of bones and organs can show how you remain unconscious of how you have structured your sense of self to please others.

**Xylophone:** Playing a musical instrument in a dream is the easy expression of your passions and feelings. Playing a xylophone represents harmony in expressing the individual areas of your life. If only one tone or one 'key' becomes the focus of the dream, you may be questioning your ability to get some aspect right so that your life 'plays in harmony.' A broken xylophone can symbolize depression. If you are dreaming about it - you might want to examine whether or not you are happy.

# Y

Seeing the letter "Y" in a dream can signify 'yes' or the answer to something you have been grappling with. The dream imagery can be telling you 'why' something is happening. It is also associated with making a choice or moving along a new path. It can symbolize feeling yoked in, or a desire for freedom.

**Yacht:**   See **Water** and **Vehicles and Places of Transportation**.

**Yard:**   Since the house represents your 'inner architecture' and ideas related to what the individual rooms represent, the yard has more of an association with how you 'go out' to meet the world in social situations. The front yard represents how you interact in social situations and what you reveal to others and cultivate in terms of appearance. The backyard is more private and can represent aspects that you keep hidden or issues you may not be confronting. Something happening in the front yard can represent changes you are making through public interaction, while something happening in the backyard can represent aspects of a more personal nature. See Front and Back Yard under **Houses and Buildings**.

**Yellow**: Yellow is a color that can represent resentment and jealousy. Associated with the color of the sun and summer – it can also represent self-actualization. See **Colors.**

**Youth:** See **People.**

# Z

Dreaming of the letter "Z" can represent the idea of boredom or not feeling connected to life in some way. As a symbol representing finality, it can be describing the end of one road or course of action. You may feel like you are going backwards, but life is a circular journey and you are always moving forward as the path zig zags in your growth.

**Zebra:** The zebra demonstrates the qualities of the **Horse** but with the added symbolism of spiritual uniqueness. See **Animals.**

**Zero:** Zero can symbolize nothing at the same time that it represents wholeness as the idea that what we think we need may not be right for us. We may need to 'zero' in on what is really important. See **Empty, Circle** and **Numbers.**

**Zoo:** A zoo is a landscape where you explore your passions and earthy drives aside from social conditioning. Since this is a place of exotic animals that are kept in cages, dreaming of a zoo can represent how you are 'visiting' the idea of natural expression, but are not expressing your urges. When an animal gets loose from a cage, this part of you is breaking free. Look up the various animals for more clues to the side of you undergoing exploration. See **Circus** and **Animals.**

Made in the USA
Middletown, DE
03 March 2021